The Ethics of Criticism

The Ethics of Criticism

TOBIN SIEBERS

CORNELL UNIVERSITY PRESS

ITHACA AND LONDON

First published 1988 by Cornell University Press.
First published, Cornell Paperbacks, 1990.

International Standard Book Number 0-8014-2128-4 (cloth)
International Standard Book Number 0-8014-9712-4 (paper)
Library of Congress Catalog Card Number 87-47820

Printed in the United States of America

Librarians: Library of Congress cataloging information
appears on the last page of the book.

⊛ The paper used in this publication meets the minimum
requirements of the American National Standard for
Permanence of Paper for Printed Library Materials Z39.48–1984.

In memory of
Marion Siebers
1919–1987

Contents

Acknowledgments

I began working on *The Ethics of Criticism* during my last months as a Fellow of the Michigan Society of Fellows, and it is with a special sense of completion that I find myself finishing the book at the University of Michigan after a three-year stay at Columbia University. Both institutions have played a major role in forming this book. The Michigan Society of Fellows provided early support for the project, and the Columbia Council for Research in the Humanities generously aided my efforts during the summer of 1985.

The trip from Ann Arbor to New York City and back measures a geographical circle that has also become a circle of students, colleagues, and friends. Much of this material received the scrutiny of my graduate students in Comparative Literature 5004 during the two years that I taught the course at Columbia University. The discussion and level of activity were intense, and I only hope that the members of the seminar profited from my remarks as much as I did from theirs. Among my colleagues and friends at Columbia, Karl Kroeber was a consistent and devoted reader of the manuscript, and I profited from his good sense and demands for clarity. Carolyn Heilbrun, Martin Meisel, Carl Woodring, Charlotte Bonica, and Susan Winnett also had their influence on particular chapters, besides providing an atmosphere of encouragement and good humor. At Michigan, Ross Chambers, Julie Ellison, and Margot Norris have been faithful commentators and correspondents. They have made their marks in these pages.

Those who have had the most influence and who have worked the hardest for me remain the people who have been within my circle of friends the longest. Eric Gans has read everything and anything that I have written, and the duration of our association has softened neither his willingness to exchange ideas nor the intensity of his criticisms. Michael Clark has played the often unpleasant role of editor and critic for this manuscript and remains a reliable and astute commentator. Finally, I owe personal and intellectual debts to René Girard, Paisley Livingston, and Gustavo Pellón. I thank them.

Life in a bustling household with my wife, Jill, and daughter, Claire, has sometimes given me less time to read, but it has made me realize again and again that literature does have to do with life. My life with them is the story that I most prefer to read and to write.

Early versions of chapters 4, 6, and 7 appeared respectively in *Modern Language Notes* (1985); Paul Dumouchel, ed., *Violence et vérité* (Paris: Grasset, 1985); and *The Psychoanalytic Review* (1986). They have been substantially revised.

T.S.

Ann Arbor, Michigan

1

The Character of
Criticism: Introduction

The character of criticism emerges in its critical choices, and the nature of critical choice reveals that literary criticism is inextricably linked to ethics. The ethics of criticism involves critics in the process of making decisions and of studying how these choices affect the lives of fellow critics, writers, students, and readers as well as our ways of defining literature and human nature. To criticize in conjunction with ethics places literary criticism at large. Its environment is no longer exclusively textual, nor is it wholly political, for politics and ethics, although related, do not reflect the same ends. To criticize ethically brings the critic into a special field of action: the field of human conduct and belief concerning the human.

It is important, then, that *The Ethics of Criticism* be understood in this particular light. *The Ethics of Criticism* does not refer to "the ethics of reading" and the idea that a linguistic imperative requires critics not to make decisions between the possible meanings of literary works.[1] Such theories are inherently un-

1. See, for example, J. Hillis Miller, "The Ethics of Reading: Vast Gaps and Parting Hours," in *American Criticism in the Poststructuralist Age*, ed. Ira Konigsberg (Ann Arbor: University of Michigan Press, 1981), pp. 19–41, "How Deconstruction Works," *New York Times Magazine*, Feb. 9, 1986: 25, and, more recently, *The Ethics of Reading* (New York: Columbia University Press, 1986).

critical, if criticism necessitates choice, although no less ethical than others, as we shall see, because their indecision has an ethical motivation. Nor does the ethics of criticism refer to the work, largely admirable, being done currently on literature by moral philosophers. *The Ethics of Criticism* focuses rather on the means by which literary criticism affects the relation between literature and human life. Its area of interest does not extend to all literary criticism, but rather emphasizes a particular line of theoretical development that many see as the main path of what is now called critical theory. Each essay collected here contributes to the sense of the whole book by examining how a particular theory or school of literary criticism has justified in an ethical way its theoretical choices. Each essay further considers the impact of theoretical choice on the relation between literature and the lives of human beings.

Possible approaches toward the ethics of criticism would seem extraordinarily varied, but I have tended to emphasize two main issues where ethics and criticism consistently join, and it is these that require introduction and definition. The first issue concerns the role of the human in literature and criticism—what might be called the character of criticism. To assess the character of criticism requires one to study the ethical attitudes behind critical claims as well as the attitudes engendered either consciously or unconsciously by particular theoretical stances. Recent critical theory has, of course, placed in question the idea of the constitutive subject of language by subordinating selfhood to linguistic structure, and this theoretical position makes the study of ethical attitudes difficult, to say the least. Theory of this kind may in fact be said to deprive criticism of its character, and consequently it effects an ethical transformation not only on criticism but on our conceptions of how human beings and literature relate. To what extent, however, does the elimination of the subject lead to an ethical dilemma, and to what extent does the gesture itself rely on ethical formulations?

Michel Foucault's work provides an exemplary case where we may begin to pose and answer such questions. His proclamation of the "death of man," in particular, articulated in the most notorious rhetoric the necessity of abandoning the human for the linguistic. The critique of the human sciences in *The Order of Things* is an attack less against science than against the human as an explanatory category.[2] "'Anthropologization' is," in Foucault's mind, "the great internal threat to knowledge in our day" (348). In the place of the human, Foucault wishes to uncover a positive unconscious of knowledge, and he isolates the idea of man as the site of his archaeology. But the archaeological dig reveals less that is positive than Foucault's paradoxical and anxious attitude toward the human, for the human is in Foucault's mind what both justifies and negates itself within a certain history of violence. Foucault therefore works to replace the human with an idea of language in which such justifications and annulments would have a less oppressive effect. It is for this reason that *The Order of Things* ends with the wager that the human face will soon be washed from our shores, leaving in its place only the discursive practices of language. Foucault's announcement of the "death of man" and of the human sciences has a precise ethical context. His struggle to eliminate the constitutive subject expresses the ethical wish to end the reign of terror that he associates with human history by turning to language as the only ethical subject; and in this respect Edward Said is correct in calling Foucault's theories "an ethics of language."[3]

Foucault's linguistic ethics, then, relies on a specific theory of

2. References to Michel Foucault, *The Order of Things* (New York: Vintage Books, 1973), are given parenthetically. See also "The Discourse on Language," in his *The Archaeology of Knowledge*, trans. A. M. Sheridan Smith (New York: Pantheon, 1972), pp. 215–237, *Madness and Civilization*, trans. Richard Howard (New York: Vintage, 1965), *The Use of Pleasure*, trans. Robert Hurley (New York: Pantheon, 1985), and "What Is an Author?" in *Language, Counter-Memory, Practice: Selected Essays and Interviews*, ed. Donald F. Bouchard (Ithaca: Cornell University Press, 1977), pp. 113–38.

3. Edward Said, "An Ethics of Language," *Diacritics* 4.2 (1974): 28–37. Said notes Foucault's allegiance to visionaries and madmen who remain exterior to repressive discursive practices, remarking his belief in the heroism of "their willingness to accept the terrifying freedom that comes from hyper-individuality" (36). Said also stresses Foucault's attention to the relation between language and judgment, that "an existing system of signs is a judgment already made that those particular signs *shall be*." "In this insistence," Said believes, "upon a judgment made both to exclude and include, Foucault therefore describes language *ethically*, in the literal sense" (35).

human character, and this theory motivates his attack on the human sciences. At the heart of *The Order of Things* is the belief that the explorations of the human sciences derive from the human urge for colonization. Foucault does not seem to believe, at first, that "the colonizing situation is indispensable to ethnology: neither hypnosis, nor the patient's alienation within the fantasmatic character of the doctor, is constitutive of psychoanalysis. . ." (377). But he concludes that, just as psychoanalysis "can be deployed only in the *calm violence* of a particular relationship and the transference it produces, so ethnology can assume its proper dimensions only within the historical sovereignty— always restrained, but always present—of European thought and the relation that can bring it face to face with all other cultures as well as with itself" (377; my emphasis). What is most proper to the human sciences, in short, is the desire to repress and oppress other human beings. In *Madness and Civilization*, Foucault refers to this desire as creating the "structure of exclusion" on which Western history rests, and in "The Discourse on Language," he argues that constraints on the proliferating meanings of language as well as the constraints of language are a kind of violence. Finally, Foucault's famous attack on the idea of authorship makes sense only as a defensive measure against human character. Foucault believes that authority is oppressive, and he fights the aggressive authority of the author by reducing it to an author-function, that is, a discursive practice in which no human being holds power. Indeed, Foucault's theory of power is more of an ethical wish than a theory: ideally, no human being should be in power, and Foucault expresses this hope by defining power as that which cannot be possessed.

The image of the tide ebbing away with the human icon remains provocative, but tells finally of what can only be called a premature burial. Theories of this kind have tended to fail, as Foucault's subsequent shift to a theory of the ethico-poetic self implies, and their supporters are usually the first to speak of the general failures of theory, when perhaps it is only one kind of theory that is destined not to succeed. The replacement of the human by the linguistic turns out to be a self-defeating gesture in every sense. For the human subject always returns in the act of writing, and to attempt its suppression in writing is ultimately an act of self-violence. Indeed, the violence directed against the concept of the self by modern theorists seems only one more version of the violence associated with human endeavors throughout history. Although critics often justify the importance of language as a means of eliminating the aggressive authority of the human subject and its history of crime, they cannot escape this same history, and they end by erecting the edifice of language on the tomb of the human self. The human face, as it were, must be washed away to make way for language. Georg Lukács's concept of "reification" explains how the modes of production in capitalism gradually strip away all signs of the human from our lives, but one is tempted to apply his idea in a noneconomic way to modern literary theory. Modern critics have fallen prey to a form of reification in their preference for language over the human: every day the idea of the human grows fainter and more distant even as theories of language become more fragmented. Modern theory consequently enacts a maddening gesture doomed to repeat the crimes that it despises the most: killing the concept of the self because the self may kill does not extricate one from the cycle of violence.

And yet the desire to eliminate the constitutive self of literature has ethical motivations that cannot be renounced, no matter how unpopular ethics may become. Whether we assert a theory of the self or deny it, we remain within the sphere of ethics, if only because the word "ethics" derives from the Greek *ēthos,* or "moral character." The idea of character reveals its double meaning when ethics and literary study converge, for we should understand that literary or critical character always implies an ideal of ethical character. The discipline of ethics remains inextricably fused to the problem of human character, and the response of a particular theory to character is usually the best place to begin an assessment of the ethics of criticism. Foucault's early elimination of the self implies an attempt to master human character, and his later *The Use of Pleasure* expresses this intention explicitly in a definition of character that privileges asceticism and self-mastery. The works of René Girard and Friedrich Nietzsche also reveal their greatest ethical pertinence on the issue of character. Both writers conceive of human psychology in a way that requires the emergence of a force other than human, Christ or the overman, to provide mankind with a moral direction. The theory of Paul de Man ties the inadequacies of the human self to the nature of linguistic structure, so that language becomes a kind of divinity and death a linguistic predicament. Finally, the psychoanalytic theories of Freud and Lacan construct a theory of the self that gives privilege to sexuality in character, but persists in seeing sexuality as an impasse in human relations. In each case, the attempt to resolve the conflicts of human character manifests a particular ethical attitude that requires more scrutiny.

The second issue important for the ethics of criticism has already been implied within the foregoing discussion of the relation between the human and ethics. Literary criticism and ethics also converge in their preoccupation with conflict. By "conflict," we need not think only and always of such phrases as "the conflict of interpretations," although these conflicts always involve human agents and may explode into a form of violence that surpasses the limits of literary criticism. Conflict of interpretations is an inescapable effect within the large field of literary theory, but only rarely do differences in opinion produce ideological attitudes that injure human beings. "Violence" is perhaps a better term than "conflict" to capture the area of concern presently shared by ethics and literary theory because it alone evokes the visceral reaction that provides a key to the stakes at issue. The word "violence" carries the sense of daily life. It evokes fear and pity, courage and sympathy, exposing those emotions that define us most as human beings. This anthropological base is central to an understanding of the ethics of modern criticism because literary theorists today, despite all claims to the contrary, are engaged in a species of argument that has startling implications for the way that we relate to and define the human world. The idea of violence carries the burden of our concern with life, and its associations best focus attention on the issues shared by criticism and ethics.

Certainly much has been made of the word "violence" in its history, and it is an easy word to invoke and to abuse, whether by victims, villains, or sensationalists. No definition will infringe upon its sensational quality precisely because of the extraordinary relevance of aggression in human affairs, but it is worth introducing a general definition nevertheless. Violence exists whenever human beings harm other human beings. Indeed, the violence most threatening to human beings is human violence. It takes many forms, arising in physical attacks or words and actions that deprive human beings of their humanity. Indeed, one must always speak of the "forms of violence," if violence is not to assume a needlessly monolithic character. The forms of violence compose a register of effects that vary in their immediate impact on human life. But ethical thought, at least since Rousseau, has been most deeply troubled by those forms of violence involving the language of human inequality and difference. Here too I am most concerned with the forms of violence that injure human beings by creating categories or ideas that risk depriving them of rights in political and psychological contexts. I will also try to isolate those moments when literary critics have conflated various ideas of disagreement with the idea of violence. Let there be no mistaking, however, the difficulty of differentiating the forms of violence. The problem of violence cannot be properly defined outside of an anthropological context, and the world of human beings is vertiginously complex. Violence is a human problem. It is never an infernal machine without a driver. It is never without a victim. If it may be called systematic, it is only so because it establishes languages and patterns of behavior that can be repeated by others.

Literary criticism would seem far removed from such matters. Its isolation in the little rooms of academia makes it a tame occupation, and many of the dangers now associated with criticism by those in search of a vicarious thrill would be laughable, given the state of terrorism and brutality in the world, if they were not so misguided. And yet language is one instrument of human violence, and in that respect literary critics have a responsibility not only to supervise their own unjust practices as critics but to think about the ways in which language carries on the work of human prejudice, racism, sexism, classism, and nationalism. Even the most ethically oriented critics must remain watchful in this regard. Lévi-Strauss, for example, in the course of making an ethical argument against social injustice, does violence to the Nambikwara by attributing to them an inhumanly noble and innocent nature, and Derrida, countering Lévi-Strauss's mistake, violates him by blaming him for the not-so-noble actions of the Nambikwara's social system. Both Lévi-Strauss and Derrida produce categories—respectively, the innocent native and the instigating anthropologist—that risk stealing the status of human being from their objects. Similarly, the American New Critics counter the prejudices of those biographical critics who believe that "the author is the style" with a vision of poetic autonomy, but they express their vision in a language that creates an analogy between poetic intentions and intentionality in murder, thereby maintaining the same association between psychopathology and poetry held by biographical criticism. Such analogies imply that poets are in essence criminal. Finally, one could mention the tendency of feminist criticism to represent the injustices against women in a form that perpetuates those very injustices and stereotypes, or the new field called nuclear criticism and its tendency to fight the terrors of the nuclear holocaust by reducing violence to a game of rhetoric, but a rhetoric that nevertheless comes back to contaminate the definition of literature with the horrors of war.

The reaction of literary critics to violence needs to be interpreted, first and foremost, as an ethical gesture performed within a human context, and in this context literary and ethical problems cannot be separated, no matter how zealous the claim for the autonomy of literature. Nevertheless, as literary critics, we flee from this human context, and above all others. The majority of critics writing today conceives of the violence involved in literary criticism as a problem in the "conflict of interpretations" or at most in terms of a feeble political idea such as the "politics of literature." These ideas stretch in the right direction, but their formulations are often so general as to miss the mark. More precisely, I am referring to the tendency in critical circles to view conflicts of interpretation as if they were essentially violent, to the view that equates acts of criticism with those of physical or ideological violence. No idea is more widespread today than the notion that language is by definition violent and that critical language risks being the most violent of all. This idea needs to be disputed, and I will return to the effects of its mistaken claim repeatedly.[4] But, for the moment, it is important to recognize that our sense of interpretive violence fits into a larger context in which literary criticism and moral philosophy converge. The symptoms of this alliance nevertheless must be read at their deepest levels to have any value for the ethics of criticism. In its sensitivity to its own violence, whether false or not, literary criticism demonstrates both its affinity with the history of ethics and its status as a human science, for it is precisely the appearance of the critical sensitivity to violence that defines literary criticism as anthropologically, psychologically, and ethically determined.

What is at stake ethically in the idea of critical violence? If critical language is by nature violent, then the act of criticism becomes ethically suspicious, to say the least, and those who engage in criticism must develop complicated attitudes and definitions of character to deal with their crises of conscience. The sensitivity of the theorist to the apparent violence of criticism contributes to the character of modern criticism, and the study of these ethical attitudes forms a part of the enterprise of the ethics of criticism. In one sense, this book attempts to write not a history of critical ideas but a genealogy of the character of modern critical theory. The idea of genealogy here does not refer to its present fashionable definition as a strategy to avoid

---

4. I have contested critical theory's rather absolutist equation between language and violence on a variety of fronts. In Chapter 4, I show how Derrida's and Lévi-Strauss's claims for the relation between violence and writing cannot account for the fact that language acts again and again to defer aggressive actions. In Chapter 5, I explain that Keats's moral philosophy undoes de Man's argument for the similarity between linguistic arbitrariness and death; and in Chapter 7, I analyze how the Freudian theory of sexuality misconstrues the ability of the unconscious to create representations that permit a recovery from violence. Finally, in Chapters 8 and 9, I argue that suffering is only a commodity, not a property of literature, and that the false analogy between literature and war created by nuclear critics endangers their ethical hopes. For an account of this problem in another register, see my "Language, Violence, and the Sacred: A Polemical Survey of Critical Theories," *Stanford French Review* 10.1–3 (1986): 203–20.

the totalizing movement of historicism. The substitution of "genealogy" for "history" today in fact represents one more attempt by critical thinkers to escape the violence of human history. Nor should genealogy be read in opposition to anthropological designs as a type of archaeological project concerned with the strata of meaning. Rather, genealogy refers to human relations and the lineage of character. For all the influence that Nietzsche has had on the modern scene, it remains difficult to understand genealogy in the sense that he uses it. Nietzsche's project in *On the Genealogy of Morals* is to study the character behind moral claims, which is why he strives again and again to describe the personalities of the man of resentment, the priestly caste, the noble Greek, the nihilist, and the ascetic.

Modern critical theory has its own cast of characters. It speaks in a discourse largely concerned with issues of language, but behind its definitions of language lie ideals of human character. The study of these attitudes can be pursued in a variety of ways. The slippage between the autonomy of human will, proposed within the moral philosophy of Kant, and the autonomy of language, found in the New Criticism and poststructuralist theory, proves a most fertile ground for interrogating the character of language. What is at stake, however, as I try to demonstrate in my readings in ethical criticism from Plato to pluralism and the ethics of autonomy is not merely the naming of a hidden ethos. The substitution of language for the self produces its own distinct moral dilemma because it has created a view of human consciousness in which ethical reflection is always destined to fail. The character of language promoted by theory today makes extremely difficult the type of consciousness necessary to moral reflection.

Here it is impossible not to discuss the influence of Freud and Nietzsche on modern ideas of both character and language. Modern critics return insistently to Freud as well as to Nietzsche because they are the most inspired students of the ethical implications of will, consciousness, and unconsciousness. But, unfortunately, the interest in them on the modern scene is rarely expressed in terms of such fundamental ethical issues. Rather, Freud and Nietzsche have become theorists of language. The contribution of psychoanalysis to the ethics of criticism remains especially powerful, for modern theorists have in many cases adopted Freud's idea of the unconscious as a model to describe linguistic structure, and consequently their idea of language both asserts and seems to displace a series of ethical difficulties associated with consciousness and unconsciousness. To understand the real influence of Freud and Nietzsche, we must restore the original context of their arguments, arguments that turn inevitably on the human self and its self-representation. Only then will the true character of their impact on the modern scene emerge.

Despite the insistence on the importance of language, then, critical theory never abandons the problem of character and self-representation. The one figure that best demonstrates this assertion is the critic. The character of the critic in modern literary theory is only and everywhere presented in ethical terms. The expression used most often is "disinterestedness." The word carries appropriately moral associations, but it underestimates the extent to which modern theory wishes to remove the critic from a world of violence and ethical dilemmas. The modern critic is literally not of this world. Even a theorist such as Edward Said, whose principal notion of late is worldliness, places the critic in a genealogy extending from Matthew Arnold's "alien" critic to his own "exiled" critic. Said insists on maintaining the persona of the exile, going so far as to describe Lukács's "transcendental homelessness" as the ideal state toward which all good literary critics should aspire.[5] Such homelessness is the

5. I cite from Gary Hentzi and Anne McClintock, "An Interview with Edward W. Said," *Critical Texts* 3.2 (1986): 6–13. Notice the religious and ethical rhetoric of the otherworldly and alien critic's "mission": "Matthew Arnold uses the word *alien* to describe the critic: somebody who isn't anchored in class but is more or less adrift. For me the figure of the exile is terribly important, because you reach a point where you realize that exile is irreversible. If you think of it in this way, then it becomes a really powerful image; but if you think that the exile can be repatriated—find a home—well, that's not what I'm talking about. If you think of exile as a permanent state, however, both in the literal and in the intellectual sense, then it's a much more promising, if difficult, thing. Then you're really talking about movement, about homelessness in the sense in which Lukács talks about it in *The Theory of the Novel*—'transcendental homelessness'—which can acquire a particular intellectual mission that I associate with criticism" (7–8).

proof that the critic is not implicated in either repression or normality, but this rhetoric also represents the critic as exclusive and different when compared to ordinary mortals.

In this characterization, Said is certainly not alone. A moral defensiveness pervades the definition of the critic's character in almost every major thinker on the current scene. Each tries to capture an aura of innocence and moral disinterestedness by cultivating personal marginality. Lévi-Strauss uses the idea of *dépaysement* to characterize the anthropologist. Foucault allies himself with the outcasts of history. Derrida appropriates Rousseau's rhetoric of marginality to develop a theory of linguistic difference that enacts a kind of morality play dependent on Rousseau's ideas of human equality and difference. Paul de Man builds on this tradition by securing with the greatest force the special ethical power that modern thought attributes to the role of the exile and victim. De Man's rhetoric ensures a perfect ethical system at an enormous cost to his idea of the critic. At the level of theory, he condones a radical idea of meaning in which the human is erased. At the level of practice, his critic attains an ethical status by embracing a logic of martyrdom, in which one turns against oneself in a gesture of moral sacrifice and self-denunciation. The theories of Nietzsche and Girard often reveal the religious and philosophical contexts of this victimary position and work to represent, with various degrees of success and failure, those strategies of willing and knowledge that oppose unconsiousness and resentful emotions. But both thinkers tend to represent the critical consciousness as exiled or marginal. Only feminist criticism, to my knowledge, has foreseen the dangers of turning marginality and suffering into a commodity or privileged claim to critical insight. The character of the feminist critic is in the main keenly and self-consciously balanced between the desire for difference and the hope of equality.

Literature is a human activity, and the character of criticism must remain as resolutely human. The power of marginality in the modern world is an inescapable fact, but this power is purchased at an enormous expense by modern critics. It places criticism in the margins of life. It expels literature as an undervalued and flawed manner of thinking, if it gives literature the status of thought at all. A marginal position may be converted into a sensational claim for literature and the critic, but its value is highly suspicious in the final analysis. It cloaks itself in mystical language to achieve a distance from the real issues of living and choosing in the world. But, in fact, living and choosing in the human world are the only true subjects of literature.

I do not deny that these essays express great concern over the ethical choices made by modern theorists, but this book is not an exposé aimed at the so-called immoral practices of critics. Its purpose remains more subtle and positive, working to examine to what extent a selected group of theorists contributes to a definition of ethical thought. No critic here detracts from this project, no matter how severe the polemics against him or her may seem. Indeed, there is finally a question whether anyone on the current scene conceives of a criticism that is not ethical. Only ethics effectively reveals the coherence implicit in the diversity of critical approaches today. Far from being a battleground of contesting ideologies, modern literary theory comprises a united front when it comes to the importance given to the ethics of criticism. There is something hopeful in that thought, and, without being sentimental, we may consider its promise.

2

Ethical Criticism: From Plato to Pluralism

If there is any agreement among literary theorists today, it may be the common observation that modern criticism is in a state of crisis.[1] According to René Wellek, literary criticism entered a state of crisis in 1914. Paul de Man fixes on 1970 as the date when Continental influences pushed critical theory into chaos. Apparently, criticism has been in crisis throughout its history. The opening manifesto of the *Stanford Literature Review* traces the origin of the present crisis to the time of Plato, and indeed Plato is often named as the beginning of our current anxieties in literary theory. What kind of crisis endures for so many years? Can a crisis be one with the tradition itself?

A crisis is a state of affairs subject to little internal coherence or consistency, unless it be the order of disorder itself. It is a period of violent instability that threatens either to shift toward another

1. Concerning the relation between criticism and crisis, see Reinhart Koselleck, *Kritik und Krise* (Feiburg: Verlag Karl Alber, 1959); René Wellek, "The Crisis of Comparative Literature," *Concepts of Criticism* (New Haven: Yale University Press, 1963), pp. 282–95; Paul de Man, "Criticism and Crisis," *Blindness and Insight* (1971; reprint, Minneapolis: University of Minnesota Press, 1983), pp. 3–19; John Freccero, René Girard, and Alphonse Juilland, Foreword, *Stanford Literature Review* 1.2 (1984): 157–58; and William E. Cain, *The Crisis in Criticism* (Baltimore: Johns Hopkins University Press, 1984).

chaotic state or to reach a state of resolution. For a crisis to be resolved, the proper pressure, the proper decision, must be applied within the untoward state of affairs. Even if one conceives of order and disorder as relative terms, or defines disorder as the dynamic passage between states of order, a question of perception still arises: how does a crisis remain in a perpetual state of crisis?

One way of addressing the apparent contradiction is to recognize that the crisis in literary theory is defined around the nature of criticism itself. The word "criticism," of course, derives from the Greek *krinein*, which means to cut, to separate, to divide, and to distinguish. On the one hand, criticism in its capacity to separate and divide would seem to be the traditional antidote to states of crisis, not the cause of disorder and lack of distinctions. It is only when the critical nature of criticism disappears that it may be said to be in crisis, for crisis turns upon the lack of those differences that criticism exists to create. In other words, criticism robbed of its differentiating talent falls into crisis. On the other hand, the current crisis in theory may have less to do with the ability to make critical decisions than with the suspicion of decision itself. Modern theory seems too aware of the relation between "criticism" and "cutting," and literary theorists have come increasingly to see critical decisions as the result of power and violence. Critical distinctions appear too arbitrary for modern tastes, and we have learned to suspect that arbitrariness conceals self-interest and aggressive willfulness. This is not an idle observation. The perception that criticism is violent is crucial to the ethics of criticism because it marks the point where literary theory and the ethical tradition begin to ask the same questions about the nature of human beings and their capacity for violence. Indeed, that the crisis of criticism derives in part from an ethical reaction to the perceived violence of the critical act reveals to what extent literary criticism and moral philosophy have a common history.

But the fact that literary criticism has an ethical dimension should shock more than it does. The wealth of critical literature on ethics and the familiarity of the problem make it easy to ignore what a philosophical puzzle is involved in the simple phrase "ethical criticism." From one point of view, there is nothing extraordinary about it, for literary criticism has been seen, ever since Plato, as serving moral philosophy. To speak of ethical criticism, however, is to fall into either redundancy or oxymoron, and as such, literary criticism does enter crisis with Plato. Either literary criticism is seen as a branch of ethics, one of the many disciplines used by ethics to exert control over different areas of thought, or criticism exists at odds with ethical requirements in its quest to chart poetic form not within the ethical domain of truth but within the strange and elusive domain of fiction. In the first case, criticism obeys the imperatives of ethics to keep literature within the bounds of moral integrity. Ethics and criticism are synonymous, and to call criticism ethical is repetitious. In the second case, criticism strives to diverge from ethical requirements to establish its own identity and objectives and to invent a unique standard of literary content and form. Here, to call criticism ethical is to commit the most perverse of oxymorons, for criticism and ethics are antonymous. Ethics is supposed to be concerned with justice, and criticism is most banal and predictable when it makes judicial claims, even in the form of poetic justice. Indeed, the moral philosopher should be threatened, or at least deeply embarrassed, by the literary critic's allegiance to fiction.

Is there not a profound error in the idea that literary criticism discovers its own nature by adhering to ethical requirements? Literary theory has tended of late to answer this question in the affirmative. The view that literary criticism is subject to ethical demands has acted within recent critical history more and more as a challenge to literary theorists to put an end to the situation. In modern times, the history of literary study almost always represents this challenge in a particular way. Criticism and literature are to be liberated from morality to ensure the freedom of the literary imagination and to allow literature to pursue the path most suitable for its individual and special development. The attack on historical and biographical criticism by the American New Critics, for example, never failed to give as its rationalization the necessity of freeing literature from the demands of external forces. The familiar opposition between "extrinsic" and "intrinsic" criticism takes for granted that literary and nonliterary standards need to be divided. Indeed, the study of "literariness" has been identified as the true object of criticism by thinkers from the most opposing schools. René Wellek defines comparative literature as the discipline that pursues the problem of literariness across national boundaries, leaving behind the narrow view of comparative literature as a study of influences between two or more countries or national authors. Jonathan Culler similarly concludes in "American Critical Debate" that "criticism advances by becoming increasingly formalistic, as linguistics does" (5); and Paul de Man states with authority that criticism pursues the study of letters and not of mankind.[2]

No doubt criticism seeks the freedom to cut its unique path. But "freedom" is not a neutral term; it belongs to the ethical tradition. To understand the crisis of criticism, one must ask from what criticism seeks to be liberated. If it seeks freedom from ethics, what is it about ethics that is so disturbing? And if modern ethics exists to guarantee freedom, equality, and nonviolence, should not ethics pit itself against the very elements that literary criticism finds disturbing in ethics? It grows apparent that the critical act does not lead to an exit from ethics at all.[3] Rather, the idea of criticism strikes to the heart of an ethical crisis concerning the nature of ethics. The rebellion of criticism against ethics belongs to the struggle of ethics with itself. The ethical substance of moral philosophy has come to be an element of scandal and a source of crisis, and critical theory today shares this element of scandal with ethics.

To chart the opposition of ethics to ethics would mean writing a history of moral philosophy. Here I can propose only a brief

2. Jonathan Culler, "Issues in Contemporary American Critical Debate," in *American Criticism in the Poststructuralist Age,* ed. Ira Konigsberg (Ann Arbor: University of Michigan Press, 1981), pp. 1–18. The paraphrase of de Man is from Stephen Greenblatt, ed., *Allegory and Representation* (Baltimore: Johns Hopkins University Press, 1981), p. viii.

3. See Murray Krieger's historical survey "In the Wake of Morality: The Thematic Underside of Recent Theory," *New Literary History* 15.1 (1983): 119–36. Krieger argues that no one on the current scene escapes membership in the "moral gang." Note also that this issue of *New Literary History* is devoted to "Literature and/as Moral Philosophy."

and necessarily incomplete overview that seeks to expose, from a literary point of view, how the critical enters the ethical, how the ethical enters the critical, and how each has tried through various means to rid itself of the other. Remarkably, each one tries to eliminate what it finds most disturbing in itself under the name of the other, and what distresses both about each other is a certain collusion with violence. In effect, ethics expels its ethical substance as the violence of critical judgment, and criticism struggles to free itself of its own violence by rejecting ethics.

Historical surveys tend to suggest exceptions more often than the rule, and I intend my remarks not as a survey of historical moments but as an overview of some case histories in which the interference between ethics and criticism is especially acute. Plato, of course, stands at the center of the debate concerning the validity of associating ethics and criticism; indeed, the history of his reception duplicates the history of the debate on ethical criticism. Those moral philosophers interested in literature as well as the great literary defenders of poetry have sought traditionally to reinterpret Plato or to use his arguments for their own purposes. This explains in part why Plato is often named as the origin of the crisis in criticism. Yet Plato did not believe that criticism was in crisis. He believed that literature and the arts were in crisis. Literature invites a pluralistic stance that threatens political regime, and consequently the moral philosopher takes a firm hold on critical tools for the purpose of making the adjustments necessary to enforce the civil requirements of justice and to bring poetry into agreement with the moral strictures of the city. Literary criticism is for Plato the unreluctant enforcer of ethical principles, and it ensures that literature provides only positive models of behavior. In fact, literary criticism remains so dependent on ethics in Plato that we speak only with difficulty of a Platonic literary theory. Historians of criticism generally agree that literary theory begins only with Aristotle.

Although Plato's argument is well known and often repeated, it apparently holds little persuasive power for the modern reader, who is inclined to see Plato's remarks on poetry and government as tyrannical. Part of the issue of ethical criticism will be to reflect on this peculiarly modern perception, and I will return to the problem. It is surprising to note, however, how little Plato's totalitarian leanings have been used against him within the tradition of poetic defense. Most of the great defenses of poetry struggle to redeem poetry within the rules set by Plato's argument. Few conceive of dismissing Plato's rejection of the poet purely on the ethical grounds that the gesture is violent and repressive.[4]

Despite the modern perception of Plato, however, his argument has no equal in its ethical influence on critical method and poetic defense. The *Republic* best demonstrates the Platonic method of practical criticism.[5] In Plato's eyes, poetry is savagely chaotic and a definite threat to the order of the republic. By encouraging acting, impersonation, and pretense to science, it imperils the Delphic wisdom of knowing oneself. Literature entices citizens to play more than one role, destroying the possibility of justice. For Plato's idea of justice depends on the neat prescription that one person have one responsibility: "justice is keeping what is properly one's own and doing one's own job. . . . Suppose a builder and a shoemaker tried to exchange jobs, or to take on the tools and the prestige of each other's trade, or suppose alternatively the same man tried to do both jobs, would this and other exchanges of the kind do great harm to the state? . . . I think you'll agree that this sort of mutual interchange and interference spells destruction to our state" (5.434).

Plato repeatedly described drama and poetry in terms of their ability to bring disorder into the order of the state. Acting especially has disastrous effects: "it is unsuitable for our state, because there one man does one job and does not play two or a multiplicity of roles" (3.397e). Plato genuinely feared artistic mimesis, as René Girard has argued, because he believed that it tempts people to appropriate each other's roles and invites com-

4. See Karl Popper, *The Open Society and Its Enemies*, 2 vols. (Princeton: At the University Press, 1966). To my knowledge, Popper is the first to remark the similarities between Plato's idea of the state and totalitarianism. His book, written in the shadow of World War II, is a remarkable example of how historical events influence different interpretations of philosophical and literary works, for Plato was usually associated, before Popper, with utopian views of government.

5. Plato, *Republic*, trans. Desmond Lee (New York: Penguin, 1974).

petition and violence.[6] Representation is, in fact, a mirror on the rampage, duplicating and reproducing its surroundings until nothing but chaos remains: "take a mirror and turn it round in all directions; before long you will create sun and stars and earth, yourself and all other animals and plants, and furniture and the other objects we mentioned just now" (10.596e).

When Plato expelled the poets from his republic, his intention was to eliminate social violence. This aspect of Plato's enterprise is rarely emphasized because it lies concealed beneath his allegories. The philosophical tradition interested in epistemology has ignored the ethical implications of Plato's expulsion of poetry and interpreted it in terms of the argument against inspiration and for true knowledge. Similarly, the Platonic equation between justice in the state and in the individual has encouraged moral philosophy to stress the idea of mental rather than social conflict, even though Plato described the antagonism between the three parts of the soul with the metaphor of "civil war." Each part of the soul, like each class in the republic, must adhere to its own role if order is to survive. No part of the soul may pretend to be another or challenge another's authority. In short, Plato's ethical and aesthetic philosophies are one. He reads Homer in the same manner that he reads society, and his final objectives, the good and the beautiful, reveal in their absolute natures to what degree Platonic philosophy serves an ethico-aesthetic ambition. What is ultimately most striking about Plato, however, is that he is more successful as a literary critic than as a social reformer. His most extended examples of what does not belong to proper conduct are based either on literary works or on analyses of political "characters."

The great question introduced by Plato is why does ethical theory continually represent social conflict in literary terms? How does literary criticism's view of literary form become an extended "allegory" for the ethical struggle with social violence and disorder? The great paradox of Plato, and it is the paradox with which both moral philosophy and literary criticism will

6. See Girard's reading of Plato in *Des choses cachées depuis la fondation du monde* (Paris: Grasset, 1978), pp. 15–18.

never cease struggling, springs from the fact that ethics expresses its concern with the violence of society in literary forms, but then rejects literature as "violent." The opposition of ethics to literature becomes a bewildered attempt to reject its own efforts to formulate a coherent ethical theory. This is why the solution to Plato is not to strip away his poetic allegories to reveal political conflicts. To expel Plato's allegory for an ethical purpose is to repeat the Platonic gesture par excellence.

Although Aristotle did not argue for an unethical criticism, he was perhaps the first to lead literary theory away from the requirements of ethical form. I do not mean to give Aristotle Kantian motivations. Aristotle's separation of ethics and literary theory attempts to undo the paradox of ethical criticism: he divided ethics and criticism so that ethics might take advantage of its literary formulations without having to judge them at the same time. But Aristotle's gesture remains incomplete, and comparing the ethics of the *Poetics* to that of the *Nicomachean Ethics*, as has been the practice of classicists recently, suggests an unusual interplay. Whereas the *Nicomachean Ethics* stresses that moral agents must aim for a mean in their conduct, Aristotle argues in the *Poetics* that the best tragedies include characters who are unable to avoid committing a murder. Tragedy fails, in Aristotle's estimation, when characters intend to do evil and reverse themselves at the last minute. Aristotle, unlike Plato, was interested in literary characters who miss the mark (*hamartia*) in their pursuit of moral excellence, and this emphasis appears to keep poetry and ethics on separate ground. The obvious exception to the rule is Aristotle's praise for the ethical plot of the *Iphigenia*, in which a recognition prevents a human sacrifice, but Aristotle's esteem for the play is not matched by equal weight in his argument, and, in the final analysis, it is *Oedipus the King*, the drama of fateful violence, that serves to define tragedy. The tragic hero, it seems, is doomed to fall short of the standard of moderation required by the *Nicomachean Ethics*, and Aristotle, like Plato, ends by defining literature as ethically troublesome. The point is not, however, that ethics and criticism have nothing in common or that Aristotle considers tragedy an unethical form. The point remains that the complicated statements of literary forms do contribute to moral philosophy because they present it with an example with which to test its laws as well as an instance of practice and particularity to temper the generalities of ethical theory.[7]

Moral philosophy in Aristotle tries not to expel its own theories in the form of literary judgments, but to retain its literary formulations in their most antithetical and threatening forms within the scope of moral philosophy. Literature, for Aristotle, reveals the instability of human existence and the difficulty of living morally in such a world. Aristotle's approach was decidedly anti-Platonic, but his goals were not. Aristotle's purpose was to discover a series of limits in order to guarantee the integrity of the city and to protect citizens from both outside and inside violence. That he refused, however, to banish literature, despite its apparently conflictual character, that he established literature as an instrument for judicial contemplation, opened the humanistic age of ethics, in which ethics advances toward the possibility of a political rather than a transcendental formation. Literature exists as the other of ethics within the boundaries of the state, and it acts continually as a reminder to moral philosophy of the need to question itself.

The classicists, who stress this interplay, have been led to suggest another interpretation of Aristotle's theory of catharsis.[8] Catharsis does not strive to purge those emotions that threaten the ethical stability of the city. Tragedy presents the city with its own political and ethical flaws in an act of clarification and self-definition, and it is this all-too-human nature that the population both fears and pities. Tragedy focuses on the political dimension of ethics. It reveals that standards of justice are the products of political decisions and not of ideal forms, thereby making it possible to debate those standards of justice.

7. Gerald Else, in *Aristotle's Poetics: The Argument* (Cambridge, Mass.: Harvard University Press, 1957), attempts to merge Aristotle's ethics and poetics, highlighting the *Iphigenia* in particular because it rewards good characters. More recently, Kathy Eden has proposed a reading of the *Poetics* that discloses Aristotle's judicial idea of tragedy. See Kathy Eden, *Poetic and Legal Fiction in the Aristotelian Tradition* (Princeton: At the University Press, 1986), pp. 25–61.

8. See the remarks on catharsis in Martha C. Nussbaum, *The Fragility of Goodness* (Cambridge: At the University Press, 1986), pp. 378–94.

And yet for all of Aristotle's achievement, and his opposition to Plato, he ends by separating ethics and literary theory, if only for the purpose of holding them together. Modern scholars may struggle to merge his ethics and poetics, but we do not know that he undertook the task himself, and his separation of poetic making and moral practice ends by affirming within the history of literary criticism not an Aristotelian but a Platonic solution: ethics and criticism join only in the mutual effort to banish each other.

In summary, then, only a minor difference exists between the combination of ethics and literary criticism by Plato and Aristotle. For Plato, literature served to promote a positive view of ethical behavior. For Aristotle, it provides the "flaw," the negative example, upon which judgment and moderation are to be based. Classical literary theory is therefore defined as the discipline that systematically collects the guidelines by which literature either enforces or contradicts ethical laws with a view to strengthening moral philosophy's vision of itself. In either case, literary criticism is deprived of an ethical substance. It has little creative role in the founding of ethical principles. Rather, its ethical motivations are supplied and judged by philosophy.

With Kant, however, ethics enters the age of criticism. Kant's critical ethics brings together critical and moral philosophy in a single objective: the resolution of conflict. Kant's project takes three forms. First, criticism, as Kant defined it, intervenes within the philosophical tradition as a means of breaking the long-standing opposition between dogmatism and skepticism. It works to bring controversy to an end by detecting its sources and presuppositions. Second, the application of practical reason, or the ethical, is designed to resolve the conflicts implicit in ethical choice. Finally, Kant worked to resolve the conflict between ethics and aesthetics. In *The Critique of Judgement*, he departed from the classical tradition by giving aesthetics a creative role within the practice of ethics, for "Beauty is the symbol of morality" (§59).[9] The accent must be placed on the word

9. Immanuel Kant, *The Critique of Judgement*, trans. James Creed Meredith (Oxford: At the University Press, 1957). My reading of Kant draws inspiration from Hannah Arendt, *Lectures on Kant's Political Philosophy* (Chicago: At the

"symbol," as Ernst Cassirer understood, because art affects morality in purely representational terms.

If Plato and Aristotle described literature in its capacity to symbolize violence and competition, Kant broke with them by making literature the symbol of freedom. In Kantian philosophy, literature creates its own domain and elevates it above the clash of the world. The freer the work of art, the richer it is for taste. For "*Taste* is," Kant explained, "the faculty of estimating an object or a mode of representation by means of a delight or aversion *apart from any interest*" (§5). Literature excites the idea of a world free of interest, competition, and violence, and as such, it provides the image of the goal toward which ethics should strive. Only literature captures the inscrutability of the idea of freedom upon which the entire program of Kant's moral philosophy rests.

Kant's aesthetics and ethics always return to the idea of freedom, for the paradoxical "duty" of art is to provide the ideal image of autonomy to the willing subject. Kant's emphasis on freedom demonstrates the degree to which he departed from Plato's vision of society, even though he stressed his debt to Platonic idealism. Kant differed from Plato in holding that the freedom of art no longer risks introducing chaos into the governing body, but instead designs the model for a world of free personalities, a republic of self-sufficient subjects purposively united. For Kant, art is the production of freedom by freedom, not the lie of inspired and insipid poets; it designs the ideal form of ethical practice. Most important, Kant's idea of beauty cannot exist, as Plato's and Aristotle's can, within the totalitarian state. In Plato especially, literature is denounced because it introduces a frightening plurality into his hierarchical regime. Contrarily, Kant required that "pluralism" be part of the state, but he defined it not in terms of a multiplicity of interpretations, as modern literary critics do, but in purely human terms. Pluralism, as

Kant explained in his *Anthropology*, represents the attitude of not being occupied with oneself as the whole world but regarding and conducting oneself as a citizen of the world.

Kant's idea of pluralism is inseparable from his anthropology. His moral philosophy demands a radical anthropology because he refused to conceive of freedom apart from human activity and willing. Freedom in Kant always refers to human liberty, not to a freedom of objects or interpretations. Kant proceeded from the nature of the human, and his critical philosophy assumes that nature provides the conditions of possibility for ethical freedom and action. Similarly, human nature guarantees aesthetic communication by ensuring that all people share an equal capacity for experience. Kant required that judgments of taste be valid not egotistically but pluralistically. Art cannot exist without morality, most significantly because beauty is communicable only provided that there is human equality or, as Kant expressed it, "the subjective conditions of this faculty of aesthetic judgement are identical with all men" (§38). The universal communicability of taste requires the human context that Kant called "universal subjectivity," that is, the common ground of cognition and autonomy shared equally by all individuals.

Kant's idea of freedom, in both the ethical and the aesthetic senses, depends on the ability to make impartial judgments. The categorical imperative legislates that personal interest cannot become the rule for general ethical conduct. One may universalize one's desires only if they are in everyone's interest because truly selfish interests once universalized would destroy personal freedom once and for all. If thieves present their behavior as a universal code of conduct, for example, they guarantee that others will steal their goods, and private property will cease to exist. Similarly, aesthetic judgment requires complete impartiality of interest. "Every interest," Kant concluded, "vitiates the judgement of taste and robs it of its impartiality" (§13). If an object of contemplation has a personal interest for the judge, it cannot be defined as beautiful. Both aesthetics and ethics require human beings to renounce purely individual interests in favor of universal principles.

What is at issue in Kant's description of aesthetic impartiality?

It is again a matter of freedom from social violence, for Kant was interested in describing how freedom places constraints upon itself. At the most fundamental level, the renunciation of personal interest acts to defer conflict over objects. Here Kant returns to his classical origins. Plato expelled artistic representation because he associated it with an excessive freedom and disorder; he believed that art encourages citizens to compete over roles and responsibilities. The difference remains, however, that Plato laid the foundations of totalitarianism by assuming that some individuals have a superior knowledge of how a people's freedom must be limited in order to free them from personal interests. Kant held that the universal interest of free subjects dictates naturally which personal interests have to be sacrificed in the interest of freedom.

The problem of moral and aesthetic disinterest, however, does introduce a paradox into Kant's critical ethics. The categorical imperative demands that personal interest be renounced for the sake of ethical conduct; yet the realm of moral practice is ultimately one of interest, albeit common interest, because its objective is perpetual peace. A similar problem arises in matters of taste because aesthetic disinterest eventually implies the intervention of moral interest. At first glance, the satisfaction that determines taste seems devoid of interest, for Kant concluded that any judgment tinged by the slightest interest will be partial. Beauty possesses a purely symbolic purpose based on the "analogy" between ethical and aesthetic autonomy. It exists to give the pleasure of freedom that is universally communicable without being based in concepts, and literature must remain free of moral demands if it is to fulfill its promise. Nevertheless, aesthetic judgment cannot escape a certain interest because aesthetic disinterest symbolizes the moral freedom in which humanity places the greatest hope. The paradox can be summarized as follows. Literature represents the image and conditions of possibility for the ethical, but it must be isolated from morality in practice to remain the image of the ethical. Simply put, literary criticism must expel morality to guarantee the ethical purity of literature.

Ethics cannot be practical if it relies on the fact of freedom. To have any value, however, moral philosophy must be practical, and therefore its purest elements must be compromised to have any impact in the world of human action. Kant's solution to the paradox remained purely symbolic, and it has received varied acceptance by subsequent thinkers. Kant once more relied on the creative dimension of art to disclose a new path. He argued that the paradoxical designs of ethics are united in the feeling of art: in the free play of the powers of the mind, nature appears to the perceiver *as if* it were a work of freedom. The solution is only an image, an aesthetic judgment, but it allows individuals to pass into teleological judgment and a synthesis of ends. The end is the mental principle of union that judgment applies to the totality of experience. It manifests itself in the idea of a formal purposiveness in nature and in art. The concept of something that is its own end, however, belongs purely to the idea of freedom, not to the realm of nature. Only aesthetic judgment permits us to transform nature into the image of freedom, into the hypothesis of freedom's conditions of possibility. The "peculiar causality" of the end in itself designs the circle of the will's freedom, but Kant allowed art to share in that freedom; and in the fact that freedom belongs to willing and art uniquely lies the unity upon which Kant based his hopes for the emergence of his "culture of moral feeling."

Influenced strongly by Kant's claim for art, the Romantic generation gave literature an even more creative role in ethical understanding. Poetic language serves as the instrument through which the Romantic poet teaches others the essential moral nature of mankind.[10] Two problems arise, however, with the Ro-

---

10. In *A Defence of Poetry*, Shelley insisted that "poetry acts to produce the moral improvement of man" (487). Although Shelley broke with Plato in his essential description of poetic inspiration as false, he realized the potential for moral education that Plato ascribed to literature. To reconcile his allegiance to Plato and to Rousseau's democratic ideals, he inverted Plato and gave literature the moral capacity to envision human equality and freedom. In this regard, the Romantic love of metaphor becomes a cipher for the democratic ideal of equality. In the *Defence*, Shelley claimed that early human language was vitally metaphorical, serving to mark the "before unapprehended relations of things" (482). Shelley's definition of "relations" is essentially democratic. "Relations" means "similitudes," what Bacon referred to as "the same footsteps of nature impressed upon the various subjects of the world" (482). And these "relations"—in the largest

mantic project. As creators of poetic language, poets risk isolating themselves from their equals as either hierophants or martyrs to a holy cause. The uniqueness of genius, which Kant counterbalanced with the common sense of taste, proves an attractive temptation for the aspiring poet, and the majority of Romantic poets made a point of remarking that their special gifts set them apart from others. The cult of the artist undermines the principles of equality and freedom whose cause first stirred the poetic imagination of the nineteenth century. As Schiller expressed it in *On the Aesthetic Education of Man*, poets metamorphose through their craft and return to their own age as alien figures, not to gladden it, but to cleanse it.[11]

---

sense, human relations—afford the motives of equality, diversity, unity, contrast, and mutual dependence according to which human beings act and will within society. The great secret of morals and poetry is love, because Shelley's idea of love realizes the essence of relation: love is in his mind "a going out of our own nature, and an identification of ourselves with the beautiful which exists in thought, action, or person, not our own" (487). Wordsworth, in the Preface to the *Lyrical Ballads* (1800), similarly ascribes the pleasure received by the mind from metric language to the perception of "similitude in dissimilitude" and the reverse. This perception, Wordsworth believed, is the great spring of the human mind, enlivening sexual appetite, human conversation, and moral feelings. Love and metaphor in Romantic theory provide mankind with the moral sympathy necessary to find identity in difference and to stand in another's place. If poets are the unacknowledged legislators of the world, it is because they enact with their art and language the fundamental principles of a free social existence. It is only a matter, as Shelley said, of stripping away the "temporary dress" of the poet's creations to discover "the eternal proportions of their beauty" (487). See Percy Bysshe Shelley, "A Defence of Poetry," in *Shelley's Poetry and Prose*, ed. Donald H. Reiman and Sharon B. Powers (New York: Norton, 1977), pp. 478–510.

11. Schiller's *On the Aesthetic Education of Man* is often named as using Kant wrongly to enshrine art, but Schiller's inclinations were largely those of his contemporaries. Schiller gave aesthetics an even more active role in ethics than did Kant, arguing that mankind must pass through the aesthetic condition, from the sensual, to reach the ethical. Literature restores mankind to itself after the fall. It reintroduces human beings to freedom, for Schiller believed that "Art is a daughter of Freedom" (26). Most important, beauty is not merely a symbol of freedom, as Kant described it; "it is through Beauty," Schiller explained, "that we arrive at Freedom" (27). The risk in imposing any moral system remains that it may destroy the plurality of nature: the essential equality of people that the Romantics associated with emotional compatibility, human sympathy, and the nature of sensibility. Schiller's solution was to propose that literature has the ability to mediate between the two distinct realms of nature and culture by

The second danger to the Romantic ethical project concerns poetic language itself. As language acquires greater power to embody the ethical, it also assumes greater responsibility for moral success and failure. If language partakes of the moral, it can be guilty of spreading immorality, and here the Platonic theory of poetry receives a renewed vigor. Wordsworth, for example, admitted with many others that the violence of his day revitalized poetic language, but he felt increasingly guilty that his poetry took substance and inspiration from the power of violence. In "Upon Epitaphs (3)," Wordsworth confessed that "words are too awful an instrument for good and evil, to be trifled with; they hold above all other external powers a dominion over thoughts. . . . Language, if it do not uphold, and feed, and leave in quiet, like the power of gravitation or the air we breathe, is a counter-spirit, unremittingly and noiselessly at work, to subvert, to lay waste, to vitiate, and to dissolve" (129–30).[12] Just as the unique genius of poets (à la Plato) makes them responsible for the immorality of their work, the awful instrument of language exerts a special duty in ethical affairs. Language in Romantic theories possesses the capacity to vitiate and reorient thought, and it must be used responsibly if its potential for violence is not to be unleashed on human society.

The Romantic shift from moral action to language is admittedly subtle, but it has an enormous impact nevertheless. It prepares the way for the importance given by some modern philosophers and literary critics to language over human action. In twentieth-century Anglo-American philosophy—in the work of C. L. Stevenson, for instance—the idea of linguistic autonomy supports the belief that moral philosophers may discuss only the language of ethics, not conduct itself. Similarly, literary critics have tended to interpret the autonomy of literature not as a symbol of ethical freedom but as a property of literary repre-

---

lending to the unity of physical society the plurality of nature. See Friedrich Schiller, *On the Aesthetic Education of Man*, trans. Julius A. Elias (New York: Frederick Ungar, 1965).

12. William Wordsworth, "Upon Epitaphs (3)," in *Wordsworth's Literary Criticism*, ed. Nowell C. Smith (Oxford: At the University Press, 1925), pp. 123–43.

sentation. The famous gap between the signifier and signified discovered by semiology ensures the belief that language is distinct from other phenomena. Among the New Critics and poststructuralists in particular, the principle of linguistic autonomy underlies the special status given to "poetry" and "textuality" and contributes to the idea that no form of language can be grounded in external phenomena.

The shift between human and literary autonomy is a peculiar feature of both modern ethics and literary criticism, and it derives its strength from the emerging importance of language as the interpretive category of modern thought. Most important, the shift ends by radically altering Kant's idea of pluralism, robbing it of its human context and transforming it into an issue of language. Indeed, the worse offense that one can commit today is to ground a literary interpretation in an anthropological bias. Nevertheless, the fact that linguistic autonomy and plurality in interpretation are defended with such moral enthusiasm suggests that they may yet carry the symbolism that Kant afforded them. Even among the most strident opponents of ethical criticism, the fight to preserve the autonomy of literature from morality can be justified only if it furthers the ends of ethics.

Before I turn to the current view of ethical criticism, however, it is necessary to consider Nietzsche's contribution to the notion of pluralism because it had a profound effect on ethics in general. Nietzsche transformed the notion of pluralism into precisely what Kant most abhorred: the idea of being preoccupied with oneself as the whole world. In Nietzsche's world, autonomy and ethics exclude each other, and the human race is composed of a plurality of radical individuals in which each person struggles with every other in a contest of wills. Moral language obeys the will to power; it is nothing but a system of representations intended to conceal emotions and to manipulate other people. Similarly, literature exists to express power and hardly differs from morality.

Since everything, in Nietzsche's view, has a common source in the will to power, he had no reason to oppose criticism and ethics. Nietzsche's singular view of metaphysics has been called an inverted Platonism, and he certainly seems to have applied

Plato's view of literature to ethics. Now ethical theory, not poetry, represents the lie of those drunk with the desire for power. Ethics is a system of inspired falsehoods designed to reverse the natural order of human might and to give power to those who possess neither real knowledge nor merit. Nietzsche may have inverted Plato, but he did not dispute that literature is largely immoral. The surprise is that Nietzsche believed that literature expresses, by virtue of its immorality, the only truth possible, that is, the untruth of ethical language. Thus literature frees itself from ethics at last by discounting ethics as mere literature.

It is currently fashionable to credit Nietzsche as the philosopher who exposed the metaphorical nature of ethical truths. Poststructuralist theorists return habitually to his essay "On Truth and Lie in the Extra-Moral Sense" to debunk the will to truth as mere anthropomorphism. Apparently, for them, Nietzsche makes it possible to pass beyond Kant's anthropological emphasis by discovering the primacy of language in human history. But Nietzsche's preoccupation with language was limited; he had literary pretensions to be sure, especially for his style, but his principal interest was ethics and not literature. Nor did Nietzsche dismiss the anthropological context, as many wish to claim. His philosophy is notorious precisely because he refused to abandon the anthropological definition of pluralism. Pluralism, for Nietzsche, refers to the inescapable isolation of every person from every other and to the inexorable need of all persons to transform themselves into gods. Nietzsche's description of the will to power derives both its great originality and its horror from the fact that he pushes human selfishness to its limit. His vision of human society is pessimistic because he cannot conceive of any form of social agreement that would not serve violence and repression. The natural result is Nietzsche's theory of the overman, a superhuman individual who regulates his desires and behavior not for the sake of others or under the compulsion of social contract but for his own satisfaction.

Modern ethics and literary criticism both preserve Nietzsche's view of pluralism, but they blind themselves to its most dreadful aspects. They accomplish the task, as I noted, largely by interpreting pluralism as a linguistic rather than human category.

The emotivists, for example, agree with Nietzsche that moral language exists only to vent emotions and to manipulate other people. Not being sufficiently Nietzschean, however, they conclude that moral language is too irrational to merit analysis. Modern critical theorists define pluralism as a literary or linguistic property, and, like Nietzsche, they view it as an expression of autonomy. Since they isolate language from its social context, however, they fail to see the inadequacy of their linguistic view of pluralism.

What lies behind the modern tendency to equate ethical behavior and linguistic pluralism? It relates in its most profound aspects to the struggle of ethics with itself over the issue of social violence. In "The Ethics of Linguistics," Julia Kristeva, although a believer in linguistic pluralism, gives a remarkably clear description of the view of ethics current in literary criticism.[13] Ethics today must take as its primary aim the dissolution of the form of ethics associated with repression and violence:

> Ethics used to be a coercive, customary manner of ensuring the cohesiveness of a particular group though the repetition of a code—a more or less accepted apologue. Now, however, the issue of ethics crops up wherever a code (mores, social contract) must be shattered in order to give way to the free play of negativity, need, desire, pleasure, and jouissance, before being put together again, although temporarily and with full knowledge of what is involved. Fascism and Stalinism stand for the barriers that the new adjustment between a law and its transgression comes against. (23)

Kristeva's political motives are stronger than those of the other pluralists present on the current scene. Nevertheless, she still

13. Julia Kristeva, "The Ethics of Linguistics," *Desire in Language*, trans. Thomas Gora, Alice Jardine, and Leon S. Roudiez (New York: Columbia University Press, 1980), pp. 23–35. This essay is not, however, a definitive statement of Kristeva's position. Elsewhere, for example, Kristeva departs slightly from her dependence on marginal ethics, expressing concern that marginality, especially that of women, is easily exploited by totalitarianism. But she still concludes that only a knowledge of the relativity of symbolic and biological existence poses an alternative to an ethics whose essence is largely sacrificial. See "Women's Time," trans. Alice Jardine and Harry Blake, in *Feminist Theory: A Critique of Ideology*, ed. Nannerl O. Keohane, Michelle Z. Rosaldo, and Barbara C. Gelpi (Chicago: At the University Press, 1981, 1982), pp. 31–54.

defines ethics linguistically, making language the source of pluralism as such. To arrive at a "linguistic ethics," literary criticism must be deflected "toward a consideration of language as articulation of a heterogeneous process" (24). For Kristeva, heterogeneity, another term for pluralism, resides primarily in poetic language, a language that frees marginal, negative, and destructive causalities. The silent causalities of poetic language subvert repressive social regimes, exploding totalitarian structures and rigid models for daily existence. Traditionally, "coercive ethics" struggles to kill poetic language to achieve its stability. "Consequently," writes Kristeva, "we have this Platonistic acknowledgment on the eve of Stalinism and fascism: a (any) society may be stabilized only if it excludes poetic language" (31).

Kristeva's description of the struggle of ethics with itself differs from current opinion only to the extent that she states openly the political dimension of her choices. Her moral and political choice is to take the side of poetic language against society as such, and her apology for poetry consists of dismissing Plato's expulsion of the poet as a fascist gesture. For Kristeva opposes poetic language explicitly to murder, death, and unchanging society. Nevertheless, she remains within the Platonic tradition insofar as she accepts its description of poetry as marginal to social and moral behavior. Her choice is Romantic because she defines ethics simply as taking the side of whatever has been excluded by society.[14] For Kristeva, ultimately, there

14. The same theoretical problems exist in the work of Michel Foucault. Foucault's allegiance to Romantic marginals, those expelled from history, reveals his history to be more anthropological than archaeological. His early ethics are explicitly transgressive, as Kristeva's are, and they focus on the freeing of desire from the forces of repression. Transgressive discourse captures the discourse *of* the subject, such as the discourse of madness explored in *Madness and Civilization*, and refuses to create a norm or to expel. Indeed, Foucault usually finds distasteful anything that recalls order, norm, or law, judging that any discourse *on* a subject in fact weighs upon and crushes it beneath a desire for discipline and order. Morality belongs for Foucault to the type of discourse that operates on subjects; it is essentially normative and regulated, and comprises finally a language useful only to order desire.

In *The Use of Pleasure*, however, Foucault seems at first glance to have abandoned this view. There he conceives of a subject of ethics who engages in an exercise of selfhood that is autonomous and free from the constraints of law. Nevertheless, upon closer inspection, Foucault's older views remain. He defines

can be no society that is not repressively Platonic because every society has its victims: "The question is unavoidable: if we are not on the side of those whom society wastes in order to reproduce itself, where are we?" (31).

I treat Kristeva at such length because she exemplifies a certain Romanticism pervasive in modern critical theory. This Romanticism admits that Plato's description of poetry as antisocial is correct, but it embraces rather than banishes poetic language as the only hope for an ethical existence. Literature and society oppose each other, and the literary critic decides to stand with the marginal forces of literature. Literature comes to represent the last avatar of freedom within a vision that imagines human society as gruesomely totalitarian. Linguistic pluralism is Romantic because it bases its hopes on the inability of society to absorb the heterogeneity and irrationality of language. In this view, poetic language may sometimes be allied with cultural violence because its codings influence human behavior, but its properly contradictory nature also means that literature may take itself as its own object, turning upon itself to explode its repressive potential and to quench its own violence.

Linguistic pluralism assumes the fundamentally polysemic and ambiguous nature of language. With the New Criticism, poetry was understood as a symbol of freedom because its ironic and paradoxical nature could not be paraphrased by ordinary (social) language. W. K. Wimsatt's "Poetry and Morals," for example, concludes that one cannot really refute Plato because "a moral code must be by its nature too rigid to accommodate, or at least too rigid to account for or specifically sanction, the widely heterogeneous concreteness of the world's recognized poetry" (89).[15] The New Critical defense of poetry explicitly inverts Plato's values by embracing literature's chaotic nature as repre-

---

"morality" as the laws of conduct and "ethics" as the practices of the self. His preference for the latter over the former preserves the taste for transgression and Romantic individuality so fervent in his earliest writings. For an extended discussion of Foucault and Romantic marginality, see my *The Romantic Fantastic* (Ithaca: Cornell University Press, 1984).

15. W. K. Wimsatt, "Poetry and Morals," *The Verbal Icon* (Lexington: University of Kentucky Press, 1954), pp. 85–102.

sentative of its autonomy. "What Plato saw as the evil of poetry," Wimsatt explains, "the mixture of its emotions and the confusion of its advice, has become now, under such names as ironic 'tension' and 'synaesthesis,' the richness of aesthetic value" (91). Poststructuralism similarly asserts that the self-reflexive quality of language maximizes free play, describing linguistic structure in terms of its differential nature or its capacity to give insight into blindness. The popular deconstructive term "differance" allows no exclusive form of judgment because it both negates itself and permits an expansive and uncontainable dissemination of meaning. Whereas Plato associated poetry with the discovery of inconsistency and strife, modern criticism appraises poetry as good only if it presents the reader with paradoxes, negativities, and ironies.

If ethical theory has traditionally struggled to pass judgments and make decisions, the new ethical criticism differs by suspending judgment and embracing all interpretations, however contradictory. Thus Northrop Frye, in "Ethical Criticism," the second essay of *Anatomy of Criticism*, defines ethical criticism as the commitment to plurality in interpretation:

> The principle of manifold or "polysemous" meaning, as Dante calls it, is not a theory any more, still less an exploded superstition, but an established fact. The thing that has established it is the simultaneous development of several different schools of modern criticism, each making a distinctive choice of symbols in its analysis. The modern student of critical theory is faced with a body of rhetoricians who speak of texture and frontal assaults, with students of history who deal with traditions and sources, with critics using material from psychology and anthropology, with Aristotelians, Coleridgians, Thomists, Freudians, Jungians, Marxists, with students of myth, rituals, archetypes, metaphors, ambiguities, and significant forms. The student must either admit the principle of polysemous meaning, or choose one of these groups and then try to prove that all the others are less legitimate. The former is the way of scholarship, and leads to the advancement of learning; the latter is the way of pedantry, and gives us a wide choice of goals, the most conspicuous today being fantastical learning, or myth criticism, contentious learning, or historical criticism and delicate learning, or "new" criticism. (72)[16]

16. Northrop Frye, *Anatomy of Criticism* (Princeton: At the University Press, 1957).

Frye's political and ethical motives are oblique, to say the least. He castigates the opponents of his "ethical criticism" not as enemies of the open society, as Kristeva does, but as academic pedants. Nevertheless, Frye's commitment to interpretive pluralism and poetic autonomy has its roots in a social context. Equating ethics with judgment rather than with pluralism risks Plato's cultural repression and violence. "As soon as we make culture a definite image of a future and perhaps attainable society," Frye writes, "we start selecting and purging a tradition, and all the artists who don't fit (an increasing number as the process goes on) have to be thrown out. So, just as historical criticism uncorrected relates culture only to the past, ethical criticism uncorrected relates culture only to the future, to the ideal society which may eventually come if we take sufficient pains to guard the educating of our youth" (346). Literature fights repressive regimes by freeing the imagination and making a liberal education possible. This is in itself ethical, according to Frye: "The ethical purpose of a liberal education is to liberate, which can only mean to make one capable of conceiving society as free, classless, and urbane. No such society exists, which is one reason why a liberal education must be deeply concerned with works of the imagination. The imaginative element in works of art, again, lifts them clear of the bondage of history" (347).

I do not want to dispute Frye's contention that the purpose of a liberal education is to liberate. What is disturbing about Frye's embrace of linguistic pluralism is the implication that judgment by definition cannot be ethical. The modern view of ethics tends to translate freedom of choice into freedom from choice, as if suspending judgment places one on the side of a higher morality and liberates one from the chains of social existence. If literature exists solely above the clash of the world, it has no value for the human race. A freedom defined apart from social reality, as purely literary, cannot be the model for freedom within society. One might even venture to suggest that it cannot be understood.

Not surprisingly, the problem of incomprehensibility has become part of the ethics of criticism. That language and literature are baffling is now commonly assumed by critical theory. Their incomprehensibility is necessary to the desire to separate art from the everyday world, to promulgate, apparently against Platonism, the Platonic gesture itself. No single theorist can be singled out as the unique proponent of this view. In this sense, none of the poststructuralists is original. The major figures rarely use the word "ethical," no doubt for fear of being unethical, and they usually do not make the association between the undecidable nature of language and ethical motivations. When critics do refer to ethics, it is almost a foregone conclusion that they mean some form of linguistic pluralism.

J. Hillis Miller's "The Ethics of Reading" is a good case in point.[17] Miller represents the mainstream view of deconstruction in America, and he is not embarrassed to make its ethical assumptions clear. As Kristeva does, he opposes his ethics to the one that values truth. To dream of unification in matters of truth is hopeless, and neither humanism nor the nihilistic challenge to the value of humanity proceeds ethically when one insists on its own truth to the exclusion of the other's. Rather,

17. J. Hillis Miller, "The Ethics of Reading," in *American Criticism*, ed. Konigsberg, pp. 19–41. In this context, I also recommend the "Limits of Pluralism Debate" among Wayne C. Booth, M. H. Abrams, and Miller in the pages of *Critical Inquiry* 3.3 (1977), even though none of the participants really venture beyond the linguistic definition of pluralism. Miller's position remains similar to that in "The Ethics of Reading." Abrams's essay is essentially an attack on deconstruction and its claims to infallibility. Booth argues that the limits of pluralism are plural and focuses on the core of agreement shared in textual interpretation. More recently, however, Booth has turned explicitly to the study of ethical criticism. He stresses in particular the ethical motivations hidden in the "professedly anti-ethical and apolitical stances of modern aesthetic movements" and criticizes their attempts to forego judgment (49). See "Freedom of Interpretation: Bakhtin and the Challenge of Feminist Criticism," *Critical Inquiry* 9 (1982): 45–76.

For a special contribution to the debate over linguistic pluralism, see René Girard's "Violence and Representation in the Mythical Text," *To Double Business Bound* (Baltimore: Johns Hopkins University Press, 1978), pp. 178–98. Girard argues that not all texts can be interpreted pluralistically and proposes as an example what he calls the "texts of persecution," or documents of scapegoating, such as texts of medieval anti-Semitism, written from the perspective of the persecutors. According to Girard, linguistic pluralism and autonomy here succumb to morality, for "even the most rabid exponents of a textuality detached from any referent and entirely closed upon itself will relent when confronted with the texts of persecution. They will not only confess that a referent is in order, but they will identify that referent if asked to do so" (193).

Miller argues that ethics must be modeled after epistemology and the fact that meaning is pluralistic and self-contradictory. Following Paul de Man, Miller insists that the most distinctive property of language is its tendency to unravel itself. The ethical stand par excellence, therefore, is to subject oneself to the words on the page and follow their example. The ethics of reading requires that readers make no decision to support any specific interpretation but that they allow the paradoxical and undecidable character of textuality to shape and coerce them. The necessity of this coercion obeys what Miller calls, after de Man, the linguistic imperative: "*Es ereignet sich aber das Wahre*," or "What is true is what is bound to take place" (41). If the linguistic imperative permits any truth, it consists in the requirement that reading "go against the grain of what one would want to happen in the name of what has to happen" (41). "The ethics of reading," Miller concludes, "is the moral necessity to submit in one way or another, whatever one says, to the truth of this linguistic imperative" (41).

Miller's belief that the ethics of reading consists in the necessity of submitting to linguistic structure does not permit a great deal of freedom for literary critics. Indeed, it places them in what he calls the "cage of language." The formulation calls to mind a series of equally troublesome ideas. One thinks of Hegel's reproach against Kant that he subjected the "is" to the "ought," revealing to what degree the aesthetics of the third *Critique* relies on morality. Hegel's preference for the "is" or "what is bound to take place" made it easy for him to become the philosopher of Frederick William's Prussian absolutism. Miller's devotion to necessity also summons Aristotle's view of the teleology of character—that one can become only what one is— an idea that meant in terms of Greek society that slaves must remain slaves, and aristocrats, aristocrats. Finally, does not Miller's idea of necessity invoke what Freud also called "Necessity," that is, *Ananke*, the inescapable imperative of human violence and death?

I do not want to suggest that Miller supports totalitarianism. I have already stressed, perhaps excessively, that linguistic pluralism evolves as an ethical response to the perception that so-

cial language is repressive and violent. My point remains, however, that the creation of an isolated linguistic morality robs
ethical theory of its social context and renders ethics ineffectual.
Linguistic undecidability really amounts to a Romantic strategy
designed to confront what is perceived to be the differentiating
capacity of literature and language. It tries to turn a dangerous
element into one that is self-reflexive and self-destructive in the
hope that what is violent and threatening in language will
defuse itself without any effort on our part. That language is
necessarily ethical merely because it does not permit judgments
(that it defers differences) is an idea whose absurdity will become increasingly apparent as time goes by. What the proponents of this view really desire is to return to primal chaos, to
some pure state of nature, where men and women are mutes,
and language does not exist to impose order or to corrupt. But
the theorists of linguistic pluralism will never be free. Language
has become their ruler, and they enslave themselves to it, making it their prison keeper and giving it powers in theory that
mean their destruction in practice. They resemble the community of frogs in the fairy tale who regret having made the stork
their master, after it becomes apparent that the bird is interested
in dining on them rather than with them.

Pluralism may be applied through language, but it cannot
have value solely as a linguistic category. If pluralism were defined in society the way literary critics define it, society as we
know it would die. The judicial system would simply collapse in
indecision, and every element abhorred by society would rise to
power. As Kant understood, pluralism can have no value outside of an anthropological context.

Society can be a dangerous domain, as Romanticism has never tired of repeating, but man is and will no doubt remain a
social animal. Moral philosophy as a result has been concerned
throughout its history with purging from the borders of the city
the disorder and violence that the city was born to contain. The
process has not been necessarily just or simple. The philosophical tradition in particular has tended to occult how unsteady the
progress of ethical ideas has been from their earliest concerns to
the latest. In the earliest times, cultural forms were not rigidly

associated with violence, as they were by Romanticism, but were described as a response to violence. The first meaning of "virtue" in Homer, for example, refers to performance in battle to preserve one's society. This is why Achilles' refusal to enter the Trojan War is such a radical act; and the *Iliad* traces as its plot the efforts of the Greeks to restore peace to their ranks so that they may defeat their enemies. In the end, Greek victory is assured only by redirecting Achilles' wrath against Agamemnon toward Hector, thereby restoring the difference between the inside and the outside and permitting the Greeks to have an enemy once more.

Ethics in modern culture is more political, however, in the sense that it is concerned more with the justice of its own civility than with the morality of its enemies. Romantic ethics created this focus. The Romantics formulated the problems of social existence in terms of civilization and its discontents, and they belong to the modern phase of ethics insofar as only modern culture has the time to examine its own inadequacies and injustices. That modern culture remains discontent with itself is, ethically speaking, its most redeeming feature.

The modern emphasis on undecidability could no doubt be traced to such impulses, and liberal education has implicitly accepted the task. Because liberal education, as Frye remarks, is concerned with liberation, it chooses to look at the crisis of ethics from an inside view. It enters into crisis as a means of understanding it. Yet the project casts aspersions on the humanities. That the liberal arts are in crisis represents a serious threat to the humanists' claim that they make a contribution to modern life and education. The inability to make decisions, for example, marks literary studies as a soft discipline in an age that demands hard facts, and opinion increasingly gathers that the liberal arts have fallen behind the times. But the human sciences are not obsolete. That criticism is in crisis signals not that it is behind the times but that it has entered an advanced stage in the ethical concern with social violence. The present crisis in literary criticism reflects the tendency of modern ethics to turn its focus inward to the interpretation of its own laws and the nature of interpretation as such. In fact, it represents a characteristically modern impulse, for modern culture may be defined as a period of anxious concern over its own arbitrariness, that is, over its tendency to control violence arbitrarily in the manner of violence itself. It follows, incidentally, that the modern theory of the arbitrariness of the sign is not generally responsible for placing critical language in doubt. The theory became possible only because modern thought is preoccupied with arbitrariness as the method of violence.[18]

Modern literary critics are almost unanimous in the belief that the act of decision is violent. They understand that decision, like criticism, requires that a cut be made. But decision is not immoral by definition, and ethical theory is hardly served by rejecting the responsibility for making judgments. Indeed, the essential principles of ethics cannot be preserved without the capacity to make decisions. Totalitarianism abolishes as its first step toward power the right to judge for oneself. The totalitarian state understands only too well that freedom and decision are inextricably bound to each other.

Similarly, literary criticism cannot endure without the freedom to make judgments, and modern theory urgently needs to regain the capacity to decide. Criticism requires the right to judge in favor of a single interpretation in order that many interpretations may exist. Begin by rejecting all interpretation, and one ends by accepting any interpretation. As it stands, modern criticism has lost its sense of purpose. Perhaps its greatest failing has been its refusal to judge the difference between literature and life, for this activity is the definitive characteristic of crit-

18. By "arbitrariness of the sign," I refer to the modern idea that the correspondence between sign and object is wholly arbitrary and motivated only by convention. That language is arbitrary is certainly an ancient idea: it may be found at least as early as Plato's *Cratylus*. Nevertheless, in every case, the doctrine of arbitrariness is compromised by some transcendental guarantee that language will refer despite its arbitrariness. Michel Foucault follows this tendency historically in *The Order of Things* (New York: Vintage, 1973), demonstrating to what extent most theories of the sign depend on metaphysical assumptions. The modern discourse of arbitrariness, however, is much more radical in its views. Only use establishes guarantees against arbitrariness, and when human use becomes subordinated to linguistic laws, as it is in modern criticism, use is not a strong guarantee. The gap between sign and object yawns, as language becomes more autonomous.

icism. Entering into the conflict between life and literature does not necessarily mean dividing them. Literary criticism best evolves by installing itself in the space between literature and life not to hold them apart, but to bridge the gap. The conflicts that arise between life and literature, and between rival interpretations, comprise the dialogue in which it is the business of criticism to engage. Criticism properly understood means an end to the Platonic and Romantic belief in the marginality of literature, for it accepts the task of examining to what extent literature and life contribute to the nature and knowledge of each other.

Criticism cannot endure by keeping one eye nervously on society while continuing to focus on the autonomy of its pursuits and language. The critical desire to free literature from ethics is an ethical gesture that must fail if it is to succeed. Criticism needs rather to admit its role as a mediator between life and literature and to accept the ethical responsibilities of its judgments in both domains. Once the task has been accepted, ethics and criticism can no longer be divided. Literature cannot be free in an immoral climate, for ethical principles guarantee the freedom of literary expression. Nor can ethics develop or maintain itself without the creative spirit of literature. Ethics and criticism are inseparable. At its best, literary criticism is always ethical, and the best form of ethics is relentlessly critical.

For the critics who fear that all criticism is violent, the attempt to restore decision to literary theory will be seen as a restrictive and aggressive project. Those who decide to defer judgment, however, can escape neither the hypocritical pretense of indecision nor the ethical injustices of their choices. Nor can criticism be stripped of its teeth by proclaiming that theory is really literature, for literature is hardly free of violence and ethical decisions. Literature merely sublimates its judgments and aggression in plot and characterization. Kierkegaard said that the instant of decision is madness. He was referring to the choice between ethics and aesthetics, and no doubt he understood that the decision itself is ethical as only decision can be. The crisis of criticism belongs to the nature of this decision, and criticism cannot exist without it. The inescapable fact remains that criticism always makes decisions, if it is criticism, and therein lies its monstrous character for an age that views the instant of decision as madness.

3

The Ethics of Autonomy: Biography and the New Criticism

The New Critics gave poetry an independent status, liberating it from historical, biographical, and psychological requirements. They argued that the poem inhabits its own space, without support from either the author or the reader. This curious property is usually called "poetic autonomy," and historians of literary criticism generally note that the New Critics found the idea in Kant's *Critique of Judgement*. That Kant elsewhere defined the idea of autonomy in relation to human intention and freedom rarely figures as part of the story. Kantian ethics requires that human beings be treated as ends in themselves, as autonomous subjects, not as mere instruments to satisfy another's personal desires. In contrast, poetic autonomy is usually described in terms of the formal requirements of New Critical practice, and not as it relates to moral philosophy and human subjectivity. Two questions, then, arise for the ethics of criticism. Are there ethical motivations behind the shift from human autonomy to poetic autonomy, despite the New Critical disinterest in extrinsic issues? And to what extent, if any, does the idea of human autonomy secretly direct the character of the New Criticism?

Recently, Frank Lentricchia and Gerald Graff have argued that the aesthetic ideal of poetic autonomy prevents literary critics from engaging in political and moral reform. The argument against the New Criticism's lack of social involvement turns most frequently on the issue of autonomy, but the ethical reasons behind the shift from human to poetic autonomy have received no sustained attention. The lack of interest may be related to the fact that recent critical theory also stresses a shift from the human to language. The poststructuralist theory of intertextuality challenges the autonomy of the lone poetic text, although not in a manner that dissents ultimately from the spirit of the New Criticism. The poststructuralists isolate language for study in the same way that the New Critics isolated the poem. For the poststructuralists, language is itself autonomous. The "death of man" leads to the question of language, just as the "death of the poet" led the New Criticism to the question of poetry. While disputing the privileged status of poetry, poststructuralism offers no serious threat to the doctrine of autonomy; it merely broadens its influence. Nor does it offer assistance in understanding the ethical basis of either poetic or linquistic autonomy.

In spite of its late theoretical formulation, the desire to escape the affective and intentional fallacies represents the essential impulse upon which the New Critical doctrine of autonomy rests. The fallacies fail to separate the concerns of the reader and the author from those of the poem, threatening in the New Critic's eyes to destroy the independence of poetic meaning.[1]

1. See the definitions of W. K. Wimsatt and Monroe C. Beardsley at the beginning of "The Affective Fallacy," in Wimsatt, *The Verbal Icon* (Lexington: University of Kentucky Press, 1954), p. 21. Frequently cited works will be noted parenthetically in the text. They include Monroe C. Beardsley, "Intention and Interpretations: A Fallacy Revisted," *The Aesthetic Point of View* (Ithaca: Cornell University Press, 1982), pp. 188–207; Ananda K. Coomaraswamy, "Intention," *American Bookman* 1.1 (1944): 41–48; T. S. Eliot, "Tradition and the Individual Talent," *Selected Essays* (New York: Harcourt, Brace, 1932), pp. 3–11; E. D. Hirsch, *The Aims of Interpretation* (Chicago: At the University Press, 1976) and *Validity in Interpretation* (New Haven: Yale University Press, 1976); W. K. Wimsatt and Monroe C. Beardsley, "Intention," *Dictionary of World Literature*, ed. Joseph T. Shipley (New York: Philosophical Library, 1943), pp. 326–29; W. K. Wimsatt, "Genesis: A Fallacy Revisted," in *Issues in Contemporary Literary Criticism*, ed. Gregory T. Polletta (Boston: Little, Brown, 1973), pp. 255–76; Wimsatt and Beardsley, "The Intentional Fallacy" and "The Affective Fallacy," in *The Verbal Icon*, pp. 3–18, 21–39.

Wimsatt and Beardsley define the intentional fallacy as a confusion between the poem and its origins: it tries to derive a standard of criticism from the psychological causes of the poem, but ends in biography and relativism. They describe the affective fallacy as a confusion between the poem and its results: it tries to derive a standard of criticism from the psychological effects of the poem on the audience, but ends in impressionism and relativism.

The affective fallacy, however, has long lost the ability to intimidate the critical imagination. Theorists of reader response and of reception criticism thrive today in great numbers, attacking the prohibition against the affective fallacy from all sides. Jane Tompkins represents the essays in her *Reader-Response Criticism* as a direct assault on the New Criticism, and the volume attests to the significance that literary theory now accords to the reader. The resistance to the intentional fallacy, on the other hand, deserves to be called the defining feature of the New Criticism, and it has retained even today the force of a sacred taboo. The rejection of human intention remains for most critics, with the exception of E. D. Hirsch and a few others, a stable law of literary interpretation.

Intention, however, does not depend solely on questions of interpretation. The issue of intention represents one of the areas where the idea of the human as an ethical and anthropological category is most hotly contested by modern literary critics, and most often intention has survived as a theoretical principle only when it has been stripped of subjectivity. In American theory, for example, John Crowe Ransom, the most ontological of the New Critics, salvaged the idea of intention only by suggesting that poetry is directed by "poetic intentions." Separating the poet from intention, Ransom writes that the "total intention of the poem is something, but not an intention known to the poet at the moment when he begins to work up his logical content into a poem."[2] In phenomenology proper, this form of intention goes by the name of "intentionality." Maurice Merleau-Ponty,

2. John Crowe Ransom, *The New Criticism* (Norfolk, Conn.: New Directions, 1941), p. 224.

Jean Starobinski, and the Geneva School in general redefine intention as a type of consciousness in language. Similarly, structuralist and poststructuralist theorists tend to empty intention of its human content. Edward Said defines intention as "an appetite at the beginning intellectually to do something," and "the net result is to understand language as an intentional structure signifying a series of displacements."[3] Finally, Paul de Man charts the enduring influence of the intentional fallacy on theory today when he argues that the structuralist critic strives to demonstrate the discrepancy between sign and meaning for the expressed purpose of eliminating the constitutive subject.

It was through the denial of intention, in fact, that the New Critics most forcefully maintained the rhetoric of the poem's autonomy, and the effect of that rhetoric remains a dominant force in theory to this day. Rightly or wrongly, the doctrine of the intentional fallacy has, in effect, forced critics to make a choice between human and poetic autonomy; and, as such, the idea of intention has a special importance for the ethics of criticism. This does not mean that a new argument for or against intention is necessary to address the ethics of the New Criticism or of literary criticism in general; the question of intention has a long history and will continue to be a major issue for many critics. Rather, it is a matter of reading anew the most significant discussions of intention in a manner that clarifies the relations among intention, autonomy, and the hidden ethical motivations of the critics in question.

Against "Biographism"

The pervasive use of such terms as "speaker," "narrator," and "persona" is generally considered to have emerged as a means of avoiding reference to the author's life and personality. Indeed, current narrative theory holds that all texts have narrators, and scholars from the most opposing camps now accept the critical use of such vocabulary as a caution against in-

3. Edward W. Said, *Beginnings: Intention and Method* (New York: Basic Books, 1975), pp. 12, 66.

judicious identifications between an author and a text. Unfortunate is the uninitiated reader who dares to attribute a statement in a work to its author. Only if the attribution is too tempting to avoid may the clever theorist save face by accusing the writer of being too weak to hold a mask in place.

Critical doctrines often evolve in response to each other, and the popularity of the "persona" during high New Criticism aptly met the threat of the intentional fallacy. Indeed, Wimsatt calls the persona a "token of *im*personality," impersonality being the "required condition for the kind of criticism that hopes to escape the 'intentional fallacy.' "[4] Yet the use of such vocabulary may have had a related purpose now obscured by fifty years of formalism. Its appearance in critical discourse may protect poets from unfair identification with their characters and works. To assert that the New Critics were concerned with protecting poets, or concerned with them at all, may seem farfetched, but it opens the way to an unremarked dimension of the New Criticism. Poetic autonomy is not merely an aesthetic notion; it possesses an ethical dimension, for the separation that it creates between the poet and the poem acts to shield authors from aggressive criticisms.

"The Intentional Fallacy" by Wimsatt and Beardsley begins by attacking a paraphrase of the biographical critic's slogan: "In order to judge the poet's performance, we must know *what he intended*" (4). The "judicial" approach of the biographical theorist focuses on the poet with a critical eye, and the New Critics reacted to the tradition.[5] Sainte-Beuve, for example, described authors in relation to their race, country, times, family, education, and environment, highlighting their associates, first suc-

---

4. W. K. Wimsatt, "Eliot's Weary Gestures of Dismissal," *Massachusetts Review* 7.3 (1966): 584–90, 585, and "Genesis: A Fallacy Revisted," p. 257.

5. See Stanley Edgar Hyman, *The Armed Vision* (New York: Knopf, 1948), pp. 11–12. Jacques Barzun, in "Biography and Criticism—a Misalliance Disputed," *Critical Inquiry* 1.3 (1975): 479–96, also touches without great emphasis on the accusatory dimension of biographical criticism. Frank Cioffi, "Intention and Interpretation in Criticism," in *On Literary Intention*, ed. David Newton–De Molina (Edinburgh: At the University Press, 1976), pp. 55–73, argues that Wimsatt and Beardsley mean biographical data when they refer to the design and intentions of the author and their relation to interpretation (50).

cesses, and first moments of disintegration. He paid particular attention to the author's peculiarities of mind and body and placed special emphasis on weaknesses. Taine, Brandes, and Brunetière followed in the tradition, thereby institutionalizing the already long association between the work of art and the artist's irregularities. In Germany, there is a lengthy history of referring poetry to disease, and such writers as Goethe, Schopenhauer, Thomas Mann, and Nietzsche have related art to suffering and sickness. Freud forever established the special connection between the artist and illness by tracing the origin of art to neurosis, and once imported into literary criticism, psychoanalysis focused on the artist's weaknesses, producing the massive psychobiographies (of Poe, Goethe, and others) popular in the literary criticism of the middle twentieth century.

"Biographism," as the New Critics derisively called it, moves increasingly toward the idea that a writer's abnormality will be the major feature in determining the character of the poem. The natural outcome of such theories is a "judicial" criticism in which the poet is judged not merely for eccentricities but for a faulty character and criminal intentions. The opposition of the New Criticism to psychoanalysis, Marxism, and nineteenth-century biographical criticism in general derived from their enthusiastic identification of personality and poetry.[6] We seldom remark that the New Criticism's antagonism constituted a genuine awareness of the accusatory dimensions of such identifications and as such concealed an ethical motivation in addition to the aesthetic ones normally associated with the movement. The moral thrust of the New Criticism against biographical criticism has become lost in the debate over how meaning is to be determined. But in fact the real source of dispute between New Critics and intentionalists was more ethical than semantic. The ideas of meaning held by the New Critics and the early intentionalists

6. Some of the strongest examples of biographical accusation appear in the age of the New Criticism. Van Wyck Brooks stresses the artist's personality or lack thereof and theorizes that the critic's selection of a topic is never accidental, but a secret confession of an affinity with the writer. Mark Van Doren tries to expel Whitman from the pantheon of democratic writers because of his homosexuality.

were not so very different: both believed in one meaning for one text, and both poised themselves again and again against relativism.

Poetic Execution

An attack against biographical criticism similar to the New Critics' is captured in Benedetto Croce's critique of the notion that "the style is the man." It "seemed impossible," Croce explained, "that a man who gives expression to generous feelings should not be a noble and generous man in practical life; or that the dramatist whose plays are full of stabbing, should not himself have done a little stabbing in real life. Artists protest vainly: 'Lasciva est nobis pagina, vita proba.' They are merely taxed in addition with lying and hypocrisy."[7] That the style may be the author perpetuates the idea that poetic and real execution have qualities in common. If poets write about murder, apparently they are murderers—if not in reality, at least in intention. The biographical emphasis of psychoanalytic theory characteristically takes such tendencies to great extremes. In "Dostoevsky and Parricide," for example, Freud asks in a discussion of criminal behavior "why there is any temptation to reckon Dostoevsky among the criminals." "The answer is," Freud concluded, "that it comes from his choice of material, which singles out from all others violent, murderous and egoistic characters, thus pointing to the existence of similar tendencies within himself, and also from certain facts in his life, like his passion for gambling and his possible confession of a sexual assault upon a young girl" (178).[8] When poets appear in biographical criticism, they appear to be attacked. The ethics of the New Criticism emerges in its denial of the identification between the author and poem. A formalist writing in another tradition, Roman Jakobson, attacked this identification with an analogy much in the spirit of the New Criticism. He maintained that "to incriminate the poet

7. Benedetto Croce, *Aesthetics*, trans. Douglas Ainslie (New York: Macmillan, 1922), p. 53.

8. See Sigmund Freud, "Dostoevsky and Parricide," *The Standard Edition*, ed. James Strachey, vol. 21 (London: Hogarth, 1961), pp. 171–96.

with ideas and feelings" from his or her works "is just as absurd as the behavior of the medieval public which beat up the actor who played Judas."[9] The New Critics and Russian formalists both negated the role of the author, but only to preserve it, to protect authors from the violence of biographical criticism.

The New Critics opposed the notion that the critic is a judge imposing a sentence. The metaphor of the trial is hardly extraneous, for it recurs in both the New Criticism and biographical theory, suggesting a perceived association between literary intention and criminal guilt. In "Intention," the earliest sketch of the intentional fallacy, Wimsatt and Beardsley note that poets should not stand trial, but may be admitted as witnesses to meaning: "The author must be admitted as a witness to the meaning of his work, and one may even grant special validity to idiosyncratic associations of the author. . ." (327). Later Wimsatt and Beardsley expand upon this idea, excluding it from the precinct of biographical criticism. They argue that the author's sense of a word contributes to the history of its meaning, not to biography, and must be studied in that light. Their objective, therefore, is not to estrange the author from the meaning of the poem but to eliminate the notion that meaning resides in authorial intention, a notion that retains a decidedly judicial coloring.

Intention is one of the major concepts of criminal justice. If we doubt that judicial and literary intention are related, we may simply recall the role of intention in those countries where political censorship rules. The preoccupation with the writer's ideology throughout the history of Russian literature represents a fine example of the ethico-political dimension of intention and its stake in political and critical violence. In "What Is an Author?" Michel Foucault defines the penal function of authorship in these very terms, remarking that "speeches and books were assigned real authors . . . only when the author became subject

9. Cited by Leon Trotsky, *Literature and Revolution*, trans. Rose Strunsky (Ann Arbor: University of Michigan Press, 1960), pp. 165–66. Trotsky objects to Jakobson's use of "incriminate," arguing that poets write in the language of their school and that poems involve a "complex system of psychological transmitting mechanisms in which there are individual, racial and social elements" (167).

to punishment and to the extent that his discourse was considered transgressive" (124).[10] The author-function in Foucault's view brings a false principle of coherence to the troublesome language of fiction. It tames the craft of lying and limits its hazards, but it accomplishes the task at the author's expense.

The metaphor of the trial emerges most dramatically in a critical response to the early dictionary article of Wimsatt and Beardsley. The response by Ananda K. Coomaraswamy in "Intention" comes to represent the idea of intention that Wimsatt and Beardsley most oppose in their late writings. Coomaraswamy claims in contradistinction to Wimsatt and Beardsley that criticism exists to find fault. "Criticism," he writes, "never presupposes that a work is faultless, and I say that we can never *find* fault unless we can distinguish what the author meant to say from what he actually said" (45). Finding fault with the poem soon leads criticism into the courtroom: "an evil intention need not result in a poor work of art; if it miscarries, it can be ridiculed or ignored; if it succeeds, the artist (whether a pornographer or a skilful murderer) is liable to punishment" (47). Although Coomaraswamy states that evil intentions need not result in poor literature, he immediately contradicts himself: evil intentions that fail should be mocked and those that succeed call for judicial action. The implication remains that good intentions determine good poetry, and if the poetry is not good, at least the poet's intentions should be. To lessen a charge or to acquit the poet standing trial for bad poetry, the critic, like the good lawyer, proves that the poet's intentions were at least innocent.

The New Critics were indeed the new apologists for poetry. Faced with the threat of judicial criticism, however, they became apologists for the poet. The insidious analogy between the expert murderer and the skillful poet figures in both the early and the late views of intention as conceived by Wimsatt and Beardsley, and it reveals that an ethical sensitivity to violence lurks beneath the debate over poetic autonomy. In "The Inten-

10. Michel Foucault, "What Is an Author?" in *Language, Counter-Memory, Practice: Selected Essays and Interviews,* ed. Donald F. Bouchard (Ithaca: Cornell University Press, 1977), pp. 113–38.

tional Fallacy," they appear to confront the identification between murder and poetry, but actually use it as another occasion to reiterate their view of objective or artistic criticism.
Astoundingly, they do not deny the analogy; rather, they work
within it, providing the means to distinguish poetry from
murder. To make this distinction, objective criticism asks
whether the act (or poem) "ought ever to have been under-
taken" and "whether it is worth preserving," not "whether the
artist achieved his intentions" (5–6). The name "artistic criticism" is properly given to the inquiry that asks whether the
work should be preserved. Ostensibly, Wimsatt and Beardsley
think of judicial and literary intention as different species, but
the apparent distinction actually conceals their fear of all forms
of intention. Artistic criticism, they suppose, does not need a
theory of intention; it judges the work itself. Judicial criticism, in
contrast, has already passed judgment on the "work" and must
determine the murderer's responsibility for his or her action.
Whenever intentions are raised, Wimsatt and Beardsley fear,
severe judgment of the poet follows.

Over twenty years later, the problem still haunts Wimsatt and
Beardsley. In "Intention and Interpretation: A Fallacy Revived,"
Beardsley turns repeatedly to images of murder and lying. Specifically, he uses the example of accusation to define intention,
and illustrates his discussion of how intention relates to failed
performative gestures with the case of firing a gun and missing
the target. In "Genesis: A Fallacy Revisted," Wimsatt argues that
"we may indeed be likely to assign a kind of merit" to the successfully planned and executed murder, "but it should be understood as referring to the artist himself (who was 'skillful'
enough to do what he aimed at doing) rather than to the work—
which may be a murder, a robbery, a libel, a silly lampoon"
(266). Still trying to separate themselves from the intentionalists,
Wimsatt and Beardsley nearly fall into their camp. Now a skillful
murderer is an agent whose intentions and deeds correspond.
Their position rediscovers that of the intentionalist critic who
argues that "we can never *find* fault unless we distinguish what
the author meant to say from what he actually said."

The response of Wimsatt and Beardsley to the metaphor of

the skillful murderer reveals a lapse in their argument, although it does not represent a complete acceptance of intention. Judicial intention is arguably as complex as literary intention, but Wimsatt and Beardsley separate them with little effort. The New Critics simply cannot dispose of intention in the case of murder because social responsibility is at issue. Poetry, after all, is not murder, even though some critics treat bad poets like assassins. Morse Peckham similarly notes that Wimsatt and Beardsley have different theories of intention for poetic and ordinary language: in ordinary language, unlike poetry, intention determines meanings (141–42).[11] These two slips have no impact on New Critical practice, but they do expose the limits of its antiintentionalism and its preoccupation with ethics.

Yet a major difference remains between the intentionalist and the New Critic. Whereas the intentionalist trusts the statements of authors, Wimsatt and the New Critics remain skeptical. Wimsatt claims, first, that it is not feasible "to illustrate all kinds of evidence (or supposed evidence) that may be adduced from an author's plan outside the poem." Second, he denies that the critic can trust statements of intention: "when does the witness mean what he says?" Furthermore, in the case of poetry, unlike that of murder, it must be determined whether statements of intention were written before or after the poem, or whether "testimonies written before the poem might well have suffered by change of intention while the poem was being written." Wimsatt's vocabulary—"evidence," "witness," and "testimony"—implies that the New Critic has not yet left the courtroom of judicial criticism, but his refusal to condemn even the "skillful murderer" betrays a reluctance to sit in judgment of the poet ("Genesis" 266).

"Genesis" finally makes clear Wimsatt's distinction between the "biographical" and the "objective" critic. The biographically oriented critic "will find a correspondence between life and work an explanation of either goodness or badness in the work, as he happens to find the work itself good or bad" (260). In

11. Morse Peckham, "The Intentional? Fallacy?" in *On Literary Intention*, ed. Newton–De Molina, pp. 139–57.

short, the biographical critic blames the poet's life for the quality of the poem. Contrariwise, Wimsatt's objective critic learns "to discipline his efforts unless he wishes to surrender to the flux, the gossip, the muddle and the 'motley' " for which the biographical critic so earnestly yearns (275). Objective criticism, in Wimsatt's view, cannot rely on gossip and accusation.

The New Critics clearly saw intentionalism as a species of gossip and consequently referred the intentional fallacy to the Romantic conception of the poet. Romantic artists sacrificed themselves on the altar of beauty and poetry, laying claims to extraordinary sensitivity and intuitions. Their passwords were "spontaneity," "originality," "individuality," and "feeling." In Romanticism, personality became the greatest work of art, and the cult of the poet came into prominence. According to Wimsatt and Beardsley, the intentional fallacy unwittingly participates in Romantic "bardolatry," whereas the New Critical doctrine of poetic autonomy refuses it. Nevertheless, the New Critics never stopped defending the poet. Herein lies the essential quandary of the New Criticism: to oppose bardolatry, but to defend the poet—all without falling with an embarrassing crash between the two chairs.

The quandary is genuine and reappears in different guises. The New Critics, for example, deal roughly with the critics who try to appropriate poems for their own. It is not unusual to find the New Critics attacking an idiosyncratic or highly individualistic critical reading, and by today's standards the New Criticism appears quite conservative. Yet they did not agree with those who would defend against aggressive misreadings by taking recourse to authorial meaning. "The poem," argue Wimsatt and Beardsley in their famous article, "is not the critic's own and not the author's (it is detached from the author at birth and goes about the world beyond his power to intend about it or control it). The poem belongs to the public. It is embodied in language, the peculiar possession of the public, and it is about the human being, an object of public knowledge" (5). Even "a short lyric poem is dramatic, the response of a speaker (no matter how abstractly conceived) to a situation (no matter now universalized). We ought to impute the thoughts and attitudes of a poem immediately to the dramatic *speaker*, and if to the author at all, only by an act of biographical inference" (5). The idea of the speaker, however, merely embraces the contradictions of the New Criticism. It saves the author from criticism, but places language in the service of the human subject. It makes poetry impersonal and personal at the same time.

The New Critical view of inspiration pivots on a similar contradiction. The New Critics attacked the Romantic concept of inspiration, but they asserted that everyday language is more abstract than poetry, for poetry conveys meaning ontologically and sensuously: "A poem should not mean but be." They refused to relinquish the special status of poetry and poetic inspiration. Wimsatt and Beardsley turn to Plato's famous attack on poetic inspiration to condemn Romantic bardolatry, but they end by admitting that Socrates "saw a truth about the poetic mind which the world no longer commonly sees—so much criticism, and that the most inspirational and most affectionately remembered, has proceeded from the poets themselves" (7). On the one hand, they praise the message of the poet as more exciting than the critic's, although they doubt its validity. On the other hand, they admit that tranquillity inspires poetic expression, whereas scholarship does not, and criticize Eliot and modern poets in general for reading and planning too much. The New Critics differed from Plato in the final analysis. They did not wish to expel the poets from the state. They preferred to direct criticism away from them. Yet poets were still inspirational, if not in Plato's sense, at least in a modern one. Although the New Critics sometimes affirmed the poetic quality of the critical act, they nevertheless preserved the privileged status of poetry and its traditional primacy over literary criticism. Simply put, the "judgment of poems is different from the art of producing them" (9). When Wimsatt and Beardsley conclude "The Intentional Fallacy" with the ironic caveat, "critical inquiries are not settled by consulting the oracle," we understand that they are placing to rest bardolatry and the intentional fallacy, but less completely than they may have wished. Ironically speaking or not, they still attribute to the poet the inspirational power of the oracle.

Impersonal Poetry

The New Critics formed strong alliances with modern poets, and it may seem especially odd that so many poets joined the critical movement generally held responsible for removing the poet from center stage. Yet the poets themselves expressed the wish to escape the focus of criticism. Sketching the doctrine of autonomy that Wimsatt and Beardsley were later to institutionalize, T. S. Eliot argues in "Tradition and the Individual Talent" that "to divert interest from the poet is a laudable aim: for it would conduce to a juster estimation of actual poetry, good and bad" (11). Ransom, the poet and New Critic, agrees with Eliot and describes his theory of poetry with the notorious word "autotelic," thereby establishing the standard for the New Critical doctrine of autonomy. He also calls Eliot a "historical critic," but not to situate him among the historical and biographical thinkers whom the New Critics detested. Whereas Eliot is a "historical critic," the members of the old guard are "historical scholars."

Ransom has in mind Eliot's notion of tradition and the individual talent, a theory that displays the New Criticism's characteristic ambivalence toward the poet. Not surprisingly, Eliot's view of impersonality and tradition, like the intentional fallacy, both negates and celebrates the poet. He theorizes that great poets possess a historical sense not only of the pastness of the past but of its presence as well. They write not with their own generation in mind but with the whole of literature before their eyes. In the poet's mind, the whole of literature has a simultaneous existence and order that permit artists to be aware of both their place in time and their contemporaneity. Thus, poetic impersonality lessens the particular achievements of individual periods, poets, and poems by enmeshing them in a great weave of textuality, for Eliot defines "poetry as a living whole of all the poetry that has ever been written" (7). But we have not yet arrived at the poststructuralist theory of intertextuality, which describes a text not as a unified writing but as a set of relations with other texts, that is, as a fragmentary set of voluntary and involuntary borrowings. The poststructuralists attribute the workings of intertextuality to writing itself, whereas Eliot submits that the substance of tradition is melded through the catalytic power of the poet's mind.

The talented poetic mind sublimates itself in the tradition. Like Wimsatt and Beardsley, Eliot struggles to define poetry without making recourse to the poet's personality. He claims that his denial of the poet is a reaction against the Romantic cult of personality that was responsible in part for the growth of biographical criticism. Nevertheless, Eliot's descriptions of poetic impersonality take many motifs from Romanticism, especially its ideals of sacrifice and suffering: "The progress of an artist is a continual self-sacrifice, a continual extinction of personality" (7). Eliot seems to underestimate the extent to which the rhetoric of self-sacrifice contributes to the Romantic cult of the poet, as any careful look at the lives of the great Romantic writers will demonstrate. Michel Foucault, on the contrary, gives special status to the sacrificial character of authorship. In his view, the defining feature of authorship from Flaubert to Kafka is the link between writing and sacrifice. Modern works of art, Foucault explains, are born by murdering their authors, and authors represent themselves as the victims of their own writing. The death of the author has as an immediate result the questioning of the unity of the literary work, which prepares the scene for the arrival of the theory of intertextuality.

Eliot's concept of self-sacrifice pivots on an ambivalent view of the poet. The more perfect the artist, the more completely separate in the poem will be the person who suffers and the mind that creates. Eliot dares to argue that what matters to poetry is not the intensity of emotions but the pressure under which fusion between poetry and emotion takes place in the poet's mind. As "mind" replaces "poet," Eliot's theory of impersonality emerges. The poet does not express personality in the Romantic tradition. Rather, the poet is a "medium," in which "impressions and experience combine in peculiar and unexpected ways" (9). Eliot still accents peculiarity, but he expects that novelty will somehow emerge without casting its light of strangeness on the writer. The poet's mind here is not the celebrated filament of platinum but some type of alchemical vessel, a caldron from which poetry boils. Eliot seems to exclude the poet from his description of mind, but the concept of inspiration lingers in his metaphors. Even though he specifically opposes the Romantic view of poetry as a spontaneous overflow of emotion, the alchemical images reintroduce it. Finally, in Eliot's most celebrated description of poetry, the poet continues in the Romantic tradition to occupy center stage, although the role is expressed obliquely. Like the critic, the poet directs attention away from the poet toward poetry: "Poetry is not a turning loose of emotion, but an escape from emotion; it is not the expression of personality, but an escape from personality." The ideal of self-sacrifice reaches perfection, but the poets remain in power, for only they have the need and will to sacrifice themselves. Poetry is an escape from personality, Eliot explains, "but, of course, only those who have personality and emotion know what it means to want to escape from these things" (10–11).

If the emotion of art is truly impersonal, why does Eliot preoccupy himself with the poet's personal sacrifices and sorrows? Wimsatt argues that Eliot views suffering as indispensable to poetry, despite the doctrine of impersonality, and notes that "few poets have been treated less impersonally" than Eliot ("Eliot's Weary Gestures" 585). Moreover, few poets express themselves less impersonally. As Eliot transforms the Romantic cult of personality into a cult of personal impersonality, it grows apparent that impersonality serves merely as a mask to preserve personality. Only the poet who has personality knows to seek the security of impersonality. No matter how strongly Eliot asserts the doctrine of impersonality, personality returns like a bad dream, and no doubt with its bad dreams. In a word, Eliot defines personality as that which tries to escape personality. To arrive at the Romantic view of personality, we need only substitute "personality" for "progress" in his phrase "The progress of an artist is a continual self-sacrifice, a continual extinction of personality."

Eliot's early denial of personality prepares for its overt return in his late writings. In "Impersonality in Blanchot," Paul de Man reminds us that the askesis of depersonalization in Blanchot, which conceives of the work as an autonomous unity, prepares the way for the reappearance of subjectivity, which has never in fact ceased to be present.[12] Similarly, personality never disappears in Eliot; it merely moves underground for shelter. As a rule, the interplay between personality and impersonality serves a protective function. It only remains to ask what poets seek protection from, and the answer surfaces in Eliot's earliest formulation of poetic autonomy. Poetic autonomy guarantees poetic anonymity, and anonymity remains the best defense against the animosity of biographical criticism and the gossip of the press: "Honest criticism and sensitive appreciation are directed not upon the poet but upon poetry. If we attend to the confused cries of the newspaper critics and the *susurrus* of popular repetition that follows, we shall hear the names of poets in great numbers; if we seek not Blue-book knowledge but the enjoyment of poetry, and ask for a poem, we shall seldom find it" (7).[13]

The New Intentionalists

The New Critics deplored the aggressive instincts of biographical and intentionalist theory, and this ethical thrust combined with their strong literary interest in poetry to direct criticism away from the author and toward the work. Although some forms of biographical criticism may indeed treat the author unkindly, it is nevertheless unwise to accept the New Critical rejection of intention merely for ethical reasons, for intentionalist theory also possesses ethical hopes. Here the recent writings of E. D. Hirsch provide a fine counterexample to the New Critical view of intention, since they privilege with unabashed zeal the role of ethics in interpretation. Hirsch argues that authorial

12. Paul de Man, "Impersonality in the Criticism of Maurice Blanchot," *Blindness and Insight* (1971; reprint, Minneapolis: University of Minnesota Press, 1983), pp. 60–78.

13. On the motivations for impersonality, see "Interview with Harold Bloom," *Diacritics* 13.3 (1983): 57–68, where Bloom remarks that Eliot's statement about the impersonalized role of poets is "a self-serving defense," but one directed against his poetic precursors and not against the academic attitude toward poets.

intention is the best standard for validity in interpretation not because original meaning is most valid, but because it represents an ethically superior choice for the critic. The moral imperative of language demands that the critic "respect an author's intention," which explains "why, in ethical terms, original meaning is the 'best meaning'" (*Aims of Interpretation* 92). Hirsch's theories openly challenge the New Critical doctrine opposing the intentional fallacy. Yet his style and manner often recall those of the New Critics, and for all his polemics, he never makes a direct frontal assault on Wimsatt and Beardsley. When their names arise, his criticisms soften. Indeed, *Validity in Interpretation*, the book in which he argues the case for authorial intention, is dedicated to Ronald S. Crane and William K. Wimsatt. Intentionalist theory and the New Criticism make strange bedfellows, but given that Hirsch enjoys disclosing areas of agreement shared by apparently opposing theories, perhaps he has found common ground for friendship. In fact, in their concern with ethics, the New Critics and the new intentionalists are brothers under the skin.

Hirsch is admirably frank on the issue of ethics in interpretation. In *The Aims of Interpretation,* he supplies the ethical dimension missing from his argument in *Validity in Interpretation*, transposing the ethics of language into a golden rule of critical interpretation. Critics must not disregard the original intentions of writers, he insists, if they wish their own intentions to be honored. Hirsch bases the golden rule on a general maxim of ethical behavior, advising that individuals treat each other equally. "When we simply use an author's words for our own purposes," he writes, "without respecting his intention, we transgress . . . 'the ethics of language,' just as we transgress ethical norms when we use another person merely for our own ends" (90). Hirsch concludes that individuals should be conceived as "ends in themselves" and not as instruments of others. By refusing to admit the intentions of an author's words, the critic loses the "soul of speech" and succumbs to a form of interpersonal violence. "To treat an author's words," Hirsch explains, "merely as grist for one's mill is ethically analogous to using another man merely for one's own purposes" (91).[14] In this light, the New Critical denial of intention appears particularly ruthless, as ruthless, I suspect, as biographism seems to the New Critics.

It is clear that Hirsch views the critic's appropriation of the author's meaning as a perverse act of will, and he tries to subvert New Critical anti-intentionalism largely through the rejection of poetic autonomy. Autonomy, for Hirsch, is not a formalistic idea but part of a program of evaluation based on intrinsic categories. The New Critics feared that literature would lose its essential character when viewed in historical and biographical contexts. As a consequence, Hirsch argues, they developed categories especially appropriate to literature. Poetic autonomy strives to represent literature as literature and not as an instrument for historical and psychological documentation. It is clear that Hirsch, although atuned to ethical issues, views the New Criticism as merely an aesthetic movement. For Hirsch, the New Critics showed no desire to protect poets, and he finds the aesthetic doctrine of autonomy to be inadequate, skeptically inquiring, "what lies behind tautological formulations like the injunction to consider a poem as a poem?" (129).

Hirsch discovers the origin of poetic autonomy and the literary study of literature in the Romantic period. Wimsatt and Beardsley similarly argue that the intentional fallacy and bardolatry are Romantic inventions. Whereas Wimsatt and Beardsley make Romanticism responsible for the disappearance of poetic autonomy in criticism, Hirsch holds Romanticism responsible for its appearance and proliferation. More specifically, Hirsch claims that the Romantics mistakenly created an ethic of individuality to preserve the sovereignty of the particular from the domination of the general. As each culture becomes a note in the divine symphony, the ideal of cultural relativism emerges, and to preserve pluralism, each individual, culture, and text must be judged in its specificity.

Can Romanticism be responsible for both the decline and the

14. Cf. Jack Meiland, "Interpretation as a Cognitive Discipline," *Philosophy and Literature* 2.1 (1978): 23–45. Meiland objects that using a work of art for purposes other than those the author intended does not infringe upon his or her individual freedom, since that freedom was exercised in the creation of the work.

rise of autonomy as a standard of criticism? The defining ethic of Romanticism, from Rousseau through Kant to its modern equivalents, is the preservation of equality over the human impulse to judge individual differences as the proof of inequality. The Romantic idea of individuality represents each person and object as individual unto itself, but maintains as well that all are equal in their individuality. Despite their idea of equality, however, the Romantics placed the greatest stress on individuality, and cults of the individual sprang forth as a result. But there can be cults of individuality for both authors and texts. The New Criticism struggled to protect the individuality of the poem and denigrated the presentation of an author's individuality as bardolatry. The new intentionalism strives to preserve the individuality of the author and disdains the cult of art for art's sake.

Both criticisms derive their principles from the Romantic ideal of sovereign individuality. And it is no coincidence that Hirsch has recourse to Kant (and the *Nicomachean Ethics*) in order to formulate his golden rule of criticism. Acknowledging the influence of his teacher John Crowe Ransom, Allen Tate also describes his critical education as a composite of "Kantian aesthetics and a philosophy of dualism, tinged with Christian theology, but ultimately derived from the Nicomachean ethics" (616).[15] The principle of autonomy lies beneath both positions. By autonomy, I mean that an author or poem is its own instrument and not that of another writer or discourse. Autonomy in its purest form is not necessarily a sound philosophical principle. It is an ethical ideal, an ideal discovered by Romanticism, compatible with cultural and critical relativism, but incompatible with collective and normative enterprises, whether social or linguistic. Individuals cannot act by their own rules in society any more than speakers can speak by their own rules in language. There must be a system of mutual definition between the particular

15. Cited by Russell Fraser, "My Two Masters," *Sewanee Review* 91.4 (1983): 614–33. Fraser also captures the New Critical position on biography: "All roads led back to form. The academic community denied this, and dissolved the poem into biography and history. It offered a pretext for the study of the sexual life of the poet, maybe of the reader, or of anything else that Professor X, pursuing his own vagaries, wanted to study" (632).

and the general. Consequently, Kant, unlike Rousseau, seeks to preserve order by placing certain restrictions on individual freedom. The autonomy of individuals is sacred only on the condition that they respect the autonomy of others.

Frank Lentricchia, in *After the New Criticism*, remarks that the doctrine of poetic autonomy held by Northrop Frye and the New Critics would be unimaginable without Kant. In *The Aims of Interpretation*, Hirsch refers specifically to Kant to establish the ethical ideal that individuals should be conceived as ends in themselves. The primary issue is whether and how these two forms of autonomy relate. Hirsch's attack on the politics of the New Criticism introduces a context in which the connection between poetic and human autonomy is dramatically exposed. He contends that the superiority of the New Criticism in the public mind springs only from the privileged ring of its rhetoric; and to debunk the myth of the poem in itself, he compares it to the myth of man as the privileged category: "The 'literary study of literature' has a privileged ring to it, like 'the proper study of mankind is man'" (129). Hirsch's debunking of the ideal of "literature as literature" depends in part on the New Critical and structuralist debunking of "man as man," and it brings him into his opponents' camp. He means to deflate the New Criticism with the comparison, but risks undermining his argument for authorial intention. The main support for the superiority of authorial intention is Hirsch's ethical requirement that all people be recognized as unique and autonomous on the basis of their shared humanity. If he attacks the status of autonomy in the New Criticism, it cannot stand within his own work.

Hirsch's comparison is possible only because the New Critics and intentionalists converge on the issue of autonomy. Indeed, Hirsch discovers the equation whereby formalist critics replace "man" with "literature" and maintain for poetry the special status of human autonomy. But Hirsch misses the opportunity to enter the New Criticism's secret home of subjectivity. He fails to understand that the real reason for the New Critic's love of poetic autonomy is not the preservation of aestheticism but the protection of individuality, whether in the form of the poet or of the poem. Instead, he advances the explanation that the Popean injunction to study literature as literature conceals the aesthete's conflation of art and literature, whereas literature in fact cannot be privileged as a linguistic act. In Hirsch's opinion, "literature has no independent essence, aesthetic or otherwise. It is an arbitrary classification of linguistic works which do not exhibit common distinctive traits, and which cannot be defined as an Aristotelian species" (135). Hirsch's attack on "literature" sounds remarkably like Foucault's attack on the "author." "Literature" and "author" are viewed by Hirsch and Foucault respectively as false unities that distort their objects by representing them as essentialistic. "No critical approach can," Hirsch writes, "without distortion, make essentialistic claims upon literature" (135). Nor can a critical approach make essentialistic claims upon an author without risking distortion, which explains why the New Critics reject the two extremes of biographical theory: judicial criticism and bardolatry.

The battle cry "autonomy" permits any poem to enter the canon of literature because any poem can be established if it is judged intrinsically according to its own categories; and Hirsch worries that the literary study of literature will pervert ethical and aesthetic principles.[16] The ideal of autonomy may be held responsible for the perversion of standards because it risks separating literature from life, but it also depends on an ethical motivation. Hirsch, whose main interest lies with ethics, might be expected to understand what is at stake. Just as bardolatry and anonymity allow poets to transgress normative standards and to infuse poetry with individuality, the principle "literature" places texts beyond the reach of criticism and frees the individualizing impulses of writers and critics. The battle cry "autonomy" transforms the domain of literature into an island, like

16. The heterogeneity of the literary curriculum in American universities, which includes such course titles as "The Literature of Fantasy," "The Black Man in Literature," "Women in Literature," and "Patristic Elements in Anglo-Saxon Literature," provides Hirsch with an example of such perversions. The term "literature" in such titles is for him a "mere concession to academic propriety," and his rejection of them is ethically disturbing within the context of his ethical quest. The titles can indeed be explained by the principle of autonomy, but they also reveal the ethical foundation of critical relativism. See *Aims of Interpretation*, p. 136.

Rousseau's Saint-Pierre, made safe for the poet. "Literature" is an ethical category, an invention of Romantic ideals used to protect the integrity and particularity of authors and works against colonization by politics, mores, and alien ideologies in general. Thus the Chicago critic R. S. Crane, although suspicious of the New Criticism, could write in defense of poetic autonomy that "no literary work is other than it is or better or worse than it is because of any circumstances of its origins or of any personal peculiarities of its author or of any filiation that it may have with other works or of any reflection in it of the philosophical doctrines or the economic interests of its age" (658).[17] In short, Crane claims that the knowledge of authors should not bias criticism against their work but should serve to eliminate prejudice and to preserve diversity. The ideal of poetic autonomy is fused inextricably with the ethics of human autonomy.

Literary criticism preserves, more often than not, the hesitations surrounding the judgment and condemnation of human beings, and if critics forget their relation to the human world, they risk misunderstanding the nature of their own judgments. A startling example has recently emerged. In their argument against theory, Steven Knapp and Walter Benn Michaels define theory as the supposition that literature is free of intention and assert that meanings without intentions are meaningless as well. Knapp and Michaels are correct in their assertions, but they obey the same inclinations as those whom they attack. A clearer way of making this argument would be to define theory as the belief that literature can be other than a human creation. But anthropological concepts remain so unfashionable at the present time that most critics avoid them even at the expense of clarity.[18]

Both the New Critics and the intentionalists fall into this trap, endangering the bond between literature and life. In Hirsch's case, the idea of the human acts to exclude the idea of literature;

17. Ronald S. Crane, "History versus Criticism in the University Study of Literature," *English Journal* 24, College Edition (1935): 645–67.

18. Steven Knapp and Walter Benn Michaels, "Against Theory," *Critical Inquiry* 8.4 (1982): 723–42.

his admirable desire to protect the rights of authors leads him to treat works of literature as if they were people. But reading a work incorrectly is not like misinterpreting a person, as long as a critical misinterpretation does not become the basis for unfair judgment and violence. Authorial autonomy is best exercised in the creation of a work and not in the writings of critics. In the final analysis, Hirsch takes a Platonic and marginal view of literary meaning. He decides to reject "literature" in favor of "the human" and ends by making the interpretation of poetry a risky enterprise at best for the ethically minded.

The New Criticism falters as well because it substitutes "literature" for "the human" in a way that banishes the human subject in the very act of protecting it. New Critical theory tries to dispense with human intentions, but it ends by giving language the multiple and human character of being. Indeed, the ontological characteristics of poetry were so strong for the New Critics that any attempt to reduce the language of paradox to facts or statements risked destroying the "life" of the poem, and such fears soon turned the New Criticism against its own method of close reading. The New Critics believed that it is impossible, without committing an act of violation, to paraphrase a poem, but all criticism is by definition a form of paraphrase. Cleanth Brooks's "The Heresy of Paraphrase" states the issue clearly. The essay begins by attempting to place the individual poem or poetry in general within an inviolable domain of signification, but it is only a short step to the position that all criticism perpetuates violence against poetry. "If we allow ourselves to be misled by the heresy of paraphrase," Brooks cautions, "we run the risk of doing even more violence to the internal order of the poem itself" (202).[19] Brooks ends by arguing for the need to protect poetic language from critical violence, much as Hirsch and the new intentionalists argue for the need to preserve the author's meaning from aggression.

The New Critics and intentionalists are both ethical in principle, despite their apparent differences, because they desire to

---

19. Cleanth Brooks, "The Heresy of Paraphrase," *The Well Wrought Urn* (New York: Harvest Books, 1947), pp. 192–214.

free criticism from violence. Each prefers to choose freedom over aggression. Indeed, the embrace of autonomy, whether concerned with the author or the work, reveals a more than tacit awareness of the role played by human conflict in the creation of meaning and the writing of criticism, and such awareness is the mandatory first step for an ethics of criticism. But the knowledge of violence will have no meaning for any school of criticism if it has only words to save. The ethics of criticism cannot endure when it abandons the world of human meaning and questioning. Literary criticism, as the New Critics understood, needs a theory of language, but no viable theory of language can exist in the absence of a human ethics. Both the New Criticism and the new intentionalism try to divide literature and the human to avoid the violence of their own criticisms. But ultimately neither one can really separate ethics from criticism or the question of the human from that of literature. For "all questions," even W. K. Wimsatt has to admit, "lead to the master question, 'What is Man?'"[20]

20. Wimsatt, "Eliot's Weary Gestures," p. 588.

4

Ethics in the Age of Rousseau: From Lévi-Strauss to Derrida

Structuralism exists, Lévi-Strauss claims in the shadow of Rousseau, to return human beings to nature, and deconstruction makes its debut as a challenge to structuralism—most specifically, to the structural anthropology of Lévi-Strauss. Derrida dedicates *Of Grammatology* to a critique of the "age of Rousseau," the age of anthropology, in which the concept of the human reaches its greatest power as an explanatory category. Structuralism is in Derrida's view only the latest phase in Western logocentrism, and his early essay "Sign, Structure, and Play in the Discourse of the Human Sciences" attacks the notion of structure with which Lévi-Strauss hopes to reconcile nature and culture. The central issue in the disagreement between Lévi-Strauss and Derrida is the explanatory status of "man."[1] Much has been

1. General references to Derrida and Lévi-Strauss will be given parenthetically in the text. They include Jacques Derrida, "Differance," *Speech and Phenomena*, trans. David B. Allison (Evanston, Ill.: Northwestern University Press, 1973), *Of Grammatology*, trans. Gayatri Chakravorty Spivak (Baltimore: Johns Hopkins University Press, 1974), *Positions*, trans. Alan Bass (Chicago: At the University Press, 1981), and Claude Lévi-Strauss, *L'Homme nu* (Paris: Plon, 1971), *Le Regard éloignée* (Paris: Plon, 1983), *Tristes Tropiques*, trans. John and Doreen Weightman (New York: Pocket Books, 1977), and *La Vie familiale et sociale des Indiens Nambikwara* (Paris: Société des Américanistes, 1948). Translations, unless otherwise indicated, are mine.

written about their debate, but its ethical dimension has been largely ignored. The declared Rousseauism of Lévi-Strauss is not merely an idiosyncratic preference for one historical figure but the acknowledgment of an awesome intellectual debt, for in many ways Rousseau founds modern anthropology. Rousseau's bequest is not methodological, however, as much as it is ethical. Indeed, the name of Rousseau can hardly be mentioned without either alluding to the science of ethics or passing a moral judgment on the man himself. His greatest contribution to ethics is his vision of human equality and difference. The most anthropological works, *The Discourse on Inequality* and *The Social Contract*, examine the origins of inequality and equality in culture, or contract, as opposed to the ethical tendency of nature to give equal value to human beings on the basis not of their sameness but of their specific differences. The autobiographical works, *The Confessions* and *The Reveries*, take a personal and aesthetic, although consistently ethical approach to Rousseau's own differences. They record the history of a unique individual, whose originality is demonstrated on the basis of his exclusion and isolation from the rest of humanity.

If the opposition between "inside" and "outside" surfaces repeatedly in the writings of Lévi-Strauss and Derrida, it is because of the legacy of Rousseau. The age of Rousseau defines a period of brooding over those divisions that tend to establish inequality among human beings. In *Le Regard éloigné*, Lévi-Strauss provides a definition of anthropology that reproduces Rousseau's struggle with and against oppositions. Anthropology aspires to seize its object "humanity" in its most diverse manifestations, and that is why "humanity" retains the mark of ambiguity. In its generality, "humanity" seems to reduce to a unity those differences that the anthropologist works to isolate as particulars. The great test of anthropology is to reconcile the postulated generality of the human condition with the incomparable diversity of its particular manifestations.

Good scientific methodology certainly lies behind the desire to reconcile the two extremes of the anthropologist's quest. To focus only on scientific method, however, would be to overlook the anthropologist's ethical motivation and the profound influence of Rousseau. For to rank peoples according to separate categories, placing some closer to nature through the use of terms such as "primitive" and "savage," ends by refusing them the constitutive qualities of human beings. Anthropological theory is more ethically than scientifically motivated insofar as the hypothesis of a general human condition erodes the impact of those particulars and differences that lay the foundation for the violence of prejudice and racism. Its appeal as a hypothesis may in fact owe more to ethics than to scientific objectivity. Anthropological methodology, in its attention to the particular, leaves no avenue to a universal hypothesis without attracting the accusation of incompleteness. Moreover, the anthropologist's fascination with human differences always risks the accusations of prejudice and racism, especially when this fascination appears in writing, for ethnography presents individual human beings as objects of discourse to a public. Perhaps the Rousseauism of the modern anthropologist is not nostalgic but a solution to the ethical problem of representing particularity in any scientific system. Rousseau's innovation is to attribute the perfect reconciliation between the general and particular to the state of nature. In nature, Rousseau proposed, individuals are equal in their differences and distinctive autonomy. Culture establishes the divisions among people that must be healed through social contract.

Here is the key to the similarity between ethnocentrism and logocentrism in the respective views of Lévi-Strauss and Derrida. For Lévi-Strauss, ethnocentrism is the name for the anthropologist's inability to write about particular groups of people without abandoning general and ethical theories. Such is the curse of a disabling culture that strives to reach the methodological purity of Rousseau's nature. For Derrida, logocentrism replaces ethnocentrism as the name for the debasement of writing and the use of "writing" as a category to rank peoples. "Actually," Derrida observes, "the peoples said to be 'without writing' lack only a certain type of writing. To refuse the name of writing to this or that technique of consignment is the 'ethnocentrism that best defines the prescientific vision of man' . . ." (*Of Grammatology* 83). Oddly, antilogocentrism, if possible, would be an ethical position akin to Rousseau's perfect state of nature, where proper names, for example, could circulate through the general population without damaging their propriety.

Rousseau's stand on opposition also has a uniquely private dimension. His aesthetic and ethical system attains its historical eminence through his identification with the victims of exclusion and violence.[2] The autobiographical works record a remarkable understanding of the ethical superiority of the victim in history and end by contributing more to anthropology than do the writings on social contract. Like his view of nature, Rousseau's status as victim reconciles the inside and outside, but in a highly personal manner that leads ethics into the realm of aesthetics. To call it a paranoid system underestimates his vision of interpersonal aggression as well as the power of discovering a unique position of marginality at the center of society. To become the example and outcast of humanity, "to make an example of oneself," is to resolve methodologically a certain division between victim and victimizer as well as to achieve a uniqueness extremely beneficial to aesthetic goals.

That ethnography increasingly takes the form of the confession reveals both its debt to Rousseau and the ethical superiority of placing oneself among the ranks of cultural others. The identification with the outcast is made possible in anthropology by the essential requirement that all students do fieldwork. Although the requirement was conceived for other reasons, anthropologists benefit ethically from their identification with their subjects, and anthropological literature has achieved an aesthetic status within Western culture. In addition, the easy solution to the accusation of ethnocentrism is to identify with the victims of ethnocentrism. This identification begins as an ethical response to the existence of ethnocentric behavior, but it may

2. See Eric Gans, "The Victim as Subject: The Esthetico-Ethical System of Rousseau's *Rêveries*" and "*René* and the Romantic Model of Self-Centralization," *Studies in Romanticism* 21 (1982): 3–31 and 22 (1983): 421–35. Gans situates in the writings of Rousseau the origin of the ethical and aesthetic system that recognizes and strives toward the historically significant position of the victim. It is this system, furthermore, that accounts for the configurations of character in the Romantic novel as well as its ability to reflect upon its ethical heritage.

evolve into a rhetorical maneuver having little to do with the existence of genuine ethnocentrism. Rather, it concerns the campaign to preserve the appearance of anti-ethnocentrism and the anthropologist's marginal status in Western culture.

As anthropologist in the age of Rousseau and philosopher in the age of anthropology, Lévi-Strauss and Derrida both take advantage of Rousseau's rhetoric of marginality. *Tristes Tropiques* laments the awkward position of the anthropologist, whose profession isolates him from his own culture without establishing him in another. Among the Indians of South America, Lévi-Strauss lives as an outcast, and often among the outcasts of the tribe. He tells us that he shares a hut with a Bororo *bari*, a shaman who acquires his skills by making a pact with the community of evil, and with an elderly widow who has been abandoned by her relatives and stung by the loss of five consecutive husbands. According to Lévi-Strauss, *dépaysement* is the definitive affliction of the anthropologist, and the chapter entitled "A Little Glass of Rum" further enhances his feelings of estrangement by identifying him with the victims of the French guillotine. *Of Grammatology* records Derrida's adventures among the wilds of theory, where he forges the impossible science of writing. Its perilous object is contemplated at risk, and its "future can only be anticipated in the form of an absolute danger" (5). Derrida's metaphors consistently heighten the threat to the grammatologist, who has become a latter day anthropologist risking his person within the forest of symbols.

A Writing Lesson

The use of Rousseau's rhetoric by Lévi-Strauss and Derrida would be of minor importance if it did not cut to the heart of their philosophical presuppositions. The influence of Rousseau survives most dramatically in the stubborn equation between violence and writing found throughout structuralism and poststructuralism. For Rousseau, writing is the carrier of death. Compared to an innocent nature, writing insists on the fallen state of culture. Differences among human beings that are superficial in nature are exaggerated by culture to an unjust degree, and inequality and violence erupt within institutions. In effect, Rousseau initiates the line of questioning concerning the relation between the language of inequality and the performance of violence that has become the central issue in civilization's struggle with its ethical discontent.

Lévi-Strauss's "A Writing Lesson" in *Tristes Tropiques* would seem to be a stunning example of Rousseau's ideas put into practice. Such, at least, will be Derrida's point of departure for his critique of structural anthropology. As Lévi-Strauss distributes pencils and paper to the Indians, the writing lesson begins, and it produces the expected results. The leader of the band immediately aligns himself with writing in order to consolidate his power over the others:

> No doubt he was the only one who had grasped the purpose of writing. So he asked me for a writing-pad, and when we both had one, and were working together, if I asked for information on a given point, he did not supply it verbally but drew wavy lines on his paper and presented them to me, as if I could read his reply. . . . Was he perhaps hoping to delude himself? More probably he wanted to astonish his companions, to convince them that he was acting as an intermediary agent for the exchange of the goods, that he was in alliance with the white man and shared his secrets. (333–34)

Derrida attacks Lévi-Strauss's conclusions as naive because they represent the Nambikwara as innocent and peaceful when many incidents contradict that view. Moreover, Derrida concludes that Lévi-Strauss's Rousseauistic and ethnocentric image of the tribe actually does it a disservice by further widening the gulf between Western and non-Western cultures. The bond between Rousseau and Lévi-Strauss is most visible, according to Derrida, on the issue of writing's relation to violence, a relation that Derrida wishes not to dispute but rather to explore in its most radical expressions. Opposed to the apparent innocence of the Nambikwara, those "without writing," Lévi-Strauss situates the Western anthropologist, whose use of writing carries the seeds of political oppression. For Lévi-Strauss, writing holds the essence of cultural politics. He makes it responsible for the creation of unjust laws that enslave the many at the hands of the few. "Writing is a strange invention," he begins; "it seems to have favoured the exploitation of human beings rather than their enlightenment" (336–37). Writing is indispensable to a centralized authority. It does not consolidate knowledge, but strengthens dominion. "My hypothesis, if correct," Lévi-Strauss concludes, "would oblige us to recognize the fact that the primary function of written communication is to facilitate slavery" (337–38).

At first glance, there would seem to be no need to pursue a reading of "A Writing Lesson." The relation between Rousseau and Lévi-Strauss seems undeniable. Moreover, Derrida's extensive reading of the episode appears to allow no escape from the conclusion that Lévi-Strauss is hopelessly unoriginal in his adherence to Rousseau. Yet Derrida does agree with Lévi-Strauss on a significant point. Indeed, the major source of agreement among Rousseau, Lévi-Strauss, and Derrida is their belief in the violence of writing. Derrida makes his agreement absolutely clear: "Rousseau and Lévi-Strauss are not for a moment to be challenged when they relate the power of writing to the exercise of violence. But radicalizing this theme, no longer considering this violence as *derivative* with respect to a naturally innocent speech, one reverses the entire sense of a proposition—the unity of violence and writing—which one must therefore be careful not to abstract and isolate" (106).

The relation between violence and writing is the central issue. All three writers affirm and develop the correspondence. Rousseau defends the primitive as the noble savage, a breed yet free from the constraints of writing, culture, and violence. Nearly two centuries later, Lévi-Strauss further honors the "savage mind" by revealing and defending its sophisticated turn of thought. Finally, Derrida exposes the "ethnocentrism" of both men in their tendency to deny the possession of writing to non-Western peoples and to consider this as the proof of their nonviolent nature. Derrida's judgment of the Nambikwara differs considerably: "But above all, how can we deny the practice of writing in general to a society capable of obliterating the proper, that is to say a violent society? For writing, obliteration of the proper classed in the play of difference, is the originary violence itself . . ." (110).

Derrida tries to escape the ethnocentrism characteristic of the thought of Rousseau and Lévi-Strauss. He neither segregates "primitive" from "modern" peoples nor insinuates that anyone is without writing. According to Derrida, writing is present in the differential system of kinship relations, and as such no culture is without writing. Despite Derrida's redefinition of writing, however, it grows apparent that he maintains essentially the same position on writing and violence as do Rousseau and Lévi-Strauss. In short, Derrida uses a radical terminology but not a radical argument. He still argues that writing is the violent sword separating nature from culture.

I will return in a moment to the agreement among Rousseau, Lévi-Strauss, and Derrida concerning the irrepressible unity of violence and writing. First, we must finish our reading of "A Writing Lesson" by examining how it strays from the theories of Rousseau. Lévi-Strauss cannot help admiring the chief's ingenuity in "recognizing that writing could increase his authority, thus grasping the basis of the institution without knowing how to use it" (339). But the anthropologist soon laments his introduction of writing to the "virtuous savages" and blames himself for perverting the innocent politics of the tribe. For Lévi-Strauss, it is the presence of writing that corrupts the chief. Yet it might be argued that writing is only the medium through which the chief acts to ally himself with the mysterious secrets and economic powers of "the white man." Had Lévi-Strauss chosen to introduce another aspect of Western life to the Indians, would not the chief have imitated this practice as well in order to cement the bond between himself and the powerful anthropologist? If the tribe's politics are perverted, it is due not to the introduction of writing but to the arousal of the chief's desire to share the social prestige of the Western anthropologist. The chief's genius consists in his ability to recognize Lévi-Strauss's difference and to transfer some of it to himself.

That writing is responsible for separating natural and civilized peoples is also placed in doubt by the central tenets of structuralism. Lévi-Strauss's most original contribution to modern thought is perhaps his theory of myth. Opposed to the disorder of ritual, he explains, myth creates order. Myth organizes the raw data of nature into binary oppositions, providing a world order for believers. Before Lévi-Strauss, few anthropologists had ever held this view: ritual was defined as the originator of order and opposed to the deceitful and imaginative powers of myth. Linguistic structuralism reduces language to the structural disposition of oppositional patterns, and in Lévi-Strauss, myth reproduces the elementary structure of language as such. Language and myth, in effect, betray nature by creating oppositions where none existed before. It would seem only a short step from Lévi-Strauss's theory of myth to the nature-culture opposition invented by Rousseau. We need only read "opposition" with Rousseau's sense of paranoia to see that myth becomes a device for falsifying opposition in nature, just as culture imposes disturbing inequalities among human beings.

What critics often call the paranoia of Rousseau's system is in fact a rather acute sensitivity to intersubjective violence. It is also a strategy for placing the self at the center of social life, and it may represent Rousseau's greatest influence on modern critical thought. Lévi-Strauss shares this paranoia, as does Derrida, but to overemphasize it at this moment misses the opportunity to see the extent to which both Lévi-Strauss and Derrida struggle to free themselves of Rousseau.

Lévi-Strauss's theory of myth defines language as the source of the "false" oppositions organizing the natural world, but structuralism would be untrue to its goal of reconciling nature and culture if this definition remained unquestioned. For Rousseau, there is no guaranteed return to nature after the emergence of culture, and states of reconciliation with nature are maintained only with difficulty in his writings. The idyll of *Julie* is shattered. The model of *The Social Contract* seems impossible, and the love between Emile and Sophie is eroded in Rousseau's unfinished sequel, *The Solitaries*, in which Emile is parted from his beloved and reduced to solitude and nostalgic reveries. In Rousseau's mind, opposition in the form of social hierarchies dominates culture; but the existence of nature establishes the hypothesis that we may yet be able to overcome forms of social inequality and violence. The heroism of civilization is defined by the struggle within social contract toward the ethical purity of natural equality.

For Lévi-Strauss, structuralism is the insight that easily restores humanity to nature, if not to innocence. For "binary distinctions do not exist solely in human language" (*L'Homme nu* 617). Structural analysis reveals the profound organic truth of opposition; it "can arise in the mind only because its model is already in the body" (*L'Homme nu* 619). It appears that binary oppositions permeate both the body and the mind, and with this revelation, the barrier between nature and culture crumbles. Natural innocence is a myth, and human divisiveness only a shadow of nature's pattern. A profound coherence now unites humanity and nature, but this unity is based on a negative property common to culture and nature.

The value of "A Writing Lesson" as an example of Lévi-Strauss's Rousseauism pales in this light. The episode demonstrates the profound influence of Rousseau, but gives ultimately a distorted picture of Lévi-Strauss's larger concerns. The philosophical implications of the episode contradict the theory of structuralism. The separation between the Nambikwara and the anthropologist created by the critique of writing maintains the nature-culture distinction that structuralism struggles to eliminate. For the major thrust of *The Savage Mind* and other writings is to assert the similarity between Western and non-Western thought in general. Lévi-Strauss's "Rousseauistic" critique of writing acts unwittingly to decenter the rest of his theoretical system.

Derrida's reading of the scene now acquires added dimension as well. He does not agree with Lévi-Strauss's estimation of the relation between writing and political oppression. Nor does he readily disagree. Rather, he concludes that Lévi-Strauss's statements are the answer to a meaningless question, which means that "A Writing Lesson" is apparently not germane to the real link between writing and violence. Just as Lévi-Strauss's theory of binary distinctions destroys the myth of nature by exposing the deep structure of opposition, Derrida's deconstruction of Western logocentrism and the subsequent "radicalizing" of writing end by eliminating the hypothesis of natural innocence. Deconstruction, in effect, tears down the barrier between nature and culture, fulfilling the goal of structuralism as Lévi-Strauss defines it. "Deconstructing this tradition," Derrida says of Western logocentrism, "will therefore not consist of reversing it, of making writing innocent. Rather of showing why the violence of writing does not *befall* an innocent language. There is an originary violence of writing because language is first, in a sense I shall gradually reveal, writing. 'Usurpation' has always already begun" (37).

In the context of their other writings, Derrida's view of "A Writing Lesson" parallels that of Lévi-Strauss. It represents his ongoing struggle with the legacy of Rousseau and the nature of political contract. But Derrida will soon turn from the potential aggression of writing in politics to the essentially violent nature of symbolic forms as such, thereby devising the theory of writing now associated with deconstruction. The theory establishes an absolute association between violence and writing that ends in the kind of "radical Rousseauism" expressed by a certain Nietzsche and by the tradition that denies the possibility of any ethical action within social institutions.

"A Writing Lesson" plays no more than a thematic role in the exposition of both structural anthropology and deconstruction. The scene is important, however, for two reasons. First, it defines the point where Lévi-Strauss and Derrida appear to take Rousseau's ideas most seriously. Both maintain a momentary political emphasis that opens the way to the ethical theory of "nature." Second, it defines the point where both Lévi-Strauss and Derrida swerve away from the possibility of an ethics. In Lévi-Strauss, the reconciliation of nature and culture by structuralism requires the departure from the political meaning of "A Writing Lesson" and the ethical hypothesis of nature.[3] In Derrida, the swerve occurs in the form of the thematic subordination of "The Battle of the Proper Names" and "The Battle of the Poisons" to "A Writing Lesson." Despite the deconstructive view that writing eschews presence, Derrida gives primary em-

---

3. In his response to Derrida's initial reading of *Tristes Tropiques*, Lévi-Strauss denies constructing any form of systematic thought and accuses Derrida of reading with too much philosophical rigor the "daydreams of an ethnographer in the field." He also reaffirms his belief that "the idea of a just society is inconceivable." See "A propos de 'Lévi-Strauss dans le xviiie siècle,'" *Cahiers pour l'analyse* 8 (1967): 89–90.

phasis to the scene in which writing *appears*. The remainder of
his analysis is devoted to defining writing by deconstructing the
myth of a natural innocence and speech—in short, the myth of
nature that represents the possibility of an ethical hypothesis in
Rousseau's system.

The Battle of the Proper Names

"What links writing to violence?" Derrida begins his reading
of *Tristes Tropiques* with this question, but it is the question with
which he might begin any of his writings, for it inspires his
deconstruction of Western metaphysics. According to Derrida,
metaphysics acts to contain the disorderly and explosive force of
writing, and his project struggles to release the constraints on
this force and to free its dissemination. Derrida's essential quarrel with structuralism focuses on its love of the binary opposition, since "all dualisms . . . are the unique theme of metaphysics . . . " (71). The binary opposition, as a product of
metaphysics, constrains writing by imprisoning its power in hierarchies, and Derrida agrees with Lévi-Strauss that language is
the principal manifestation of hierarchy. Like the structuralists,
Derrida believes in a correspondence between language and
myth because both orient through the creation of false oppositions. The oriented structure of language is therefore a disorientation: "Language is a *structure*—a system of oppositions of
places and values—and an *oriented* structure. Let us rather say,
only half in jest, that *its orientation is a disorientation*. One will be
able to call it *polarization*" (216).

In Rousseau, evil takes the form of difference, and in Lévi-
Strauss, myth and language are at the surface oppositional or-
ganizations of a chaotic nature. Similarly, Derrida's view of language is possible only within a context that perceives opposition
as disorientation. In *Positions*, when Derrida describes the economy of deconstruction, it is in response to the oppositional patterns discovered by structuralism. Notice how "oppositions" becomes a metaphor for violence: the *"general strategy of
deconstruction . . . is to avoid both simply neutralizing* the binary
oppositions of metaphysics and simply *residing* within the

closed field of these oppositions, thereby confirming it." For "in a classical philosophical opposition we are not dealing with the peaceful coexistence of a *vis-à-vis*, but rather with a violent hierarchy. . . . To deconstruct the opposition, first of all, is to overturn the hierarchy at a given moment" (41).

The neologism "differance" represents Derrida's essential tactic to intervene in the oppositional patterns of metaphysics. It is an "undecidable" in the sense that Derrida calls undecidables those verbal elements that cannot be included within "philosophical (binary) opposition, resisting and disorganizing it" (*Positions* 43). Differance "holds us in a relation with what exceeds . . . the alternative of presence or absence" ("Differance" 151). Only by viewing differance as a strategy to overcome "violent hierarchies" may we begin to see the role of violence in Derrida's work. Rousseau's sense of paranoia lurks in every writing of the words "opposition" and "difference" in Derrida's text, for Derrida perceives them as representing the "violent hierarchies" that perpetuate social inequality. Danger hides in differance itself, for the notion contains both the assertion and deferral of difference, just as Derrida's other major terms— "pharmakon," "supplement," "hymen"—merge polarities in confusion. Often the word "differance" cannot be distinguished at all from "difference," for all differences are in flux and all risk erupting in violence. The introduction "now and then," as Derrida says in "Differance," of the *a* of differance serves only to expose the true nature of all difference.

As such, Derrida's theory of differance is a strategy against itself. Just as he opposes the violent hierarchies of structuralism, he militates against "the violence of difference" by stressing its postponement. Differance is difference written under erasure, and we must understand that Derrida wishes to erase "differences" because he associates them with the violence of forced inequality. Herein lies Derrida's fundamental attachment to Rousseau. Despite his attempts to break free of Rousseau's hold by disrupting the nature-culture opposition, Derrida cannot escape the sensation that writing is violent simply because it creates differences. To some extent, therefore, the nature-culture division remains intact, even though Derrida refuses to mark the origin of its separation. Writing, in Rousseau's mind, introduces the false differences that make exclusionism, prejudice, and political oppression possible, and Derrida offers his agreement in his definition of man: "Man *calls himself* man only by drawing limits excluding his other from the play of supplementarity" (*Of Grammatology* 244). The idea of man is therefore based on a violent hierarchy whose very existence disorients and falsifies what we might call the dream of nonopposition, here Derrida's "play of supplementarity."

It might be objected that this reading has dealt only with the metaphor of the "violence of the letter." The objection would be essentially correct, although my strategy represents an appropriate entry into a theory that enshrines the metaphoricity of all argumentation. My point so far has been to demonstrate to what extent violence lurks in Derrida's metaphors of writing and how some of his ideas may be better understood as attempts to deal with his awareness of the fact. To the question "What links writing to violence?" Derrida provides only a metaphorical response, most specifically because he believes that no other response is possible. Yet this very belief may itself be a symptom of his desire to defer the violence of difference. The belief in the closure of representation has the effect of containing violence within the realm of the metaphysical, that is, beyond the concrete concerns of human beings, society, and politics.

Derrida debunks Lévi-Strauss and the social sciences in general by exposing their complacency with the violence of metaphysics. The social sciences are inappropriate to the study of writing because they are implicated in its aggression. Moreover, all forms of knowledge extend the forces of exclusion and opposition. At the same time, however, Derrida believes in a profound relationship between writing and "interpersonal violence": "If it is true, as I in fact believe, that writing cannot be thought outside the horizon of intersubjective violence, is there anything, even science, that radically escapes it? Is there a knowledge, and, above all, a language, scientific or not, that one can call alien at once to writing and to violence? If one answers in the negative, as I do, the use of these concepts to discern the specific character of writing is not pertinent" (*Of Grammatology* 127).

Since the opening of any question—"What is writing?" for example—departs from the closure of self-evidence and creates a system of oppositions, knowledge in Derrida's view necessarily takes the form of errancy. But his recognition of error is an ethical judgment, not a judgment of fact, for Derrida is concerned not with the "reality" of opposition but with its linguistic nature. His definition of errancy depends on the Rousseauistic contention that such "opposition" is false and unsupportable. Strangely, it is precisely the domain of ethics, of social character, that Derrida refuses to discuss openly in his work, despite his affirmation of the relation between writing and intersubjective violence.

Derrida enumerates, in fact, three types of violence. The first violence is to give names; "such is the originary violence of language which consists in inscribing within a difference, in classifying. . . . To think the unique *within* the system, to inscribe it there, such is the gesture of arche-writing: arche-violence." The second stage of violence, Derrida continues, "is reparatory, protective, instituting the 'moral,' prescribing the concealment of writing and the effacement and obliteration of the so-called proper name. . . ." This is the violence of prohibition that Derrida stresses in his critique of Lévi-Strauss's naive belief in the Nambikwara's innocence, for those who prohibit the proper name are by definition implicated in the aggression of concealment. Finally, out of the "arche-violence" of language and its prohibitions, "a third violence can *possibly* emerge or not (an empirical possibility) within what is commonly called evil, war, indiscretion, rape; which consists of revealing by effraction the so-called proper name, the originary violence which has severed the proper from its property . . ." (112).

Derrida gives the most emphasis in his writings to the first two forms, naming and the prohibitions surrounding naming, because "empirical violence" merely repeats the scene of these earlier infractions. As such, Derrida's exposition of the three forms of violence owes a great debt to the logic of psychoanalysis. Just as Freud wishes to trace the origin of war neurosis to the Oedipus complex, Derrida gives precedence to the violence of the letter over physical violence. War in both deconstruction and psychoanalysis would be merely the product of the return of the repressed.

This is an interesting swerve away from the earlier assertion that writing cannot be conceived outside the horizon of intersubjective violence. The distinctions between forms of violence reduce the effect of this insight by encouraging us to view intersubjective violence on a much more abstract level, equating it with naming and prohibitions before thinking of it in terms of rivalry and war. It also takes for granted that language makes physical violence possible and ignores the alternative that human aggression may in fact exist in a reciprocal relation with language, generating representations that may either contain its escalation or determine the focus of more violence.

Derrida's argument is played out in the thematic subordination of "The Battle of the Proper Names" and "The Battle of the Poisons" to "A Writing Lesson." His interest in proper names, of course, derives from the parallel between their circulation among different individuals and the slippage of language in general over and about the referent. Despite his interest in the proper name, Derrida chooses to focus on "A Writing Lesson" as the example that exposes the cooperation between writing and violence. His choice is puzzling given the relative sterility of the scene in comparison to "The Battle of the Proper Names" and "The Battle of the Poisons." Lévi-Strauss's distribution of writing implements causes little commotion: only one individual attempts to imitate the anthropologist's writing skills. Consequently, the scene occupies little space in Lévi-Strauss's first sketches of Nambikwara life. His thesis, *La Vie familiale et sociale des Indiens Nambikwara*, places "A Writing Lesson" in a totally different context. There the episode appears in the description of the Indian chief, A-1, who feigns the knowledge of writing. It is a scene that bears upon the dilemma of proper names as well. In the thesis, directly after the account of "The Battle of the Proper Names," Lévi-Strauss triumphantly announces: "On a day of great confidence, A-1 gave us the names of his parents and great-grandparents so that at the final count the list of proper names recovered a total of five generations" (38). In *Tristes Tropiques*, Lévi-Strauss suppresses the fact that A-1 helps him to complete the list of proper names. In short, the squabble among the young girls of "The Battle of the Proper Names" is not the only incident in which the prohibition is broken.

Lévi-Strauss's self-satisfaction with this day of amazing confidence is greatly undercut, however, by the absence of A-1's name from his list. Apparently, for all his trust and willingness to reveal his relatives' names, A-1 still gave some credence to the superstition against pronouncing one's own name.

Thus, all paths converge on the usage of the proper name and "The Battle of the Proper Names." The episode, perhaps more than "A Writing Lesson," unfolds within the horizon of inter-subjective violence, revealing an astounding dynamic between aggression and language. I cite the version in *Tristes Tropiques*:

> One day, when I was playing with a group of children, a little girl who had been struck by one of her playmates took refuge by my side and, with a very mysterious air, began to whisper something in my ear. As I did not understand and was obliged to ask her to repeat it several times, her enemy realized what was going on and, obviously very angry, also came over to confide what seemed to be a solemn secret. After some hesitation and questioning, the meaning of the incident became clear. Out of revenge, the first little girl had come to tell me the name of her enemy, and the latter, on becoming aware of this, had retaliated by confiding to me the other's name. From then on, it was very easy, although rather unscrupulous, to incite the children against each other and to get to know all their names. After which, having created a certain atmosphere of complicity, I had little difficulty in getting them to tell me the names of the adults. When the latter understood what our confabulations were about, the children were scolded and no more information was forthcoming.
>
> (312)

A little girl slaps another, who in turn breaks the prohibition against uttering a proper name. Derrida's reading of the episode will not be without irony; in fact, it typifies his method of reading in general. He reads over Lévi-Strauss's shoulder, repeating and exaggerating the anthropologist's own arguments to the point of absurdity. Nevertheless, a certain moment arrives when parodic imitation merges with its object; especially in those instances where the device advances Derrida's own position, we should not hesitate to strip away the exaggeration and to read a passage seriously. Derrida declares that the breaking of the taboo exceeds all other forms of violence, and given his attitude toward language, the reaction is predictable. He adds a touch of hyperbole to the anthropologist's sorrow at pitting the girls against each other, but the hidden message of his words serves his own argument that the originary violence of naming and prohibition precedes physical acts of aggression. The fact that a blow incited the transgression seems to mean very little: "That one of them should have 'struck' a 'comrade' is not yet true violence. No integrity has been breached. Violence appears only at the moment when the intimacy of proper names can be opened to forced entry" (113).

The violent catalyst of transgression literally disappears in the din of language created by the little girls and Derrida. The slap is not perceived as an authentic act of violence. Transgressing the prohibition works admirably, for it fools Lévi-Strauss, Derrida, and the Nambikwara children. The play of language turns the Indians and the critics away from the violence of the blow.

"The Battle of the Proper Names" illustrates with perfection the notion of differance, but only if we understand that the object of deferral is violence. Here the system of writing hinders the escalation of physical aggression. The transgression defers the blow into a representational domain. The difference between the blow and the transgression is the reduction of violence in the latter. The real violence of the slap is channeled into a cultural representation that subdues it. Instead of responding blow for blow and provoking a cycle of reciprocal violence, the victim retaliates through a cultural system of exchange. She avenges her injury by exposing her adversary to a less sure and less immediate form of violence. The transgression, unlike the blow, is not a private but a social and public form of reprisal. Its violence depends on the judgments of the tribe and the whims of hazard.

What is the role of hazard in the episode? It is well-known

that there is no such thing as an accident among "primitive" people. Every effect has its cause, and every cause, its effect. How may hazard serve to dissipate violence?

The easiest way to understand the role of hazard in the scene is to think of the little girl's transgression as a curse. If we consider the magical import of language among the Nambikwara, it is not surprising that they fear the proper name. In their estimation, names invoke presence. The name of a god, if uttered, may make that vengeful god materialize. Curses do indeed cause accidents. Among the Nambikwara, the proper name is considered to be a double of its possessor. To know another's name gives one power, and to speak a name carelessly is to manhandle and expose its bearer to attacks and enemies. In a society where speaking someone's name may place its bearer under the power of an enemy, such an outburst is truly a curse. Unless we believe in magic, however, an accident must follow the curse for it to work.

In this sense, "The Battle of the Proper Names" is a good case in point. The little girls remain in excellent health despite the transgression. The scene has no ramification other than the scolding. Yet another situation is easily imagined. If the plague preceding "The Battle of the Poisons" had appeared directly after the transgression, the curse might have been considered more effective. Moreover, Lévi-Strauss's role would have become more complex. Lévi-Strauss already occupies a marginal and somewhat mysterious position among the Nambikwara, as he repeatedly tells the reader. Indeed, "A Writing Lesson" presupposes that the chief can win power by allying himself with the "white man" and "his secrets." The structures of the two scenes are remarkably similar, and "The Battle of the Proper Names" in effect complements "A Writing Lesson" by providing a clearer example of Lévi-Strauss's liminal relation to the tribe. Remember that the girls seek reprisal by "whispering" the names to the anthropologist. As the new possessor of the tribe's proper names, Lévi-Strauss might have been blamed for the plague and, in retrospect, for having instigated the original transgression through sorcerer's gifts for the purpose of obtaining the means of harming the tribe.

Since no accident calls forth this logic, that is, demands to be explained at the anthropologist's expense, Lévi-Strauss escapes the potential accusations. At least temporarily. Derrida discovers the scene much later and blames Lévi-Strauss for having antagonized the children. He transforms (admittedly playing upon Lévi-Strauss's guilt) the scene of observation into a crime of sexual violation, narrating the story almost as an advocate for the tribe would to acquit the girls of all blame. Notice how Derrida retells the story, infusing it with the drama of sexual attack: "It is the anthropologist who violates a virginal space so accurately connoted by the scene of a game and a game played by little girls. . . . The mere presence of a spectator, then, is a violation. First a pure violation: a silent and immobile foreigner attends a game of young girls. . . . The eye of the other calls out the proper names, spells them out, and removes the prohibition that covered them" (113). After remarking the scolding received by the children, Derrida continues in the same vein: "The true culprit will not be punished, and this gives to his fault the stamp of the irremediable . . ." (114).

Lévi-Strauss, not the blow, apparently incites the initial transgression. Derrida views the violence of the girls in an innocent light to demonstrate the anthropologist's ethnocentric interference in tribal life. His emphasis is confusing because a major aspect of his critique is devoted to Lévi-Strauss's Rousseauism. Derrida goes to great lengths to quote every incident in *Tristes Tropiques* that exposes the turbulent nature of the Nambikwara and contradicts Lévi-Strauss's belief in the tribe's peacefulness. The only time that he allows them to maintain their natural innocence is when it is necessary to his attack on Lévi-Strauss's ethnocentrism.

The Battle of the Poisons

One example of the Nambikwara's fierceness is "The Battle of the Poisons," which Derrida automatically parallels with "The Battle of the Proper Names." The latter stresses the virginal innocence of the Nambikwara children and the lascivious desire of the anthropologist. "The Battle of the Poisons" supposedly reverses the scheme, highlighting an incident in which the anthropologist refuses to take part in tribal violence. The episode further clarifies the logic of "A Writing Lesson" and of "The Battle of the Proper Names," and it reflects so strongly on the present argument that it is well worth recounting. Lévi-Strauss provides the most complete account in his thesis:

> During our stay, poison was again to play a role in A-6's existence. In August of 1938, we were visiting a neighboring band (a-2), and relations became strained so quickly between A-6 and our hosts over what was undoubtedly a question of women that he acquired the habit of coming to my camp in search of a more cordial atmosphere. He also shared my meals. The fact was quickly noted. One day a delegation of four men came to see me, asking me in a menacing tone to mix some poison (that they had brought with them) into the next dish I offered to A-6. They estimated that it was essential to remove him quickly because, as they told me, he is "very mean" (*kakore*) and "not worth anything at all" (*aidotiene*). I had great trouble getting rid of my visitors without offering a refusal that would expose me in turn to an animosity against which I had just learned it was best to protect myself. I decided that the best alternative was to exaggerate my ignorance of the language and to feign incomprehension obstinately. After many attempts, my visitors left greatly disappointed. I warned A-6 who disappeared right away. I was only to see him again four months later. (124)

The episode opens with an outbreak of an infectious eye disease. Lévi-Strauss's wife catches it and goes home for treatment. The disease establishes an atmosphere of unrest and irritation among the Indians, and Lévi-Strauss leaves to continue his journey. In trying to escape the disorder of the plague, however, he stumbles into a more dangerous situation. He encounters a very angry group of Nambikwara, whose principal target, unfortunately, is A-6.

The space in which the conflict unfolds is just as important as the events themselves. A-6 tries to avoid the tension by going to Lévi-Strauss's camp for meals, and the anthropologist once again finds himself in the company of one who enjoys a marginal status with regard to the majority. A-6's behavior reveals more about Lévi-Strauss's status than about his own. The anthropologist's camp serves as a kind of neutral ground or sanctuary. A-6 appears to stand beyond the reach of his enemies, but not for long because they also have a mind to exploit the neutral territory of the outsider's camp. The delegation arrives and calls A-6 *kakore*, a word designating a dangerous substance, or the evil and nefarious nature of certain people. They request that this *kakore* be removed through the application of *kakore*, their poisonous devices. Any one of the Nambikwara, a group of talented poisoners, would have been able to perform the un-savory task. Why do they approach a foreigner who has no experience in poisoning? Why do they ask Lévi-Strauss to murder A-6?

The Nambikwara appeal to Lévi-Strauss precisely because he is not a member of the tribe. The anthropologist, the outsider who lives within, is known by everyone, but he has no blood ties to the tribe. Even his nearest relative, his wife, has been sent away. The arrangement is coldly logical. If a member of the tribe performed the poisoning, A-6's relatives would seek him out to avenge the murder, an act that would in turn incite further retribution. The potential feud would be avoided, however, by taking advantage of the neutral space of Lévi-Strauss's camp, by bringing in an "outside man." The cycle of revenge would stop with the anthropologist because he has no blood relatives in the tribe. Within tribal society, the use of Lévi-Strauss to murder A-6 would be the perfect crime.

The striking resemblance between this scene and "The Battle of the Proper Names" (perhaps what urged Derrida to give them similar titles) reveals the hidden motivations of the Nambikwara children. The little girl whispers the proper name to Lévi-Strauss to give the stranger possession of the *kakore*. If the little girl had shouted out the name, ignoring the presence of the anthropologist, the subsequent blame would have been placed on her head. The situation would have evolved normally, de-pending on the play of hazard and tribal justice. As it is, how-ever, the girl dictates a narrower frame within which hazard and justice must unfold. Like the delegation of poisoners, she has "tempted" the stranger to commit her crime. Whether the an-thropologist has "succumbed" to the temptation turns on the future health of the tribe. If the plague breaks out, the an-thropologist may be suspected of causing it.

The girl's actions are aggressive not because the transgression is itself violent, as Derrida suggests, but because her selection of Lévi-Strauss as the medium of her reprisal constitutes a recognition of his difference. Her violence concerns the attempt to use the anthropologist as a weapon, in effect, to bring in an "outside man." This logic is not open to scrutiny, but it is implicit in the code of behavior.

"A Writing Lesson," "The Battle of the Proper Names," and "The Battle of the Poisons" reveal similar patterns. "A Writing Lesson" singles out Lévi-Strauss as a unique individual whose power may be appropriated. Lévi-Strauss's personal feelings of guilt about his involvement preserve the uniqueness that the Nambikiwara attribute to him, and Derrida eventually criticizes him for being more concerned with his own humility and unacceptability than with the damage done to the tribe. "The Battle of the Proper Names" reproduces the same configuration. But in this case, it is the little girl and Derrida who imply the anthropologist's difference to serve their own ends. Finally, "The Battle of the Poisons" casts light on the social processes hidden in the other two episodes by making an explicit association between the difference attributed to the anthropologist and intersubjective violence.

The startling similarity between the Nambikwara's behavior and the explanations of Lévi-Strauss and Derrida disposes of any sense that Western and non-Western cultures are significantly different. Each episode progresses by holding one particular element responsible for the violence, be it the presence of the anthropologist, the transgression of a prohibition, or the special status of "writing." The transgression of the taboo against the proper names contains the violence of the children within a system of prohibitions. The Nambikwara warriors attempt to escape retribution for their murderous plot by shifting the blame to someone outside the cycle of tribal revenge. Lévi-Strauss holds himself responsible for the corrupt behavior of the Nambikwara chief and the mischief of the children. And, finally, Derrida accuses Lévi-Strauss for the girls' transgressions and then blames writing in general for being the source of cultural violence.

In point of fact, the eruption of violence cannot be traced to any one source. The anthropologist does not cause the violence any more than writing does. Violence evolves within the context of interpersonal relations and the attempts of society to regulate the focus and discharge of aggression. The Nambikwara divert their own violence toward the anthropologist and the system of proper names in order to externalize it. In the first case, the cause of violence is located in someone outside the tribe. In the second, the violence is contained through representation. In both cases, the containment is mistaken for cause. Whatever dissipates violence and is identified as its last resting place is always seen as its source. Lévi-Strauss and Derrida remain within this logic when they claim that the anthropologist and writing have the power to bring about the tribe's misfortunes.

If the value of such logic lies in its tendency to hinder the escalation of intersubjective violence, one must admit as well that the system includes the potential of directing violence against individuals or ideas in the effort to control it. In short, ethical systems are capable of producing their own violence even as they move to eradicate other forms of violence. We describe as ethically advanced the cultures that have turned their efforts toward the forms of violence that they create in addition to the forms whose insistence first sparked the need for an ethics as such.

The Nonethical Opening of Ethics

The term "ethnocentrism" arises as an ethical attempt to prohibit the unjust treatment of other peoples. It acts to deter the rivalry created by the clashing of two systems of belief, that of non-Western groups and that of anthropologists. The majority of the first anthropologists placed themselves among "primitives" in a "missionary" capacity. They arrived fully armed with a system of beliefs, coming not so much to be taught as to teach. They guarded themselves against the "savage mentality" of their subjects by asserting their own ideologies. Their methods of study translated their observations into Western languages, subject to Western comparisons, contrasts, and judgments. This disposition is found among anthropologists as recent as Lévy-

Bruhl, who keeps "modern" and "primitive" human beings on totally separate ground. It also accounts for the campaign of Lévi-Strauss to overcome past mistreatment of non-Western groups and to consider "early" and "modern" human beings as equals.

Derrida equates the anti-ethnocentrism of modern anthropology with the spirit of Rousseau. In Derrida's estimation, Lévi-Strauss's critique of ethnocentric behavior is concerned less with the spread of prejudice than with the anthropologist's desire to contrast the innocence of the native with his own sense of guilt and unacceptability. "Lévi-Strauss's writings would confirm," he claims, "that the critique of ethnocentrism . . . has most often the sole function of constituting the other as a model of original and natural goodness, of accusing and humiliating oneself, of exhibiting its being-unacceptable in an anti-ethnocentric mirror" (114). Derrida's reading of Rousseau's rhetoric of marginality is accurate, and no doubt the gesture of anti-ethnocentrism may at times be directed more toward gaining prestige than toward defending subjects of anthropological study. Moreover, Lévi-Strauss's emphasis on the Nambikwara's innocence contradicts his larger view of the "savage mind," as it derives more from the influence of Rousseau than from his own theories. "A Writing Lesson" presents the Nambikwara as a symbol of ethical innocence, as the hidden path leading back to the ethical domain of nature. The tribe represents the hypothesis of an ethical state of affairs, which may be either steeped in nostalgia and made the subject of utopic dreams or registered in social science as the possibility of social reform and action. In the case of Rousseau, it would have been impossible to write *The Social Contract* if the hypothesis of the "noble savage" had not been explored seven years earlier in the second *Discourse*. Indeed, critics of his idea complain typically about the presence of the first work in the second: they dispute the possibility of social contract among individuals who are not already civilized. The general will necessary to contract is said to be a social contract a priori.

In Lévi-Strauss, the desire for an ethics arises in the momentary concern with the influence of writing on the Nambikwara's political system, only to die as structuralism matures and strives to realize the reconciliation of nature and culture. The motivation for the reconciliation comes from Rousseau, which explains why he occupies such an honored position in Lévi-Strauss's thought, but the only reason in Rousseau for reconciling nature and culture is to recuperate the ethical hypothesis of nature. The driving force of both Rousseau's aesthetic and ethical writings is his acute sensitivity to the violence among human beings. Structuralism tries to reconcile nature and culture, but it achieves the effect at the expense of Rousseau's ethics, which denies the only reason to bring about the reconciliation.

Derrida repeats Lévi-Strauss's exclusion of Rousseau's ethics with a double gesture. First, he calls the spirit of anti-ethnocentrism a cliché of Rousseau's thought and exposes the cruelty of the Nambikwara in order to shatter the hypothesis of natural innocence. By implication, he also reduces the anthropological critique of ethnocentrism to the selfish desire to attain the status of ethical superiority in Western cultures, thereby limiting seriously any form of altruistic behavior on the part of anthropologists. Second, he translates "ethnocentrism" into "logocentrism." The former exists at the level of social interaction within the checks and balances of ethical behavior as well as within the aggression of mutual accusation, as when Derrida accuses Lévi-Strauss of being ethnocentric in his belief that the Nambikwara are anti-ethnocentric. "Logocentrism" is, in effect, a theory of language that equates representation with a certain prejudice for presence. To posit an antilogocentrism would be an ethical and nonprejudicial gesture, but Derrida reminds us continually that such a desire means thinking the unthinkable. Similar to Lévi-Strauss's theory of mind, Derrida's idea of logocentrism identifies thought itself with the creation of violent hierarchies, oppositions, differences, and structures of exclusion. In practice, the faithfulness of both Lévi-Strauss and Derrida to Rousseau's equating of writing and violence is belied by the extremes to which they take it. Both create an absolute identity between culture and violence, or writing and violence, that the author of *The Social Contract* would have energetically denied because such an identity precludes the ethical hypothesis that all of his work strives toward.

At the end of his reading of *Tristes Tropiques*, Derrida at last turns to the topic of ethics, and it is significant that the discussion occurs in a chapter entitled "The Violence of the Letter." Derrida defines Rousseau's ethics in terms of the "ethic of speech," claiming that it is nothing but "the *delusion* of presence mastered" (139). Its ethical failing may be found in its dream "of a presence denied to writing, denied by writing" (139). Derrida has been arguing that violence is writing and its exclusion of presence; and ethics, by definition, cannot exist apart from the violence of writing: "There is no ethics without the presence *of the other* but also, and consequently, without absence, dissimulation, detour, differance, writing. The arche-writing is the origin of morality as of immorality. The nonethical opening of ethics. A violent opening. As in the case of the vulgar concept of writing, the ethical instance of violence must be rigorously suspended in order to repeat the genealogy of morals" (139–40).

Ethics emerges as a defense against the violence of human relations, but Derrida understands that the primary oppositions that it establishes to bring about order are also a form of violence. Consequently, the opening of ethics is nonethical and violent. The problem of an ethics is to move from one term of opposition to the other while maintaining their sameness, their equality. Ethics creates a hypothetical sameness called equality to achieve its ends. But the idea of equality does not end in moral relativism. Evil exists in the caricatural presentations of good and evil created by hatred, human violence, and rivalry. Evil is the pact of violence that humanity designs in its dedication to the forms of prejudice and persecution threatening this world.

Derrida's allusion to Nietzsche's "genealogy of morals" is not without significance in this regard. Nietzsche attempts to move beyond good and evil and to deny the fundamental divisions established by ethics because he believes that oppositions are the product of resentment, rivalry, and excessive will—that evil is the mythology used by the "man of resentment" to define his goodness. On the one hand, Nietzsche remains a moralist and a disciple of Rousseau because he struggles against those differences and oppositions that lead to nationalism, racism, and prejudices of all kinds. The eternal return affirms the sameness inherent in apparent oppositions, thereby advancing toward Rousseau's hypothesis of nature. Nietzsche's radical Rousseauism, and perhaps his madness, on the other hand, lies in his late abandonment of the belief that ethical behavior is possible and in his stubborn affirmation of his own will to power, despite his early descriptions of its self-serving and self-deluding nature. Nietzsche's characterization of the nonethical mythologies of culture as a "prison-house" reveals both his despair and the source of his rationalization for the tyrannical willfulness of his final madness.

Derrida is most often associated with the late Nietzsche, and he does little to discourage the correspondence between the view of interpretation as will to power and his definition of writing. Derrida would not be a radical disciple of Rousseau if he did otherwise. Nevertheless, the theory of differance, which is ultimately a theory of language, may be said to contradict Nietzsche in his essential description of the "prison-house of language." For differance describes a linguistic activity that disrupts those very differences and oppositions that form the bars of Nietzsche's prison. "Is not the whole thought of Nietzsche," Derrida writes, "a critique of philosophy as active indifference to difference, as a system of reduction or adiaphoristic repression? Following the same logic—logic itself—this does not exclude the fact that philosophy lives *in* and *from* differance, that it thereby blinds itself to the *same*, which is not the identical. The same is precisely differance (with an *a*), as the diverted and equivocal passage from one difference to another, from one term of opposition to the other. . . . It is out of the unfolding of this 'same' as differance that the sameness of difference and of repetition is presented in the eternal return" ("Differance" 148–49).[4]

Differance conducts within language toward the "sameness that is not identical." In other words, differance leads within language toward equality. Language is necessary to invent the

4. For an intriguing reading of recent French thought in terms of the opposition between "the same" and "the other," see Vincent Descombes, *Modern French Philosophy*, trans. L. Scott-Fox and J. M. Harding (Cambridge: At the University Press, 1980), originally published as *Le Même et l'autre* (Paris: Minuit, 1979).

principle of equality because only language provides a space for the ethical hypothesis holding that differences may be the same without being identical. As a pure theory of language, differance makes no statement on ethics, but as a return of Rousseau's belief in the tendency of nature to guarantee the equality of individual differences, it revives Rousseau's hypothesis at the very point where his radical disciples have most threatened its existence. The theory of differance makes the structure of language not a prison-house but the ethical model and signature of a hypothetical equality based on difference and not identity. In this assertion, often denied and rarely allowed its ethical content, Derrida becomes not a radical disciple of Rousseau, but a disciple of Rousseau at his most radical.

5

Paul de Man and the Triumph of Falling

Deconstruction seeks a reversal of values, conferring a new kind of meaning on those elements of literature that critics have traditionally ignored. Whereas literary criticism has most often focused on similarities, unities, coherence, systematic ideas, and the body of the work, deconstruction draws attention to contradictions, obscurities, discontinuities, interruptions, margins, and plays of the signifier. It approaches the work of literature by reinscribing its major term within its minor one, by resetting its margins, and by subverting hierarchical and systematic elements. Deconstruction can be said to have marginalized the reading of literature.

This emphasis on the marginal, however, takes on moral overtones in its opposition to relations of power and systematic thought. Deconstructive marginalization has the ethical virtue of siding with the underdog in the system; it upsets traditional systems of power by exposing to what extent minor and marginal elements define their relations. Deconstruction acts to combat all forms of theory because it equates systematic thought with the violence of power. Paradoxically, however, this crusade grants great power to the enterprise of deconstruction, and the theory risks the same kinds of aggressions and exclusions that it associates with other systems. Some deconstructive critics have dealt with this paradox by embracing a type of philosophical martyrdom, in which they expose the violence of power, but do not partake of it, by sacrificing themselves to its fury. The martyr triumphs at the moment of falling, but does not commit the sin of enjoying the victory. What happens to this moral triumph, however, when martyrdom assumes the form of a theory, when it acquires the magnitude of a movement, when martyrdom becomes systematic?

Writing of the implicit system underlying the practice of deconstruction, Barbara Johnson strikes upon the phrase "rigorous unreliability" to characterize the methods of Paul de Man.[1] As a critical summation, it is both rigorous and reliable. The extent to which the term "rigorous unreliability" complies with deconstructive marginalization emerges when one considers alternative phrases. Johnson might have chosen "unreliable rigor," but what would that phrase have meant? "Unreliable rigor" would be an apt label for traditional literary theory as de Man sees it. Such theory strives for coherence and unity, but its striving, de Man has argued, is unreliable because of the very rigor of its attempts. Such theory depends on the power of a system that remains inherent, but that decides the conception of what is literary a priori. These theories risk violating their objects, de Man writes, for they rely on "systematic nonunderstanding and misrepresentation" ("The Resistance to Theory" 12). They are, in fact, mere "theory," if we follow de Man's definition: "by theory one understands the rooting of literary exegesis and of critical evaluation in a system of some conceptual generality" ("The Resistance to Theory" 5).

Theorizing, for de Man, falls prey to the will to system. It

1. Barbara Johnson, "Rigorous Unreliability," *Critical Inquiry* 11.2 (1984): 278–85. Frequently cited references will be given parenthetically. They include Paul de Man, *Blindness and Insight* (1971; reprint, Minneapolis: University of Minnesota Press, 1983), *The Rhetoric of Romanticism* (New York: Columbia University Press, 1984), "The Resistance to Theory," *Yale French Studies* 63 (1982): 3–20, Introduction to *The Selected Poetry of Keats*, ed. de Man (New York: New American Library, 1966), and Sigmund Freud, *The Standard Edition*, ed. James Strachey, 24 vols. (London: Hogarth, 1953–74). References to the poetry of Keats and Shelley make use of de Man's citations.

cannot escape the violence of either appropriating all diversity to its system, of imposing itself as a system, or defining its systematic nature on the exclusion of "inappropriate" elements. Consequently, de Man tries to distance himself from more traditional critics by redefining theory as an antitheoretical stance. Opposed to the theory of others, his theory at least tries to upset "rooted ideologies by revealing the mechanics of their workings; it goes against a powerful philosophical tradition of which aesthetics is a prominent part; it upsets the established canon of literary works and blurs the borderlines between literary and non-literary discourse. By implication, it may also reveal the links between ideologies and philosophy" ("The Resistance to Theory" 11–12).

De Man's ethics consists largely in his opposition to systematic thought; yet he remains systematic in his preference for moral unreliability and resistance. That he believes his position to be irrefutable further complicates matters, for the claim to irrefutability risks deploying an aggressive force far exceeding the intensity and violence of his critical opponents, who do not pretend to infallibility. De Man addresses the problem of his troublesome irrefutability in a confessional mode in "The Resistance to Theory," referring to the "correct" rhetorical method of reading associated with him: "Technically correct rhetorical readings may be boring, monotonous, predictable and unpleasant, but they are irrefutable. They are also totalizing (and potentially totalitarian) for since the structures and functions they expose do not lead to the knowledge of an entity (such as language) but are an unreliable process of knowledge . . . they are indeed universals, consistently defective models of language's impossibility to be a model language" (20).

What bothers de Man about his theory is its rigor and potential for ideology, totalization, and, most important, totalitarianism. De Man sees himself becoming a systematic thinker whose stern interpretation of the law risks dangerous generality. Indeed, he describes his views as a "universal theory of the impossibility of theory" (20). Generality is the hallmark of the kind of theory that de Man most opposes, and yet his own work has become irrefutable. De Man concludes "The Resistance to

Theory" by lamenting the permanence of theoretical systems: "Nothing can overcome the resistance to theory since theory *is* itself this resistance. The loftier the aims and the better the methods of literary theory, the less possible it becomes. Yet literary theory is not in danger of going under; it cannot help but flourish, and the more it is resisted, the more it flourishes, since the language it speaks is the language of self-resistance. What remains impossible to decide is whether this flourishing is a triumph or a fall" (20).

De Man's conclusion raises many questions. Why does he take recourse to the opposition between triumph and fall, when his theory works determinedly to scramble such polarities? What has theory become? Is his theory a triumph over other theories, or does his triumph mean that he has fallen? If he has fallen, does it represent in his eyes some kind of triumph?[2] My reading of de Man will comment on the foregoing passage, the complexity of which resounds through his entire corpus. It will lead through de Man's writings on Freud, Keats, and Shelley.

Resistances

The knowledgeable reader may start at the mention of de Man's writings on Freud. There are, in fact, no essays on Freud in de Man's published works, and the absence is curious given the status of Freud in modern critical theory. Richard Klein has noted that de Man manages to write on Binswanger, a leading figure in the history of psychoanalysis, without mentioning Freud.[3] Yet de Man's work echoes with the ideas of psychoanalysis, even though he has expressly attributed his awakening to the complexities of blindness and insight to his readings of Heidegger and not of Freud. [4] Klein locates the scene of Freud's

2. Cf. Jacques Derrida's bon mot "Whoever loses wins," in *Margins of Philosophy*, trans. Alan Bass (Chicago: At the University Press, 1982), p. 21.
3. Richard Klein, "The Blindness of Hyperboles: The Ellipses of Insight," *Diacritics* 3.2 (1973): 33–44, esp. 38.
4. Robert Moynihan, "Interview with Paul de Man," *Yale Review* 73.4 (1984): 576–602. Here de Man notes that Heidegger plays the role for him that Freud plays for Derrida in the deconstructive enterprise.

influence on de Man in "The Rhetoric of Blindness," but the closest encounter may occur in the essay "The Resistance to Theory" because the title invites a comparison with Freud's "The Resistances to Psycho-Analysis" (1925), written at the request of Albert Cohen for *La Revue Juive*.

At first glance the two essays on resistance seem worlds apart. Freud insists that the resistance to psychoanalysis depends on its sexual content, the narcissistic injury to the self in the wake of discovering its subordination to powerful unconscious forces, and ultimately to the fact of Freud's Judaism. De Man asserts that theory is resisted simply because it is a language about language. Freud's remarks, however, include a definition of the unconscious that has some impact on de Man's theories. Freud attacks the classical opposition between what is mental and what is unconscious, affirming that a philosopher will find the psychoanalytic principle that "what is mental is in itself *unconscious*" a contradiction in terms and will thus "fail to observe that in making this judgement he is merely repeating his own definition of what is mental" (19:216). Freud is criticizing the philosopher whose system interferes with observation, whose a priori suppositions determine conclusions. Similarly, Freud can attack the religious mind, the system of all systems, in *Civilization and Its Discontents* by exposing that "no one, needless to say, who shares a delusion ever recognizes it as such" (21:81).

To demystify metaphysical suppositions, one exposes the conceptions that support them, their unconscious, so to speak. But when Freud transforms the unconscious from a state of mind into a system, he disposes of the very opposition between what is mental and what is unconscious upon which such demystifications rest. Once the opposition between knowing and unknowing disappears, concepts such as "theory," "ideology," and "mythology" cannot be sharply divided. Indeed, when the unconscious becomes a system, expelling ideology and mythology risks their return in another form. A given theory may seem to expose the workings of an unconscious mythology or ideology, but the consciousness of theory cannot be maintained apart from the unconscious movements of its objects, for any theory capable of uncovering unconscious movements must supposedly be an expression of them. In effect, the philosophical implications of Freud's theory of the unconscious destroy the hopeful and constructive nature of his clinical designs. The analyst can never know more than the patient and, moreover, risks trading places with the patient at any moment. Unconscious error returns as the essence of conscious thinking.

As Freud was fond of explaining, the unconscious cannot say no, and no one can say no to the unconscious. Anyone who confronts the unconscious falls under its power, for strong opposition, especially, signals that one has already succumbed to its influence. Freud's theories certainly opened a new chapter in the rhetoric of persuasion. He discovered a nearly invincible rhetorical argument for the superiority of his views. But the basis of Freud's power is not merely rhetorical; it is ethical. Freud realized in a theoretical reversal of awesome proportions the negative image of absolute community toward which ethics has always strived. The unconscious possesses the organizing capacity and inclusiveness toward which all ethical systems reach, but it does not define its "community" on the basis of exclusions. The discovery of the unconscious is of enormous advantage to those who believe that antisystematic thought is ethically superior to the order of systems, for it gives them the impression of assaulting their antagonists systematically without partaking of the violence of a system. One might say that Freud discovered not the unconscious, but the possibility of the systematically unsystematic, for the unconscious in Freud's view remains the system to end all systems.[5]

The triumph of psychoanalysis, however, relies on its ability to be systematic and irrefutable, and here the parallels to de Man's essay grow most apparent. It is always possible, Freud

5. It may seem outlandish to argue that Freud was against systematic thought. I do not mean that Freud is a champion of delirium, as certain thinkers wish to see him. Freud is frequently most opposed to systematic thought when it is someone else's system, although to a great extent what is most admirable about Freud is his willingness to remain open to exploration, to contradict himself rather than risk missing a new perception. The dislike of systematic thought, for instance, defines his greatest criticism of Adler: "The Adlerian theory was from the very beginning a 'system'—which psycho-analysis was careful to avoid becoming" (14:52).

assures the reader, to convince the opponents of analysis in precisely the same way as one convinces individual neurotics under treatment. "The position," he confesses, "was at once alarming and consoling: alarming because it was no small thing to have the whole human race as one's patient, and consoling because after all everything was taking place as the hypotheses of psycho-analysis declared that it was bound to" (19:221). No matter how troublesome it is to be the world's confessor, Freud enjoys his infallibility. The resistance to psychoanalysis proves the truth of his theories; it is part of the theory.

De Man's rhetoric follows Freud's example. The resistance to theory is interior to theory itself, "since theory is itself this resistance" (20). The conclusion is self-resistant, for de Man's theory represents what everyone else resists, placing him in the "self-destroying" position that he associates with Romantic writers. It is also self-promoting, naturally, for de Man's definition of theory describes his own views. By identifying himself as the most rigorous proponent of theory's self-resistance, de Man creates the unique position that distinguishes him as a critic, and here de Man's essay truly merges with Freud's. Although "The Resistance to Theory" contains no sign of the overt reference to self apparent in Freud's advocacy of Judaism, de Man shares Freud's willful isolation. Freud claims that the resistance to psychoanalysis derives from his opponents' distaste for Jews, but he makes that same distaste a condition for the discovery of his theories: "Nor is it perhaps entirely a matter of chance that the first advocate of psycho-analysis was a Jew. To profess belief in this new theory called for a certain degree of readiness to accept a situation of solitary opposition—a situation with which no one is more familiar than a Jew" (19:222). Analogously, de Man's essay on resistance begins by stating how his personal theories have been resisted by the MLA, but ends by defining that same resistance as the essence of critical theory.

Accepting the marginal position, paradoxically, does not mean that either de Man or Freud will remain on the margins, outside the boundaries of the system; it is rather the first step in a triumph that will marginalize the system. But the triumph becomes a fall, if one is as antisystematic as de Man, because it also systematizes the marginal. The only possible value to be given to martyrdom consists in its refusal on ethical grounds to stand for the aggressive and exclusionary impulses of some forms of systematic thought. Once martyrdom becomes a theory, however, it fails to direct its aggression neither toward its enemies nor toward itself. It becomes a system bent on its own destruction as the first step in destroying the violence that it associates with others. Its motivations are ethical, but ethically misguided because it trades a less sure form of violence for one that strives to encompass everything. Nihilism in the modern world may be defined as the preference for nothingness over the risk of committing an act of violence. Since nihilists cannot escape the equation within the philosophical tradition between violence and negativity, however, they must accuse themselves of violence as well. General and particular, system and fragment, inside and outside merge, as one makes an example of oneself, and in the same way as one's enemies do. Such is the perverse logic called self-martyrdom.

Hyperion's Fall

Nowhere in de Man is there a fall as stern and reliable as Keats's fall. In the early Introduction to the New American Library edition of Keats's poetry (1966), de Man argues that the necessity of Keats's death is the negative moment that completes his consciousness of self. For the great Romantics, de Man insists, "consciousness of self was the first and necessary step toward moral judgment" (xxxiv). Such statements sound odd in the context of the late de Man, for whom self-consciousness is impossible and moral judgment, as traditionally defined, an infernal proposition. But the early de Man has not yet traded the search for either self-consciousness or moral choice for an ethics based on linguistic pluralism. Indeed, the Introduction argues that Keats risks losing his status as one of the great Romantic poets because his hatred of self does not permit the consciousness necessary to a complete ethics. Consequently, de Man's explicit task is to establish Keats's evolution from a disinterested sympathy toward human suffering to a sympathy based on a more mature identification between the suffering of humanity and his own suffering. To arrive at this identification, de Man submits, Keats must accept his own death without succumbing to the thrill of victorious martyrdom.

Romanticism identifies with the martyrs, the marginals, and the victims of history. It asserts the role of nature in an encompassing culture, the role of the fragmentary in the system, and sides with the outside over the inside; as a result, one can see why the ethics of Rousseau and Romanticism exerts such an influence on modern thought, including in this regard deconstruction.[6] The marginalization of the system is clearly an

---

6. The deconstructive theories of both de Man and Derrida continue the reversal of values inherent in the Romantic project. In both thinkers, however, the marginality of their positions also threatens the ethical impulses of Romanticism and its claims to knowledge. Here their respective readings of Rousseau are illuminating. De Man's interpretation is clearly the most extreme. De Man conceives of no position superior to Rousseau's own insights, whereas Derrida allows that Rousseau may be demystified (even though the task is ultimately an exercise in futility on Derrida's part). De Man's "The Rhetoric of Blindness" refuses to take Rousseau as an object by positing a definition of literature in which the literary takes itself as its own object: he calls "literary" in the full sense "any text that implicitly or explicitly signifies its own rhetorical mode and prefigures its own misunderstanding as the correlative of its rhetorical nature, that is, of its 'rhetoricity'" (136). In short, de Man underbids Derrida in the process of deconstructive marginalization. Rousseau's text deconstructs itself, de Man argues, and Derrida's reading is flawed simply because it takes an object other than itself.

De Man thus transforms into an irrefutable necessity of interpretation the conspiracy against Rousseau of which Derrida's reading is a continuation. What critics call Rousseau's paranoia becomes an inevitable fact of reading, not only of Rousseau but of all subjects. The necessity of this misinterpretation consists in de Man's assertion that "interpretation is nothing but the possibility of error" (141). To avoid the accusation of superiority and maintain his marginal position, de Man identifies himself with Rousseau. Like Rousseau, for example, he discovers the model for language in the "self-destructiveness of music." At the same time, he establishes as the universal property of all writing, including his own, the wounding self-reflexivity of Rousseau's language. For de Man, Rousseau represents the exemplary case of the "self-indictment" on which Western philosophy is founded, and de Man follows Rousseau's example by identifying this self-indictment with language itself. De Man becomes Rousseau to be himself. De Man and all writers are trapped within the position called "Rousseau."

Such self-reflexivity, however, has nothing to do with the reflections of knowledge. Indeed, neither Derrida nor de Man allows that self-reflexivity may be other than a property of blindness. Here Rodolphe Gasché, in an otherwise valuable essay, misses the point in his comparison of Derrida and de Man. He

ethical gesture on the part of Romantic poets, but the identification with the marginal threatens to create a perverse form of self-martyrdom, in which the writer plays the role of *poète maudit*. In this case, the Romantic's sympathy toward those who suffer becomes in Nietzsche's words a "mendacious form of egoism." Yet it would be a mistake not to stress the ethical impulses apparent in the gestures of even the most zealous victims of the Romantic agony. The figure of the *poète maudit* conceals, as the essence of its ethical character, a genuine sensitivity to human suffering, violence, and death.

Keats preserves a similar sensitivity to suffering, but does not fall into the lure of mendacious egoism. His great ethical achievement remains a reluctance to see himself as a martyr for literature, despite his ineluctable mortality and the power that he bestows upon the poet. Not surprisingly, the early de Man praises Keats for managing to avoid the narcissistic extremes of the *poète maudit*: "it is one of Keats's most engaging traits that he resists all temptation to see himself as the hero of a tragic adventure" (Introduction xi). Whether Keats's attitude came from his personal experience of mortality can only be surmised, but it is surely less exciting to pretend to be in the grasp of death, when death holds one firmly, and Keats's fatal illness may well have made him less enthusiastic about the poetics of suffering embraced so zealously by his Romantic contemporaries.

Most often, however, de Man has mistakenly played out the Romantic preoccupation with suffering in terms of the poet's struggle against time and impermanence. This preoccupation with time appears in de Man's early reading of Keats and re-

---

argues that de Man's emphasis on self-reflexivity is an effect of turning deconstruction into literary criticism, whereas Derrida's views simultaneously assert and undo self-reflexivity. There is only the slightest degree of difference, however, between Derrida's assertion that self-reflexivity disrupts itself and de Man's idea that self-reflexivity is its own blindness. The difference is merely one of accent. But it is important because the strong emphasis that de Man gives to self-reflexivity permits one to focus clearly on the severity of deconstruction's self-resistance. De Man's claim that literary language always blinds itself is especially self-destructive. Literature, like Oedipus, is always on the verge of suicide. See Rodolphe Gasché, "Deconstruction as Criticism," *Glyph* 6 (1979): 177–215.

mains throughout his writings, most notably in "The Rhetoric of Temporality." The theme of time opens the way to the ethical orientation of Romanticism, but continues to obscure it in the symbolism of time and nature. Repeatedly, de Man seems to take the perspective of the "Cold Pastoral," striving toward a language dispossessed of human subjectivity. The sylvan historian of "Ode on a Grecian Urn," for example, possesses beauty only because it seems to remain untouched by human misery and the chaotic scenes that it portrays: "Cold Pastoral! / When old age shall this generation waste, / Thou shalt remain, in midst of other woe. . . ." From the perspective of the urn's cold serenity, images of human woe carry no emotional or subjective content. Its surfaces display human loss, but from the urn's point of view nothing is missing, because it does not understand human suffering in the first place and its images remain intact and in time.

Similarly, de Man's theories of language perpetuate an abstract portrayal of time and nature. Human subjectivity for de Man is an illusion of language, and violence relates ultimately to the tendency of language to advance from meaning to meaning without grounding itself. De Man's theories take the modern doctrine of the arbitrariness of language to its most extreme expression, where meaning can only be intentionless, and death and love are linguistic predicaments and not human experiences.[7]

Only when the idea of human suffering sheds its abstract association with time and assumes a more concrete representation of human loss does Keats's ethics make sense. The idea of history, not merely of time, is necessary to give the ethical elements of love and sympathy their relation to human suffering.

---

7. In "Autobiography as De-Facement," *The Rhetoric of Romanticism* (67–82), de Man describes death as a "linguistic predicament" (81). And, in his last lecture, he interprets the suffering of the translator as a statement on the "specifically linguistic" nature of suffering in general (38). See "'Conclusions' on Walter Benjamin's 'The Task of the Translator,'" *Yale French Studies* 69 (1985): 25–46. Finally, de Man's early review of Harold Bloom's *The Anxiety of Influence*, collected in *Blindness and Insight* (267–76), polemically asserts that linguistic structure is the cause of subjective affects and that influence is a linguistic not a psychological property.

The early de Man understands that "the power by means of which the poet can redeem the suffering of mankind is called love" (xvii). Moreover, he stresses that love in Keats must not be linked with pure sensation, as the early detractors of Keats's love poems to Fanny Brawne argue. Sympathy is more important than sensation because it counterbalances the Romantic tendency toward excessive egotism and its mirror image, excessive selflessness. But the danger of love for Keats remains its "self-destroying" power because its sacrifices may lead to the egotism of self-martyrdom:

> But there are
> Richer entanglements, enthrallments far
> More self-destroying, leading, by degrees,
> To the chief intensity: the crown of these
> Is made of love and friendship, and sits high
> Upon the forehead of humanity.
> (*Endymion* 1.797–802)

Although Keats intends the self-destroying power of love to establish moral disinterestedness, the early de Man shows precisely to what extent self-destruction can be wholly interested. Keats's desire for communion threatens to overwhelm his sense of self, and de Man concludes that "negative capability" begins to serve not as a means of extending sympathy but as a tactic designed to escape self-reflection. Keats's self-repugnance potentially marginalizes him, removing him from the sphere of his own ethical sympathies. His ethical system remains incomplete as long as it does not include the self. Keats moves, de Man summarizes, "away from the burden of self-knowledge into a world created by the combined powers of the sympathetic imagination, poetry and history, a world that is ethically impeccable, but from which the self is excluded" (xxiv).

De Man's analysis of negative capability is striking, but it introduces a temporal warp in his own understanding: his early description of the potential dangers of negative capability applies to his late theory of deconstruction. Deconstruction, as de Man practices it, also strives for an ethically impeccable world, but it excludes the self. Deconstruction considers the self as both a great mythology and the source of aggressive impulses; yet, as de Man's early analyses conclude, expelling the self for ethical reasons leads to a mendacious form of egoism and a voracious paradox. First, it martyrs the self to give it greater luminosity and power. Second, it leads to an ethics that may seem impeccable but that achieves its faultless nature not by solving problems but by disavowing them. A moral philosophy that does not include the self may seem faultless, but its perfection rests in reality on the enormous void left by its rejection of the human. Removing the human from ethics leaves it without a basis for existence, since ethics is by definition profoundly anthropocentric.

If Keats's ethical sympathies are to survive, he must overcome the temptation to martyrdom that his hatred of self conceals. He must also overcome the temptation to see the poet as the savior of humankind. *The Fall of Hyperion* brings the historical consciousness necessary to the task. It is not about eternity, like the "Ode on a Grecian Urn," but about those who fall in history. The poem exposes the sacrificial nature of history, but it extends sympathy to its victims. Unlike *Hyperion*, it sees no new god of poetry arise from the conflict. Nor does the poet muster the resurrection of the fallen. Rather, the poet, overwrought by his own mortality, presides as the witness of the fruits of violence:

> A long awful time
> I looked upon them; still they were the same;
> The frozen God still bending to the Earth,
> And the sad Goddess weeping at his feet.
> Moneta silent. Without stay or prop
> But my own weak mortality, I bore
> The load of this eternal quietude,
> The unchanging gloom. . . .
> *(The Fall of Hyperion* 1.384–91)

The passage is notable because it represents not the triumph of the Olympians but the fall of the Titans. The poem sympathizes with the sacrificed of history, and Keats's accent on the poet's frozen mortality creates a parallel between the situations of the Titans and the poet, prefiguring the identification necessary to bring the self back into Keats's ethically impeccable world.

The Titans' fall defines the sacrificial character of history. Without it there would be no insight. Similarly, Keats's fall is necessary to prompt the self-knowledge necessary to complete his ethics. De Man locates the final scene of Keats's self-consciousness in "This Living Hand":

> This living hand, now warm and capable
> Of earnest grasping, would, if it were cold
> And in the icy silence of the tomb,
> So haunt thy days and chill thy dreaming nights
> That thou wouldst wish thine own heart dry of blood
> So in my veins red life might stream again,
> And thou be conscience-calmed—see here it is—
> I hold it towards you.

The hands clasp in a waltz of life. The image of the lifeless hand of the poet, introduced by the conditional "if," stirs the reader's desire to bring the poet back to life even at the cost of death. But the poet will not permit it and comes back from his nightmarish death to prevent the sacrifice and to join the living in love and friendship. As de Man remarks, the poet no longer saves humanity. He takes the position of the victim; and yet Keats does not succumb to the temptation of self-destruction.[8] He neither sacrifices himself for the reader by refusing to return from the world of "if" to the world of the living, nor does he simply relish death, but instead demonstrates in the offer of the final line the desire to live. The love of sympathy leads to life and puts an end to the "self-destroying" love of *Endymion*.

"This Living Hand" destroys the barriers created by modern criticism between the general and particular, between the system and fragment, and between the saved and the martyred. It

8. Elsewhere de Man makes a similar inference. Writing of Hölderlin and Keats, he insists that "what first appears as an act of intellectual growth and insight gradually takes on an ethical dimension of supreme sacrifice, of suicide in the highest possible sense. Both poets become increasingly aware of this as their meditation progresses, and their works shift from the theme of historical rejuvenation to sacrifice." Nevertheless, as de Man concludes of the poet in *The Fall of Hyperion*, "the actual sacrifice is not within his power; and the poet is merely the one who has *seen* the sacrifice, with the mind's eye, as Moneta reveals it to him." See "Keats and Hölderlin," *Comparative Literature* 8 (1956): 43–44.

refuses to end with the marginalization or self-martyrdom of poets by asserting their severe isolation from humanity. To the contrary, the poem is a moment of strict binding that excludes no one. De Man rightly associates the poem with the greatest achievement of Romanticism: "Romantic literature, at its highest moments, encompasses the greatest degree of generality in an experience that never loses contact with the individual self in which it originates" (xxxiv). Romantic literature at its best strikes outward toward the ethical gesture of inclusion with the knowledge of the dangers of generality and particularity, of the two-fold temptations of exclusive system and excluded martyrdom, and this scope of understanding makes possible what de Man calls "philosophical generality rooted in genuine self-insight" (xxxiv). It also makes possible Keats's late "philosophical" acceptance of the powers that force self-knowledge.

Hyperion Falling

Hyperion cannot be made an example or make an example of himself if he does not fall. If Hyperion continues to fall, if he is always already falling, there is no exclusive system and no excluded martyrdom. But there is also no insight, no "philosophy" in Keats's sense, except for the insight that one is falling, "falling back to nought," de Man remarks in his Preface to *The Rhetoric of Romanticism*.

In "The Resistance to Theory," de Man abandons his ethical reading of Keats's poetry. That Keats was unable to complete either *Hyperion* or *The Fall of Hyperion*, de Man concludes, "manifests the impossibility, for him as for us, of reading his own title" (16). Keats's death has nothing to do with it. Nor does Keats ever risk achieving the self-knowledge necessary to mature ethical judgment. Rather, de Man's rereading of Keats serves as an example of why resistance to theory thrives. Such resistance is a "resistance to the rhetorical or tropological dimension of language." Resistance no longer expresses subjective emotions, as it did in Freud, but merely indicates the workings of positional language; and language definitively usurps the position of the self. Indeed, the "self" in de Man is the position in language than cannot comprehend language.

No longer the product of Keats's ethical struggles, *The Fall of Hyperion* now appears as a classic example of language's resistance to language. The genitive in the title frustrates grammatical readings, de Man argues, for it could mean either "Hyperion's Fall," the story of a definitive defeat, or "Hyperion Falling," the story of an incessant falling, in which Apollo, Hyperion, Keats, and the reader are all interchangeable and constantly plunging downward. De Man also reads *The Fall of Hyperion* intertextually as a gloss on Keats's earlier *Hyperion*. The late poem tells the story of the failure of the first poem. Yet the fall of *Hyperion* does not signify the triumph of *The Fall of Hyperion* because both poems remain unfinished. De Man asks whether the title does or does not tell "the story of why all texts, as texts, can always be said to be falling" (17). The rhetoric of the poem suggests opposing grammatical readings, necessarily making the title unreadable. And the poem's unreadability parallels a crisis of understanding in which the author and reader share. "Just as Keats had to break off his narrative," de Man contends, "the reader has to break off his understanding at the very moment when he is most directly engaged and summoned by the text" (17). Nor does de Man permit a sympathy between poet and reader, of the kind found in "This Living Hand," to exist within the realm of possibility: "One could hardly expect to find solace in this 'fearful symmetry' between the author's and the reader's plight since, at this point, the symmetry is no longer a formal but an actual trap, and the question no longer 'merely' theoretical" (17).

Keats's ethically impeccable system needs only to include the self to reach perfection. When the self enters the system, the system unites the particular and the general with an ethical gesture, but de Man now associates all generalized systems with the impulse toward totalization and totalitarianism. Just as *The Fall of Hyperion* is for de Man the story of the failure of *Hyperion*, "The Resistance to Theory" becomes the story of the failure of de Man's early reading of Keats. *The Fall of Hyperion* risks letting the self arrive, and de Man's rhetorical reading deliberately suspends Hyperion in midair. De Man's sense of "Hyperion Falling" indefinitely postpones the arrival of the self. He freezes Keats's progress toward greater self-consciousness at an earlier stage, before he learns to fall and to accept his own death. Consequently, de Man also remains at an early stage.

De Man's insistence on the state of falling serves to defer the fall necessary to punctuate any system. Yet the idea of a system need not be violent, unless one believes that institutions can never escape their origins. Rather, the historical tendency of systems to create exclusions is violent. The essentially ethical impulse not to exclude therefore begins by targeting systematic thought as the worse offense. But ethics does not consist merely in this impulse. In point of definition, ethics is a system that denies those systems defined by their exclusions, and it works ideally toward an inclusive community of human beings. De Man's love of paradox remains an ethical response to the perceived violence of systematic thought, but he goes awry when he expels the idea of system as necessarily violent while constructing his own marginal system. In the end, his refusal to confront the self as well as his systematic exclusion of the self from the literary work risk, as did Keats's "self-destroying" love, the temptation of self-martyrdom and the glorification of the self through its failures. At this point, rigor mortis sets in and threatens de Man with its irrefutable necessity.

The Triumph of Disfigurement

"Shelley Disfigured" revolves around the same problems as "The Resistance to Theory" and the Introduction to Keats's poetry. De Man concludes "that *The Triumph of Life* is a fragment of something whole, or romanticism a fragment, or a moment, in a process that now includes us within its horizon" (94). As in the early essay on Keats, de Man defines Romanticism as a movement whose formulations encompass its potential criticism and redefinition. The self-resisting power of Romanticism also parallels that of theory and literary language. Romanticism begins to take shape as the most "literary" and "theoretical" movement.

Although the theories of Romanticism argued in the essays on Shelley and Keats are strikingly consistent in some ways, the meaning of *The Triumph of Life* differs radically from Keats's poetry, as de Man had previously described it. Unlike Keats's

"This Living Hand," Shelley's poem follows a trajectory of disfigurement, in which the loss of the eyes means the loss of insight. "This trajectory from erased self-knowledge to disfiguration," de Man summarizes, "is the trajectory of *The Triumph of Life*" (100). De Man's reading of Shelley disposes of every idea that had meaning for him in Keats as well as any idea that might associate Romanticism with higher ethical ideals. He insists that traditional interpretations of the poem, which seem to rely on a discarded passage where Rousseau admonishes the poet not to repeat the mistakes of his generation, cannot be supported. The interpretation "is a clear example of the recuperation of a failing energy by means of increased awareness," and when de Man discards it, he discards in effect his old reading of Keats (96). The sense of communion between poet and reader found in "This Living Hand" falters without the possibility of an identifying sympathy between them. And all sense of reciprocity between the poet and the fallen is erased. Rather, de Man bases his interpretation on Shelley's isolation of Rousseau from the other representatives of the Enlightenment. Rousseau's encounter with the "shape all light" becomes a scene dramatizing "the failure to satisfy a desire for self-knowledge" (99). Rousseau is not a "spoiler spoiled," who warns the poet not to play the role of spoiler. Instead, Rousseau laments, "I was overcome / By my own heart alone," and adopts the pose of the martyr (102).

Rousseau's insight is his blindness, his self-resistance, and his inability to attain self-knowledge. Like the other symbols of achievement, Aristotle and Plato, Rousseau becomes in de Man's reading a double figure, whose fall and triumph merge. In this sense, *The Triumph of Life* also acquires a double meaning in de Man's estimation. He identifies life with an eroding process, and once more, the theory of blindness and insight calls forth the ideas of psychoanalysis. The words of Freud, *"the aim of all life is death"* (18:38), intervene as if to pervert the victory of life, and *The Triumph of Life* becomes the triumph of death. My allusion to Freud makes sense in the contexts of de Man's theory of blindness and insight and of Romanticism. If Romanticism is the movement that prefigures and incorporates its own criticisms, the movement that cannot be transcended, it takes on the form of a historicized and all-inclusive unconscious system.

Civilization and Its Discontents seems to confirm the inference that de Man's view of Romanticism owes a debt to Freud. The same elements are in play and hold similar positions in their arguments. Like de Man, Freud pits the forces of love and death against each other. The book begins by reducing Romain Rolland's "oceanic feeling" of sympathy to narcissism, as de Man does in the case of Keats, and moves to attack other Romantic conceptions. Chapter 3 reads as a sustained critique of the Romantic notions that civilization is largely responsible for human misery, that the "noble savage" actually possesses a simpler life than others, and that science does not mean genuine benefits and advances. And yet for all of the criticisms of Romanticism, Freud seems unable to transcend the movement. *Civilization and Its Discontents* remains a fundamentally Romantic work. Indeed, its title has become the apotheosis of the Rousseauistic separation between nature and culture.

Most important, *Civilization and Its Discontents* exposes the logical link between the Keats and Shelley of de Man. The book insists on the brutal and random force of death, as does de Man's reading of Shelley. It pits the forces of necessity against those of love, as does de Man's reading of Keats. Keats's greatest temptation in de Man's eyes remains similar to the forces that destroy Rousseau in Shelley. Keats risks being overcome by his own heart alone and failing to achieve the self-knowledge necessary to his mature ethics. The key to Keats's victory rests in his ability to translate his own suffering, without succumbing to a sense of glorious martyrdom, into an identifying and conscious sympathy toward human suffering in general. The self-destroying dimension of love must be surpassed and aggression disengaged from love. Freud tells precisely the same story about civilization, and his first attempt at a conclusion duplicates Keats's findings:

> The fateful question for the human species seems to me to be whether and to what extent their cultural development will succeed in mastering the disturbance of their communal life by the

human instinct of aggression and self-destruction. . . . Men have
gained control over the forces of nature to such an extent that
with their help they would have no difficulty in exterminating
one another to the last man. They know this, and hence comes a
large part of their current unrest, their unhappiness and their
mood of anxiety. And now it is to be expected that the other of
the two "Heavenly Powers," eternal Eros, will make an effort to
assert himself in the struggle with his equally immortal adversary. (21:145)

The antidote to the self-destroying power of humankind consists of knowledge and "eternal Eros." Freud ends with Keats's
solution. But it was not Freud's final word. When the menace of
Hitler became apparent to him in 1931, he appended a final
sentence: "But who can foresee with what success and with
what result?" The statement inserts a moment of doubt concerning the triumph of Eros and departs from Keats's "philosophy."
But the phrase also returns Freud to the conclusion of "The
Resistances to Psycho-Analysis." Hitler takes the shape of the
death drive in Freud's mind and poses a special threat to the
Jewish advocate of psychoanalysis. Hitler symbolizes the conditions of isolation necessary to Freud's theories as well as the
dreaded inevitability of humanity's martyrdom at its own
hands.

De Man's reading of Shelley follows the same itinerary, pursuing the insight of self-martyrdom. First, it disposes of the idea
that Rousseau might present knowledge to the poet. In a series
of Freudian passages, de Man gives privilege to the process of
forgetting over that of consciousness. Since the repressed must
always return, Shelley's poet is condemned to repeat Rousseau's aberrations in a more violent mode (just as de Man is
condemned to repeat Rousseau more violently in "The Rhetoric
of Blindness"). Consequently, de Man believes, *"The Triumph of
Life* can be said to reduce all of Shelley's previous works to
nought" (120). Second, de Man takes exception to Donald Reiman's suggestion that the "shape all light" might represent Julie
as a figure of love. The rejection of Reiman's reading is also a
rejection of the mature love associated in the early Introduction
with Keats's moral philosophy. Instead, the "shape all light"

metamorphoses into a Narcissus figure, just as Rolland's "oceanic feeling" derives from narcissism. Furthermore, the "shape all light" in its narcissistic function exposes the self-reflexive nature of Shelley's poem and of all literature. "We now understand," de Man insists, "the shape to be the figure for the figurality of all signification" (116). *The Triumph of Life* becomes definitively the fall of life and the triumph of death, for what the figure of figurality reveals is the repressive and violent nature of language. The waning of the light-shape results, de Man holds, from "a single, and therefore violent, act of power achieved by the positional power of language considered by and in itself" (116).

Literary language illuminates the violence of language, although not in a manner that guarantees a knowledge of violence or of language itself. The insight is rather, in de Man's theory, the emergence of pure violence and power. Language is itself the manifestation of violence acting on violence, of fire consuming fire, of light making the perception of light impossible. Metaphor is as violent as the deadly Apollo, "for the initial violence of position can only be half erased, since the erasure is accomplished by a device of language that never ceases to partake of the very violence against which it is directed. It seems to extend the instantaneousness of the act of positing over a series of transformations . . ." (118–19). Apollo metamorphoses into Lucifer, and the figure of Satan against himself sinks "'below the watery floor' trampled to death by its own power" (119). Just as Freud's *Todestrieb* seems to ensure mankind's self-destruction, dreadful necessity arises in the form of language's "self-resisting" power. Language creates the conditions for our self-martyrdom. Its power corrupts absolutely, and Shelley's poem becomes de Man's morality play. Its moral reveals that knowledge and power destroy themselves and their possessors. Consequently, *The Triumph of Life* translates triumph into fall; it insists on the impassable distance between an actual victory, a "triumph," and the *trionfo*, "the pageant that celebrates the outcome of battle" (116). The triumph never arrives, as de Man's Hyperion never hits bottom; rather, the triumph remains a *thriambos*, an eternal hymn to the *danse macabre* and to the Dionysian destruction that is life.

The death of Shelley assures the triumph of death and casts an ironic pall over the poem's title. Shelley's defaced body appears in the margins of the poem in de Man's interpretation. His sole task is to textualize it. The task is easy because the abruptness and arbitrariness of Shelley's death imitate the random events portrayed in the poem. The arbitrariness of death and of language become one: "*The Triumph of Life* warns us that nothing, whether deed, word, thought, or text, ever happens in relation, positive or negative, to anything that precedes, follows, or exists elsewhere, but only as a random event whose power, like the power of death, is due to the randomness of its occurrence" (122). In the case of Keats, the power of death completes a system. It allows Keats to make more impeccable his ethical world. In the case of Shelley, the power of death ensures the fragmentation of the system, for de Man argues that its arbitrary and brutal arrival makes *The Triumph of Life* an impossible subject and a more impossible poem.

"Shelley Disfigured," however, does end systematically. First, it creates a unity between Shelley's disfigurement and de Man's theories and ends by embracing a strange form of self-marginalization. Shelley's fate becomes merely a trope in the linguistic predicament called death, and de Man cites it as a theoretical justification of his view that language and death are one. Second, "Shelley Disfigured" contains a deliberation on the problems of theory, anticipating de Man's final words in "The Resistance to Theory." In both essays, de Man contrasts those theories that ground themselves in natural relations with his own theory of rhetoric and its insistence on arbitrariness. But he cannot separate the two and refers to both with the same kinds of images: the belief in the natural grounding of meaning "functions along monotonously predictable lines, by the historicization and the aesthetification of texts, as well as by their use, as in this essay, for the assertion of methodological claims made all the more pious by their denial of piety" (122). As in the essay on the resistance to theory, de Man and his detractors achieve unity in a negative moment. His piety defines theirs by exposing the inevitability of piety.

De Man's piety is the piety of Shelley disfigured. It is the piety of martyrdom dependent upon the marginalization of systems.

"Shelley Disfigured" insists that falling and triumphing are the same process, and it aligns itself with the inevitability of fragmentation—in the form of Shelley's body, his poem, and the movement of Romanticism itself—thus promoting its own marginalization. The final lines of the essay assert the marginal values of deconstruction by writing the last lines of "The Resistance to Theory" not in the language of triumph and fall, but in a language opposed to generality and systematic thought: "Reading as disfiguration, to the very extent that it resists historicism, turns out to be historically more reliable than the products of historical archeology. To monumentalize this observation into a *method* of reading would be to regress from the rigor exhibited by Shelley which is exemplary precisely because it refuses to be generalized into a system" (123).

The lines are also a rewriting of de Man's early essay on Keats. There he defined Romanticism and Keats's place among the great Romantic poets in terms of their ability to encompass "the greatest degree of generality in an experience that never loses contact with the individual self in which it originates" (xxxiv).[9] Now that generality, which characterizes the highest moment of Romanticism, has been killed by necessity. Philosophical generality is the death of genuine self-knowledge, and history portrays nothing but the ineluctable necessity of fragmentation and the triumph of death and disfiguration. In its wake, triumph and fall, criticism and literature, insight and blindness cannot be opposed.

---

9. A final image associated with the procession of figures in *The Triumph of Life* poses an alternative to de Man's interpretation. I cite from *Shelley's Poetry and Prose*, ed. Donald H. Reiman and Sharon B. Powers (New York: Norton, 1977):

"These shadows, numerous as the dead leaves blown

"In Autumn evening from a popular tree—
    Each, like himself and like each other were,
    At first, but soon distorted, seemed to be. . . ."

                                                            (528–31)

The lines expose a merging between the general and particular similar to the identifying sympathy found in Keats's "This Living Hand" and associated with the highest achievement of Romanticism.

Falling to Nought

Rhetoric may transform Hyperion's fall into a falling or postpone for a time the brutal and definitive triumph of life. But rhetoric remains rhetoric and knows nothing of love and death. The Preface to *The Rhetoric of Romanticism* was written in the shadow of death, and it carries the signs of de Man's unfortunate and premature passing. Unlike Keats's late poetry, however, the essay does not move beyond the Romantic rhetoric of suffering toward a theory of human sympathy based on an identification between individual and general suffering. De Man seems unable, unlike the Keats of his early Introduction, to transform the knowledge of his own death into an ethical moment and still resist the thrill of martyrdom. Rather, the Preface is an exercise in rhetoric, and it makes a final statement on the martyred language of de Man's deconstructive theories.

The prefatory essay elaborates precisely those rhetorical theories, found in de Man's late writings on Keats and Shelley, that make impossible an identifying sympathy between the dying person and the rest of humanity. It enshrines the marginal values of deconstruction as well as de Man's personal failings. The only unity possible, the "false unity" of the book, is the responsibility of another: de Man insists that the essays were collected at the initiative of the editor of the Columbia University Press. No system or coherence may be found between its covers, and the associations between the essays are as random as those of the figures passing in Shelley's *The Triumph of Life.* "The fragmentary aspect of the whole," de Man admits about the book, "is made more obvious still by the hypotactic manner that prevails in each of the essays taken in isolation, by the continued attempt, however ironized, to present a closed and linear argument. This apparent coherence *within* each essay is not matched by a corresponding coherence *between* them. Laid out diachronically in a roughly chronological sequence, they do not evolve in a manner that easily allows for dialectical progression or, ultimately, for historical totalization" (viii). The movement away from totalization and generality apparent in earlier essays animates the passage, and indeed de Man is stirred by his own inability to comment on what he has done. Each essay seems to begin "from scratch," and their conclusions "fail to add up to anything" (viii). He finds himself unable to articulate "some secret principle of summation" (viii).

De Man's sense of his difference from other theorists again tries to assert itself, but it succeeds to a degree not achieved in the other essays. As such, the Preface becomes de Man's definitive statement on his own martyrdom to the system that he has created. Instead of portraying himself as being sacrificed equally with others to the "self-resisting power" of language, he stands alone in the insight of his blindness. In no way does the Preface appropriate those who resist theory to the workings of theory. Rather, it describes them as optimistic thinkers to be envied and suspected and from whom de Man feels essentially estranged: "One feels at times envious of those who can continue to do literary history as if nothing had happened in the sphere of theory, but one cannot help but feel somewhat suspicious of their optimism" (ix). The negative unity stressed by "The Resistance to Theory" is simply impossible, and de Man stamps the book with the imprint of failure: "*The Rhetoric of Romanticism* should at least help to document some of the difficulties it fails to resolve" (ix). In effect, the book's title is true to the principle that it expresses, for de Man's theory confides increasingly as it develops that the rhetoric of Romanticism reveals insight only into its own failures.

Finally, de Man makes a last attempt to achieve a unity between the level of his style and that of history. His style has been to state "the inevitability of fragmentation in a mode that is itself fragmented" (ix). And he attains unity with the ideals of Romanticism as he has described them. He aspires to the discursive elegance of those Romantic writers who teach the insight of the figurality of all signification, and like those writers, he seems to think it "a small price to pay, perhaps, compared to the burden of constantly falling back to nought" (ix). Just as *The Triumph of Life* in de Man's reading negates Shelley's previous writings, the Preface reduces all of de Man's "previous work to nought." Indeed, de Man concludes by mentioning "Shelley Disfigured" as his best effort at facing questions about history and fragmentation. There death is portrayed as the totalizing god of language, and we are sacrificed in its name.[10]

Death is, in effect, the perfect antisystem, more perfect by far than the Freudian unconscious. Its flawless negativity consumes our parodic and addled attempts to mimic its perfection in life. For de Man, the violence of philosophical generality is arbitrary and common compared to the dreadful necessity of death. Death casts its shroud on all equally and with cruel justice. It permits no escape and no insight, but it holds a special torture for those who cling in the knowledge of their blindness to the delights of martyrdom. Death defines their being, and it can be neither arbitrary nor tame. The only knowledge valued by the martyr is the inexorable fatality of blindness, for it defines the possibility of martyrdom and gives one brief insight into the triumph of falling.*

10. Only its penultimate sentence suggests another mood. This line states de Man's characteristic vision of blindness and insight, but hints that the future of criticism—and perhaps his future—"is far from clear, but certainly no longer simply a matter of syntax and diction" (ix). Whether de Man is referring to a necessity beyond grammatical and rhetorical readings is a question that those acquainted with him personally might know better than I how to answer. It remains, however, that de Man was unable in his writings to move beyond the experience of death. Elsewhere I have argued that de Man's work elaborates a rhetoric of mourning that requires the idea of death, and not absence, to create its coherence. See "Paul de Man and the Rhetoric of Selfhood," *New Orleans Review* 13.1 (1986): 5–9.

Author's note to 1990 printing: The texts of Paul de Man's wartime journalism were discovered after *The Ethics of Criticism* had gone to press. For an analysis of de Man's journalistic writings that builds upon the remarks here, see my "Mourning Becomes Paul de Man," in Werner Hamacher, Neil Hertz, and Thomas Keenan, eds., *Responses: On Paul de Man's Wartime Journalism* (Lincoln: University of Nebraska Press, 1989), pp. 363–67.

6

Resentment and the Genealogy of Morals: From Nietzsche to Girard

What does it mean to be a philosopher of resentment? It means that one is a philosopher of life, emotions, and instincts. It means that one is a psychologist who focuses on human behavior. There can be no philosophy of resentment without a theory of the human.

Being a philosopher of resentment also makes one an ethical thinker. Resentment remains a special emotion in the ethical tradition; and not merely because Nietzsche based his *Genealogy of Morals* on its place in history. "Resentment" is only the most recent word for revenge, and the problem of revenge enters the ethical tradition at its inception. The appearance of the word, in fact, marks the attempt, especially on Nietzsche's part, to establish a psychological theory of revenge and its representations. Indeed, the fear of revenge may be the emotion that underlies moral philosophy in the West. A society can survive arbitrary acts of violence; it may even withstand warfare, since battle often strengthens the unanimity of a group. But no society can withstand the premeditated and organized violence of revenge because it initiates menacing cycles of conflict from within. Blood feuds, cycles of revenge, and other forms of organized violence endure for generations; as Greek tragedy dramatically illustrates, they place a curse on the house of mankind.

Nietzsche's theory of resentment focuses on the problem of representation.[1] It explains how the weak represent the world to save themselves from the strong. The infamous "slave morality" ascribed by Nietzsche to Judeo-Christianity remains in the final analysis a system of representation. In this regard only, the French Nietzscheans are right to view Nietzsche as a theorist of language. But Nietzsche is more than a linguistic structuralist. Nietzsche saw himself as the first psychologist, and that label is meant to contrast sharply with the philological interests of his youth. Indeed, he feared that mankind would believe in God as long as it believed in grammar, and it follows that the death of God should signify the death of language, and not necessarily the death of the human, as the structuralists believe. Nietzsche cannot be a philosopher of resentment and simultaneously proclaim the death of man, and yet recent theory has used Nietzsche to grant special privilege to the linguistic over the human sciences, often rewriting his work as a grammatology. The French critics of Nietzsche find that his originality lies in his "style" or in the early theories of rhetoric positing that truth is only a fiction of the will to power. For them, Nietzsche was first and foremost a rhetorician; his object of inquiry was language, and he wanted little to do with either the social sciences or the idea of the human.[2]

1. General references to Friedrich Nietzsche will be given parenthetically in the text. They include *The Gay Science* (abbreviated as *GS* in the text), ed. and trans. Walter Kaufmann (New York: Vintage, 1974), *On the Genealogy of Morals* and *Ecce Homo* (*EH*), ed. and trans. Walter Kaufmann (New York: Vintage, 1967), *The Portable Nietzsche* (*PN*), ed. and trans. Walter Kaufmann (New York: Penguin, 1954), and *The Will to Power* (*WP*), trans. Walter Kaufmann and R. J. Hollingdale (New York: Vintage, 1968). References to the works of René Girard include *Deceit, Desire, and the Novel*, trans. Y. Freccero (Baltimore: Johns Hopkins University Press, 1965), "Strategies of Madness" (61–83), "Delirium as System" (84–120), and "The Underground Critic" (36–60), in *To Double Business Bound* (Baltimore: Johns Hopkins University Press, 1978), *Le Bouc émissaire* (Paris: Grasset, 1982), and "Dionysus versus the Crucified," *MLN* 99.4 (1984): 816–35.

I have found it difficult to express Nietzsche's thought in a nonsexist vocabulary, especially when discussing the idea of the overman. Perhaps it is best not to mask it.

2. For examples of the French influence in Nietzsche studies, see David B. Allison, ed. *The New Nietzsche* (New York: Delta, 1977); *Nietzsche aujourd'hui*, 2 vols. (Paris: Union Générale d'Editions, 1973); and "Why Nietzsche Now?" ed. Daniel O'Hara, *boundary 2* 9.3 and 10.1 (1981). An examination of Nietzsche's style may be found in Jacques Derrida, *Spurs: Nietzsche's Styles*, trans. Barbara

René Girard, the modern critic of violent desire, has recently developed an argument similar to that of the French Nietzscheans, despite his characteristic opposition to their claims. Girard concludes that Nietzsche's theory focuses on the subtle and civilized language of resentment to the exclusion of the far more dangerous desire for vengeance. In a sense, Girard accuses Nietzsche of being overly concerned with the modern representations of revenge, of which resentment is only one, and not with the real object of humanity's problems. The concern with resentment reveals that Nietzsche has been duped by a fascination with the language of revenge, whose mystifying nature always tries to lead its pursuers off the track by offering them interesting diversions. Resentment is the interesting diversion offered to modern philosophy by violence, while real vengeance advances its death grip on us in the form of nuclear politics and terrorism. Resentment, for Girard, is the spirit of revenge half suppressed. Accordingly, Nietzsche's idea that only the reemergence of revenge will call a halt to modern resentment is revenge's diabolical joke.

Human violence, be it called resentful or revengeful, is mainly an issue of representation insofar as language is the principal means through which individuals come to the knowledge of violence. The most significant question for the ethics of criticism remains whether human beings are capable of understanding their own violence; and Nietzsche's theory of resentment and Girard's theory of vengeance agree that mankind cannot penetrate the nature of its aggression. Sharp contrasts exist between their theories of knowledge, but both thinkers end by placing the knowledge of ethics beyond the reach of human intelligence. In Nietzsche, resentment establishes a slave morality that deliberately misinterprets the differences between the strong and the weak. If human difference is truth for Nietzsche, then

---

Harlow (Chicago: At the University Press, 1979). For an analysis of Nietzsche's early rhetoric, see Paul de Man, "Rhetoric of Tropes," *Allegories of Reading* (New Haven: Yale University Press, 1979), pp. 103–18. I analyze de Man's reading of Nietzsche in depth in "Paul de Man and the Rhetoric of Selfhood," *New Orleans Review* 13.1 (1986): 5–9.

its knowledge is profoundly restricted by resentment, for the slave morality strives to found a democratic and egalitarian society in which human differences are negligible. Only the appearance of the overman, the creature who has overcome humanity's intellectual limitations, preserves Nietzsche's ideal of difference. In Girard, vengeance as a form of mimetic desire creates elaborate mythologies to defeat human understanding and to perpetuate violence; it enflames its victims with the fever of superiority, giving them a special license to persecute others. The end result is self-destruction, a veritable inferno of violence, in which victim and victimizer annihilate each other.

Revenge and resentment create their own perverse mythologies of knowledge, and Nietzsche and Girard agree that they are dangerous theories at best. There are, however, some differences in the ways that Nietzsche and Girard conceive of the danger. Girard perceives an essential association between violence and desire, whereas Nietzsche defines resentment in the absence of a consistent theory of desire. As a result, Nietzsche sometimes believes that resentment can be overcome by human efforts. Another way of expressing this difference would be to say that Girard is writing with the knowledge of Freud, whereas Nietzsche has no reason to discuss unconscious desire. What post-Freudian thinkers would call desire appears in Nietzsche under other names, not because he is repressing desire but because the psychoanalytic tradition of desire has yet to be established. Nietzsche, of course, gives greater weight to the will, whereas nothing like the will can exist within psychoanalysis. The idea of the will in Nietzsche affirms his wish to posit a theory of knowledge. Freudian theory, to the contrary, insistently divides knowledge and desire, for desire in psychoanalysis works essentially on an unconscious level. Any knowledge of desire acquired by the self is always placed at the service of more desire. The light of desire makes it possible only to cast larger shadows.

Has Freud taught modern thinkers to overestimate the significance of desire in psychology? It is easy in a post-Freudian age to accuse Nietzsche of fleeing from a theory of desire for unconscious reasons. Why does no one ever ask why Freud created a theory that suppresses the will? The psychoanalytic theory of unconscious desire holds an enormous attraction for the modern sensibility, perhaps because it provides an antidote to its painful self-consciousness. Once the intellect has been reduced to unconscious motivations by modern theories of desire, individuals may disclaim responsibility for the violence of which they are only too aware.[3]

Although there is certainly no reason to doubt the existence of unconscious desires, no one has yet proved that they are either as determinant or as elusive as psychoanalysis tends to portray them. If the unconscious is unknowable, then psychoanalysis as the science of the unconscious collapses in contradiction. Either psychoanalytic theories of desire are produced by unconscious fantasies and understand nothing about desire, or psychoanalysis has a knowledge of desire that contradicts its own theory of the unconscious. Nor can one accept, without acknowledging the possibility of knowing desire, either the value of the psychoanalytic method or its evolution as a social science.

Desire is indeed central to psychology, but Freudian theory accounts for desire in Nietzsche only with difficulty. Nietzsche does not describe desire only in terms of sexual instincts; he describes the volatile passions of daily human struggle. Desire in Nietzsche is not a monolithic structure but is identified with many unbound and conflicting impulses that pertain to everyday activities and individual character: resentment, false hopes, revenge, nausea, disappointment, and emotions of defeat and victory. Furthermore, Nietzsche seems to accept that human desires can be overcome. The many drives directing humanity's emotional state continually contradict each other, establishing a

3. Recent criticism tends to exaggerate Nietzsche's relation to the unconscious by imposing a Freudian reading on it. Since Freud argues that the unconscious cannot say "No!" some theorists believe that Nietzschean affirmation may be read as a pure desire for unconsciousness. Reducing affirmation to an unconscious state denies the power of the will to determine character and to make decisions. In Freud, the existence of the unconscious acts to discharge individuals of their responsibility for violence, whereas Nietzsche views the will to power as the means for individuals to assume the responsibility for violence in a world where God is dead. What makes affirmation essentially tragic is the conscious acceptance of that responsibility and its paradoxes.

situation where the intellect must exercise its authority and choose sides. In fact, Nietzsche defines character as the ability to exercise consistent choices. It is a matter not of excluding sexual desire from Nietzsche's philosophy but of recognizing that he considers it important to understand the impact of desire on the knowledge of character and social life. For Nietzsche, there is no experience that cannot lead to knowledge. Consequently, desire includes, at least in theory, the possibility of being understood. Modern theorists make the distinction between the Nietzschean and Freudian views of desire difficult to comprehend because they always prefer the latter to the former. They may begin by arguing that Freud represses the influence of Nietzsche, but they usually end by showing how Freudian Nietzsche is, perhaps because psychoanalytic theory grants a semblance of order to Nietzsche's aphoristic thought.

Like his view of human nature, Nietzsche's idea of psychology contains an abundance of contradictions, and his theory of resentment is no exception. At its center resides the opposition between the conscious and unconscious action of willing. French critics of late have acquired the habit of referring to these types as active and reactive, but the terms need the idea of consciousness to make sense because people are reactive in Nietzsche only when they act against others rather than for themselves. Nietzsche's description of the two forms of willing is hardly just, but it is in keeping with his view of religious history. Judeo-Christianity flounders in the reactive and unconscious form of willing called resentment; its usurpation of power from the "honest Greeks" is nothing like a deliberate strategy, but an accident driven by the power of resentment itself. The Jew, for Nietzsche, is clever, but not sufficiently so to defeat the "higher man" in a fair fight.

To understand the power of resentment will require some explanation, notably because Nietzsche himself does not describe it accurately. Nietzsche tends to define resentment as an emotion always directed away from the self toward others, and he is hard put to explain why the culture of resentment has managed to crush those potential overmen who have maintained their autonomy. Suffice it to say for the moment that resentment thrives not by focusing on others but by focusing on itself in contrast to others. Resentment gives by its very structure a certain degree of strength to the resentful self because it acts to muster all the self's suffering around itself. Judeo-Christianity's characteristic belief in its own unworthiness is thus a form of self-preoccupation that gives it an advantage over other religious movements.

Despite Nietzsche's claims, the "noble man" does not differ from the Judeo-Christian in his susceptibility to resentment. The difference remains that Nietzsche's potential overman supposedly possesses the strength of will to attain consciousness of his resentment and to use it as a form of knowledge to move beyond its attractions. The overman refuses the easily gained preoccupation with the self given by resentment in favor of the more conscious striving toward perfection called the will to power. Nietzsche argues that the overman wills to be unconscious of his resentful consciousness, whereas the resentful self of Judeo-Christianity is driven unconsciously by the irritating awareness of its own inadequacy. If this attitude appears psychologically unrealistic or unsound, the reason is not merely that self-consciousness is paradoxical. Such criticisms adhere blindly to a Freudian view of desire, in which desire can never be its own theory. The problem with Nietzsche's description of resentment is twofold. The greatest difficulty springs from the arbitrary distinction created between Judeo-Christians and Nietzsche's potential overman. Nietzsche's own portrait of the man of resentment consistently undercuts this difference, because his idea of who is strongest and who is weakest never corresponds with the actual state of affairs. A second and related problem is that resentment serves knowledge in the case of the noble breed, but mythology in the case of the Judeo-Christian.

The philosopher of resentment always risks being accused of resenting those whom he identifies as the sources of resentment. In Nietzsche's case, his resentment of Judeo-Christianity is undoubtedly a reality. Nietzsche's argument for the cultural productivity of resentment applies equally to his own philosophical works, which take their energy from his feelings of insignificance in face of the awesome influence of Judeo-Christianity and the Romantic movement in his world. The seminal work on resentment, *On the Genealogy of Morals*, is Nietzsche's "polemic," but readers often forget what he is arguing against and why. They are taken in by the most superficial aspect of Nietzsche's argument and accept the work as a critique of the forms of religious representation that forsake life in favor of an afterlife. But Nietzsche is not really polemicizing against religious conscience and its denial of life; if he were, he would not try to replace it with a tragic theory that also equates life with suffering. The difference between the martyrdoms of Christ and Dionysus, as we shall see, is a matter of interpretation, but in no way does Nietzsche contest the Christian idea that life on this earth is miserable. Rather, Nietzsche is a philosopher polemicizing against the dominant Christian philosophy of his age. His immediate precursors, Kant and Hegel, both owe an enormous debt to Christian thinking. Nietzsche's revolt against Judeo-Christianity is in part a quest for intellectual power and personal distinction, and his motivations are similar to those hidden beneath his break with Richard Wagner.

Was Nietzsche so brazen as to believe that he could reverse by himself the great interpretive and philosophical power of Judeo-Christianity? He certainly entered the fray with enthusiasm, and modern philosophy now identifies Nietzsche as the grand inquisitor of religion. In intellectual circles, in fact, Nietzsche emerges as the victor, for few modern thinkers continue to believe that religion possesses any theoretical force. Atheism and intellectual life are now married, and Nietzsche has been given the credit for making the match. Yet Nietzsche was hardly an atheist, but a man passionately involved in religious thinking. The idea of the eternal return provides the strongest demonstration of Nietzsche's religious instincts. One may also consider the ease with which Max Scheler, "the catholic Nietzsche," turned Nietzsche's theory of resentment in favor of Christianity. Finally, it would have been profoundly unlike Nietzsche to choose an adversary who was not his equal or better. Nietzsche entered the battle against religion not as an atheist but as a rival philosopher of religion. Similarly, he attacked morality not as an amoralist or an immoralist but as a competing moralist.

On the Genealogy of Morals tells the story of Nietzsche's resentful antipathy toward Judeo-Christianity, itself supposedly the flower of resentment. If resentment is the emotion of Judeo-Christianity, however, Nietzsche risks being seen as a resentful Christian in his attack on the religion of resentment. To expose this paradox, however, is not to succumb to the nihilist discourse of paradox uttered today in the name of Nietzsche; it is rather to identify the debt that Nietzsche owes to the system called Judeo-Christianity. What, then, is Judeo-Christianity as Nietzsche describes it?

Girard provides a most Nietzschean portrayal of Judeo-Christianity in his writings on the Bible. The Bible is the book of innocents and victims. Girard argues that, contrary to other religious forms, Judeo-Christianity always represents and takes the side of the victim. There is never any illusion of guilt associated with victims in the Bible; scripture insists on the innocence of those sacrificed to violence. It was Nietzsche who invented the idea that Judeo-Christianity is a religion for victims. Unlike Girard, however, Nietzsche found the idea repulsive. The great strength of the Bible in Girard's mind remains its loyalty to the weak and innocent of this world. The great flaw of the Bible for Nietzsche lies in its attraction to weakness, and he explicitly rejects its victimary philosophy. Nietzsche's aversion to the images of the suicidal Socrates and of the crucified Christ turns on their presentation of victims as models to emulate. His hatred of Rousseau similarly derives from the sense that the founder of Romanticism was a coward who took delight in self-deprecation, weakness, and complaint.

In reaction, Nietzsche took up his famous warrior stance, a determined resistance to pity for all victims. Being a warrior has the benefits of attracting both wisdom and women. Unfortunately, Nietzsche's success on both counts is hotly contested. What Nietzsche did achieve was a certain courage of conviction in pursuit of self-examination. For a resentful spirit, he was remarkable for his ability to accept responsibility for his ideas and personal choices. *Ecce Homo* emerges as a kind of funereal statement on Nietzsche's acceptance of his decisions in life and work. It is curiously free of resentment, although Nietzsche never abandons his acerbic and aphoristic manner. The book demonstrates his sustained effort to combat his own weaknesses, the most pernicious being the proclivity to resentment; he emerges as a victor, at least to the extent that someone of such enormous emotions could. Perhaps his only true rival in tenacious self-confession is Saint Augustine, a man who also knew the temptations of succumbing to both self-delight and peer pressure, as the incident of the stolen pears attests.

Nietzsche's hatred of weakness and disgust for pity seem his most abhorrent traits, especially in a world of Judeo-Christianity. Such traits greatly influenced the Nazis and are responsible in part for Nietzsche's association with them in the popular mind. We tend to forget, however, that the argument against weakness and pity intends to eliminate the kinds of atrocities for which Hitler was infamous. Resentment, in Nietzsche's mind, is repugnant chiefly because it leads people to blame others for their inadequacies. A Nietzschean analysis of Nazi anti-Semitism would name the Jews as scapegoats for the Germans' emotions of inferiority and pain. The resentful self never sees itself as the reason for its sorrows, and it searches feverishly to vent its feelings in accusation. "For every sufferer," Nietzsche insists in the *Genealogy*, "instinctively seeks a cause of his suffering; more exactly, an agent; still more specifically, a *guilty* agent who is susceptible to suffering—in short, some living thing upon which he can, on some pretext or other, vent his affects, actually or in effigy" (127). The sufferer's reflex action is to deaden his or her pain, and Nietzsche surmises that this alone "constitutes the actual physiological cause of *ressentiment*, vengefulness, and the like" (127). The basis of Nietzsche's hatred of resentment is a pessimistic vision of society, in which the suffering poison themselves with their own malice, tear open their oldest wounds, and make "evildoers out of their friends, wives, children, and whoever else stands closest to them" (128).

It is therefore no accident that Nietzsche's most "psychological" work, *Thus Spoke Zarathustra*, denounces resentment and revenge as obstacles to the emergence of personal health and strength. Although the book is ultimately unsuccessful in its task because it cannot overcome its disgust for mankind, *Zarathustra* does embody Nietzsche's greatest attempt to describe the possibility of knowledge beyond revenge and resentment. It advances a measured theory concerning the psychological strategies available to defeat violent emotions. The achievement of *Zarathustra* consists in Nietzsche's ability to translate the major terms of his philosophy—resentment, revenge, the will to power, and the eternal return—into models for individual behavior. And as such, each term appears not as a cosmological or philosophical idea but as a principle serving a series of psychological tactics for the formation of character and self-discipline.

"For *that man be delivered from revenge*," Zarathustra proclaims, "that is for me the bridge to the highest hope, and a rainbow after long storms" (*PN* 211). Revenge, like resentment, is a secondary form of desire that expresses a need to direct one's view outward instead of back to oneself. But both passions have contradictory effects. They create for the self a temporal continuity between past disappointments and the expectation of violent satisfaction in the future. This temporal continuity involves a certain self-consciousness, but it is a negative self-consciousness, and revenge and resentment end by obstructing the process of self-overcoming that represents the only source of satisfaction in Nietzsche's thought. The desire for revenge may determine the self's continuity and purpose, but ultimately it corrupts the self. It promises a brief taste of honey in exchange for an eternity of bitterness.

Human beings are destined, Nietzsche concludes, to live on the back of a tiger, but they need not live in ignorance. *Zarathustra* warns about the destructive effects of high expectation, disappointment, and vengefulness. Indeed, Nietzsche believes that the person single-mindedly obsessed by a past wrong is a most gruesome sight. Future expectations are equally dangerous, for they starve to death the person who feeds upon them. In general, desires directed toward the past or future consume the self in a fever and threaten to destroy it. The most sublime seekers of knowledge try to address both their expectations and disappointments, which explains why Nietzsche considers nihilism and asceticism as psychological phases in the process of gaining strength of will. The nihilist clings to nothingness as a means of voiding past disappointments and of defending against future sorrows. Ascetics extinguish in themselves those desires that they expect will remain unfulfilled in the future. Both are partially successful in protecting themselves against adverse desires as well as in protecting others from their potential resentment. Yet nihilism and asceticism are mere "winter pranks." Like the will to hibernation, the deliberate choice to lose consciousness, they are reactionary attitudes of self-defense that strive, paradoxically, to react as rarely as possible. They are prudent but necessarily incomplete strategies. "Freedom from fever is not yet knowledge by any means!" (*PN* 402).

Knowledge and freedom appear at first glance to oppose desires for violence, revenge, and accusation, although Nietzsche argues that they represent necessary stages in the process of coming to knowledge. Revenge and accusation are the negative qualities associated with the resounding "No!" of the man of resentment. In *The Gay Science*, Nietzsche describes accusation as the strongest form of no-saying. At the same time, he embraces *amor fati* as the essence of affirmation: *"Amor fati*: let that be my love henceforth! . . . I do not want to accuse; I do not even want to accuse those who accuse. . . . Someday I wish to be only a Yes-sayer" (223). Zarathustra associates the nausea of the fool with the desire for revenge. Freedom from nausea is bought only with the courage to pass by: "where one can no longer love," Zarathustra counsels, "there one should *pass by*" (290). Or, as Nietzsche says in *The Gay Science*, "*Looking away* shall be my only negation" (223). Finally, Nietzsche respects Buddhism only because it stands firmly against revenge: "there is nothing in which his doctrine is more opposed than the feeling of revenge, antipathy, *ressentiment* ('it is not by enmity that enmity is ended'—that is the stirring refrain of Buddhism)" (*PN* 587–88). Or again in *Ecce Homo*: "Not by enmity is enmity ended; by friendliness enmity is ended" (230). The desire for revenge represents the great weakness of human character and cultural institutions. It signifies, in Nietzsche's eyes, that we are still lacking in power, that we are succumbing to frustration in the face of our poverty.

The will to power represents Nietzsche's supreme strategy for defeating resentment. Yet no other doctrine has tended more to cloud the positive aspects of his project. The confusion relates to the changing meaning of the concept in Nietzschean thought. The will to power begins as a negative trait, a lust for power. Soon, however, it acquires a psychological significance. Nietzsche describes the will to power as a process of individual development and strengthening that moves increasingly toward superior judgment and self-awareness. It is the power by which the self effects its own change. The summit of this development arrives with Zarathustra, who counsels people to stand firmly in themselves and to create over and beyond themselves. Finally, Nietzsche associates the will to power with the inexhaustible procreative power of life, which nevertheless strives, like Freud's *Todestrieb*, to discharge itself.

If the will to power were solely the unleashed procreative power of life, the individual would have little effect on its direction. There would be little space for the self-examination demanded by Zarathustra, and Nietzsche would have praised rather than attacked Darwin. The third phase of the will to power coincides with Nietzsche's emerging madness. It represents the contradictory desire to affirm his omnipotence and to sacrifice himself to cosmic forces. Yet the third phase cannot be attributed entirely to Nietzsche's madness because it remains consistent with his critique of God and *causa sui* logic. The late doctrine of the will to power does not attribute any effect to a single cause; rather, it describes the world as a complex network of forces, in which force is relational and nothing is its own cause. The totalitarianism of the will to power is dispersed into a range of conflicting impulses. The will to power becomes the essence of self-overcoming (*Selbstüberwindung*).

For Nietzsche the psychologist, the second phase of the will to power is more crucial. It should not be confused with the lust for power or the will to conquer. The Nazis invented the view of the will to power as a recipe for world mastery, and Walter Kaufmann has shown most effectively that it is really a strategy for self-overcoming and not a justification for war.[4] The will to

4. Walter Kaufmann, *Nietzsche: Philosopher, Psychologist, Antichrist* (Princeton: At the University Press, 1968), p. 200.

power is always directed toward the self, although completely within a social context. Nietzsche was too aware of patterns of prejudice and reciprocal accusations to conceive of it otherwise. In effect, the will to power represents a form of self-discipline. Cultivation (*Zucht*), Nietzsche says, requires discipline (*Zuchtigung*). Man is the embryo of the man of the future, and he requires discipline to develop. "The will," according to Nietzsche, "is precisely that which treats cravings as their master and appoints to them their way and measure" (*WP* 52). Apparently, the man of the future will be master over his own savagery and licentiousness. The desires will have learned to obey and to be useful. Consequently, the will to power does not release the libido. It strives to economize desires. Walter Kaufmann calls reason the highest manifestation of the will to power because it realizes its objective most fully.[5] Nietzsche's aesthetics bears out the image of the will as an economy of desire. It defines the ugly as a lack of coordination among inner desires. The beautiful, in contrast, holds in harmony all strong desires. It is reverence without tension, and no violent person can attain the beautiful by exertion.

Greatness of character in Nietzsche's eyes means having all affect under control, but not for the pleasure of mastery. Those who will to will strive to be equal to accidents, allowing themselves neither disappointment nor expectation. They do not pit themselves against probability. They will not to defend themselves against others as the best defense. They are not hedgehogs. They choose not to have quills, but to have open hands.

Although Heidegger's reading of Nietzsche is the cause of much confusion today, his description of the will to power may clarify matters.[6] He defines the will to power as resolute openness (*Ent-schlossenheit*). Those who will station themselves among others, but keep themselves open to them. Their traits are not seizure and agitation but an awareness of their emotions and surroundings. Heidegger's remarks cast light on the dangerous opposition between active and reactive often associated with the will to power. He suggests that the will to power is

5. Kaufmann, p. 230.
6. Martin Heidegger, *Nietzsche*, 2 vols. (Stuttgart: Neske, 1961), 1:59.

reactive, but not *merely* reactive; it does not need the accoutrements of battle. Gilles Deleuze bases his reading of Nietzsche on this opposition.[7] He defines the will to power as active and resentment as reactive. His theory is nevertheless oversimplified. Like the will to hibernation, asceticism, and nihilism, the will to power is reactive in essence. It tries, however, to differ from resentment by economizing reactions. The will to power is a principle of selection. It honors by choosing, admitting, and accepting. It reacts slowly, with a slowness bred by caution and deliberate pride. It does not believe in misfortune or guilt. Most importantly, it learns how to forget.

It is easy to be open toward the future because postponing expectation takes no great strength of will. The greatest danger to the self is the past, for disappointment may transform the will to power into the desire for revenge. The will does not easily learn to forget or to pass by. "This, indeed this alone," Zarathustra concludes, "is what *revenge* is: the will's ill will against time and its 'it was'" (252). The will has difficulty willing backward, and Nietzsche's description of the will confronted by the "it was" provides a perfect portrait of the man of resentment: "what is it that puts even the liberator himself in fetters? 'It was'—that is the name of the will's gnashing of teeth and most secret melancholy" (251).

How to will backward? This is Nietzsche's most important question, for it places the will to power and resentment in direct confrontation. It requires the heaviest thought: the eternal return. The return is the heaviest burden upon mankind not because it signifies an existential or ontological dilemma but because it requires the self to posit the eternal recurrence of the "it was," which remains the secret melancholy of the will to power. The eternal return conceives of the enormous power of memory as the engine of intersubjective violence. The man of resentment lives his past in the future; he is trapped in the "it was." How can he hope to will without directing his power toward revenge?

The answer is to give the will to power no precise center and to bind it to the eternal wheel of the return. The eternal return

7. Gilles Deleuze, *Nietzsche et la philosophie* (Paris: PUF, 1967), chap. 2.

portrays the past as a riddle for the creative will. All "it was" is a fragment, a riddle, a dreadful accident that the creative will must redeem. Redemption has a special meaning for Zarathustra. It describes the process by which the will recovers what is past and re-creates all "it was." As creator, guesser of riddles, and redeemer of accidents, Zarathustra teaches mankind to work on the future and to return for profit to all that has been. The will learns to confront the "it was" and say, "Thus I willed it! Thus I shall will it!" (310).

I am stressing the personal and not the cosmological aspects of the eternal return because Zarathustra first presents it in a psychological context, although there is ultimately little difference in effect between its psychological and religious dimensions. The eternal return prevents the will to power from succumbing to the desire for revenge. It aids the will in the process of self-overcoming, for the focus of the return is the self. What returns, what finally comes back to one who wills the return, is one's own self and those aspects of the self that have been lost in strange lands and scattered among things and accidents.

The doctrine of the eternal return portrays each moment as a gateway where the past and future meet in a decision of the present. It is therefore more than a theory to redeem the past. It places the weight of decision on each moment. "I am the first," Nietzsche says, "who is *able* to decide" (*EH* 314). The question posed for each and every moment is, "Do you desire this once more and innumerable times more?" (*GS* 274). Far from celebrating indecision, therefore, Nietzsche loads each moment of existence with the burden of judgment. The strategy of the return makes the will responsible for its own existence and power. It designs the circle of the will's necessity. The will that wills the eternal return is the will that wills itself and finds itself in the necessity of willing. Nietzsche's theory of the eternal return thus belongs to the ethical tradition, especially to the view of the will established by Kant. The eternal return represents the will as the force that orients understanding not toward a mythical past, here seen as the world of resentment and revenge, but toward an ethical future. Every action stands under the compulsion of causes that are past, while simultaneously calculated from the point of view of future ends and their systematic unity. The former sense situates willing within a series of events, whereas in the latter the will belongs to the order of obligation and ideal determination. Kant invented the autonomy of the will as part of his critical ethics, but in Nietzsche it acquires a distinctive psychological emphasis. Nietzsche has different names for the strategy; he calls it *la gaya scienza*, "tragic wisdom," and *amor fati*, but each describes a supreme affirmation of life. "If we affirm one single moment," Nietzsche believes, "we thus affirm not only ourselves but all existence. For nothing is self-sufficient. . . . All eternity was needed to produce this one event—and in this single moment of affirmation all eternity was called good, redeemed, justified, and affirmed" (*WP* 532–33).

To affirm the moment is the opposite of nihilism, which affirms nothing. To be equal to accidents is to defeat disappointment and expectation. Most important, to think the eternal return is to overcome the contempt of the human. At the end of part 3, Zarathustra's animals, the eagle and snake, compose a ditty with their master's words about the eternal return. They churn out the heaviest of all thoughts like barrel organs. Suddenly, a great disgust crawls into Zarathustra's throat, and nausea sticks to his mouth. He chokes on the idea that even the small man, the man of whom he is most weary, recurs eternally. "Alas," he groans, "man recurs eternally!" (331). Zarathustra's nausea means that he does not yet understand the eternal return. Only if he can overcome his sickly contempt for the human and begin to compose his own dancing songs will he know enough about the eternal return to be its prophet.

Nietzsche portrays Zarathrustra as a convalescent, and resentment is the illness from which he is recuperating. Zarathustra feels resentment against his betters, and he resents the small man for continuing to exist. The eternal return, by creating a gateway between the past and the future, deliberately confronts the temporal structure of resentment, presenting a homeopathic remedy for what ails both Nietzsche and his only literary character. Zarathustra begins by oscillating between feelings of superiority and inferiority and between pity and disgust for mankind, and he emerges as a self-parodist and ironist. The ass festival, as the finale of the book, presents the best illustration of who Zarathustra has become. The episode represents Zarathustra as a joyful affirmer; yet the parodic attitude directed toward the Last Supper shows that Nietzsche has never strayed far from his resentment of Judeo-Christianity. Zarathustra's great moment of originality is hardly original at all; and Nietzsche's struggle toward freedom triumphs only in the freedom to imitate what he most despises. In this sense, the doctrine of self-overcoming acquires another, more ominous meaning, one that approaches the desire for self-defeat.

The paradox of Zarathustra's "victory" exposes the fatal flaw in Nietzsche's theory of knowledge. Even though much of *Zarathustra* is directed toward a potent psychological attack on revenge and resentment, its hero never throws off his chains. Such is the case not because the notion of resentment is absolutely incompatible with knowledge—it is clear that Nietzsche presents a viable method for combating the emotions that threaten self-knowledge—but because Nietzsche's characterizations of Zarathustra and the overman are self-destructive. By attributing to them a distinctiveness of will that should belong to mankind in general, Nietzsche represents Zarathustra and the overman as special cases within human destiny. The idea of the repetition of the same remains crucial to the eternal return as Nietzsche describes it, but the overman's difference from others risks corrupting the pattern of the repetition. The overman becomes a living metaphor for the resentment and contempt of the human. Similarly, Nietzsche himself emerges as the resentful parodist of the one religious institution that he wishes to forget. A generous interpretation of the ass festival would point to Nietzsche's idea of *amor fati* and conclude that Zarathustra finally adopts the only attitude toward Judeo-Christianity possible in the world of resentment—that is, to affirm it. But Nietzsche's mocking attitude betrays his acceptance, and he remains a victim to his antipathy for Judeo-Christianity. What could be a more self-despising image of affirmation than the "Yea-Yuh" of the brainless ass? In the final analysis, Zarathustra is not able to forget, accept, or surpass Judeo-Christianity, and consequently Nietzsche is forced to emulate its victimary stance, however ironically.

The case of the overman represents only a more extreme example of Nietzsche's failure to escape the throes of self-victimization. Like Baudelaire's self-torturing Heautontimoroumenos, the overman is a contradiction in terms, which explains why Nietzsche refused to provide a clear portrait of him. Apparently the overman opposes only his equals. He stands so confident in his superiority that he does not deign to compete with the inferior men of the world. But how long will the overman be able to resist the temptation to swat the gnats flying into his lordly eyes? Sooner or later, a gnat will die under his hand, reducing him, in his own mind, to the level of those most contemptible to him. Or imagine a community of overmen, sublime in their conversation and knowledge, each maintaining their distinctive autonomy and domain. The image of the Elysian Fields comes to mind, but the shepherds of Elysia are dead, and lifeless would be the community of overmen, for Nietzsche defines life as struggle and competition. If the overmen vied with each other in Homeric contest, venting their desires for revenge when necessary, the result would be a parody of Mount Olympus. And one need only read Homer to understand that the Olympic gods are beings who thrive on vanity, rivalry, and a spirit of cruelty that takes sport in destroying lesser creatures. In the end, the overman is crushed by his own weighty desire for superiority. Either he sacrifices his own vitality to prove his mastery, or he becomes a slave to his most violent and primitive instincts.

Zarathustra and the overman emerge as victims of their own will to power, and neither one is capable of forgetting that he is a victim. Nietzsche himself appears as one of the most remarkable examples of an individual who tries to forget his own persecution in a manner that most encourages self-violence. The resentful self always sees itself as a victim, for its moral strength lies in the representation of its persecution to others. The strong relinquish their essential being because the victimary image presented by the resentful self makes them ashamed of their strength. The resentful may then use their sense of victimization to rationalize the most violent persecutions. The weak are stronger for their weakness, and the strong imitate the weak with docile acceptance. But if the resentful self gains strength merely by presenting a victimary attitude, some condition for its coming into power must already exist in human society. The victimary attitude must already possess a unique social significance, one for which both the strong and the weak are willing to vie. Nietzsche's theory of the genealogy of morals thus collapses upon itself, for how can resentment be the origin of morality if it needs as a given the special moral status of the victim? Nietzsche's theory of the will to power is at once an attempt to escape this tautology and to posit a spontaneous and sui generis desire to oppose resentment. It represents both Nietzsche's attempt to think exterior to resentment and his desire to stand forth as an autonomous individual.

The ethical significance of the victimary attitude remains the blind spot in Nietzsche's genealogy of morals. Contrary to his intentions, Nietzsche demonstrates that the weak and not the strong hold a privileged role in ethical representation. His ideas are closer to Judeo-Christianity than he wishes, and the theory of resentment emerges as an extreme reaction to the fact. The contradiction appears most evident in his notion of affects. Human suffering itself creates an ethic based on the presence of a victim, for the sufferer looks instinctively to blame his pain on another. Nietzsche makes it clear that the sufferer's logic of cause and effect requires a victim if it is to divert the responsibility for the pain somewhere else. Indeed, Nietzsche's critique of culture is based on his disgust with the morality that needs victims, but this horrified vision of human aggression and cruelty does not yet include the idea of resentment. Resentment in Nietzsche does not refer specifically to human beings' general tendency to harm each other. Resentment is a secondary emotion in Nietzsche, more characteristic of higher cultures, and it emerges as the force behind the new ethics of Judeo-Christianity.

By virtue of its self-conscious nature, resentment serves to alter through a striking process the originary ethic of persecution that Nietzsche identifies with culture. The resentful self makes itself a victim, thereby occupying the role traditionally given to the victim in ethical representation. Resentment is therefore an intuition of the significance attributed to the victim in human culture. The resentful self comes to knowledge negatively on the basis of its resentment, as Eric Gans brilliantly argues, "for what is intuitively grasped is the self-as-victim, the victim of a social distinction that condemns the self to insignificance" (61).[8] This self-consciousness makes the resentful self its own center of strength, but it is, paradoxically, a strength based on its own sense of insignificance. The resentful self discovers a secret ratio between weakness and strength, literally creating its own power out of nothing. In this center of strength, its representation of itself as victim, the resentful individual discovers the privileged status of the victim's position at the origin of ethical representation. The cultural productivity that Nietzsche attributes to resentment thus evolves by imitating with a twist the representational patterns of human violence. Indeed, Nietzsche's critique of Judeo-Christianity begins from this proposition. Resentment, he proclaims, creates its moral system by victimizing the strong and noble of the world.

If Nietzsche's genealogy of morals has begun to resemble Girard's theories of violence, it is not because I have dressed a wolf in sheep's clothing. There remain differences between Nietzsche and Girard, most notably the classic distinction established by Nietzsche between his thought and Judeo-Christianity. Rather, the resemblance exists because Girard himself acknowledges that his intellectual precursors are Nietzsche and Freud. Nietzsche especially remains deeply but paradoxically involved in Girard's attempts to illuminate the role played by violence and desire in religious representation. His most recent work on Nietzsche, "Dionysus versus the Crucified," begins by describing as an oblique and somewhat uncourageous version of a larger issue the great debate that raged after the war over Nietzsche's responsibility for the Nazis' exploitation of his writings. For Girard perceives Nietzsche's antichristian polemics, not his relation to Nazism, as the ethical issue on which his work must be either exonerated or condemned. As such, Girard's work stands at one extreme of the notorious opposition

8. Eric Gans, "The Culture of Resentment," *Philosophy and Literature* 8.1 (1984): 55–66. Gans provides an extremely clear and useful discussion of resentment in which desire and knowledge are not mutually exclusive. I have relied on his remarks throughout this essay.

between Dionysus and the Crucified, and his career may be best traced through his writings on Nietzsche, just as Nietzsche's thought is best characterized in its opposition to Judeo-Christianity. Girard describes human desire as fundamentally conflictual because it encourages the most mindless imitation. In Girard's definition, desire robs individuals of conscious choices by compelling them to repeat the actions of others, and individuals who desire collide as they vie for objects and repeat each other's tactics of appropriation. Mimetic desire distorts rivals and objects of desire, generating a form of mythology that conceals the true nature of the world. Desire always leads to an explosion of human violence, Girard explains in *Violence and the Sacred*, to those episodes of general conflict in which individuals randomly imitate each other and end by blaming specific individuals for the existence of disorder. From the heat of the conflict, a scapegoat emerges, and the mob makes him or her responsible for the chaos. The mimetic desire for appropriation metamorphoses into another form of mimetic desire. The group represents the victim as a sign of the crisis, and this representation of responsibility infuses the victim with great power, for to be responsible for an event, one must have had the power to have caused it. Such is the origin of the sacred in Girard's mind. As the sacred becomes increasingly institutionalized, victims are less arbitrary in the sense that they are bred to be sacrificed. Religion uses sacred ritual to commemorate originary scenes of disorder for the purpose of forestalling the emergence of a more random form of violence.

The knowledge of mimetic desire, however, represents the most paradoxical aspect of Girard's theories. Desire in Girard's eyes depends on mankind's unwillingness to free itself from its patterns. Even if they were to understand that the desirability of objects is symbolic only of their own desires for superiority, individuals would continue to struggle for the same object. Nor would an understanding of the blind mechanisms of persecution prevent people from making scapegoats of others. Desire remains essentially unconscious in Girard's work, and the forms of violence generated by it are unknowable in the same sense that the Freudian unconscious is unknowable. How, then, has Girard made his discoveries?

In the early *Deceit, Desire, and the Novel*, literature appears as a source of knowledge. Novels in particular take as their subject the workings of desire. All great novels, in Girard's estimation, end with a conversion, in which both hero and author discover for the first time the eternal web of desire in which they are ensnared. The novel destroys as well the false differences and mythological characteristics attributed to others in the heat of rivalry. The genius of the novel seems to repeat the epiphany of Nietzsche's *Beyond Good and Evil*, for it "transcends the rival caricatures of Good and Evil presented by factions. It affirms the identity of the opposites on the level of internal mediation. But it does not end in moral relativism. Evil exists. . . . Evil is that negative pact of hatred to which so many men strictly adhere for their mutual destruction" (192).

The remark on moral relativism refers to Nietzsche. Girard reads Nietzsche's work not as a novelistic leap beyond good and evil but as a celebration of relativism and nihilism. *Thus Spoke Zarathustra* presents a new gospel to mark the end of the Christian gospel; it proposes a new askesis to make God unnecessary. Nietzsche's philosophy is Girard's supreme example of modern thought, in which people strive desperately to fill the void left by the death of God by making gods of themselves and of each other. Modern thought turns away from the revelation of the gospel. "Christ," Girard argues, "sent men in search of God; he gave them a glimpse of eternity" (275). But the feeble fail in their efforts and turn back on humanity, bringing about the tortuous world of hatred, vanity, and envy.

Nietzsche represents the antinovelistic in Girard's early writings, and as the Christian dimension of his theories emerge, Nietzsche truly becomes the antichrist. *Deceit, Desire, and the Novel* permits an understanding of desire through the reading of great novels; it is fundamentally optimistic and revelatory in character. But Girard's recent work makes it clear that the message of the novel is made possible only through its imitation of Christ's passion. The novel dramatizes the law of antipersecution expressed by Saint Paul's Epistle to the Romans: "Therefore thou art inexcusable, O man, whosoever thou art that judgest: for wherein thou judgest another, thou condemnest thyself; for thou that judgest doest the same things" (74). Novelistic truth in Girard's description remains identical to the Word of Christ and the Bible: it teaches the law of neighborly love and the profound revelation that human beings are equal in hatred and charity.

As the light of revelation grows stronger, however, so does the dark unintelligibility of desire and violence; and Girard's most definitive statements about the unknowability of desire take Nietzsche as their example. "Strategies of Madness," in *To Double Business Bound*, reduces all of Nietzsche's thought to the blindness of mimetic desire and the rivalry with Wagner. Girard compares Nietzsche's attempts to rewrite the history of his relationship with Wagner in his own favor with the reconstruction of history found in modern dictatorships. Like all modern thought, Nietzsche's will to power encourages "the most self-defeating behavior" (68). Girard explains that the will to power always collapses into resentment because it deliberately seeks opponents whom it cannot defeat; if the will to power cannot find an insurmountable rival, it will be crushed by indifference. "There is always enough indifference in the world," Girard writes, "to destroy the most powerful will to power" (73). Nietzsche's will to power obeys the theory of mimetic desire, and as such it characterizes the inability of any theory to escape the web of desire. Desire is already its own theory, but its insights return inexorably to desire: "desire learns more and more from its own defeats, but . . . it puts this knowledge in the service of more desire, making even more catastrophic defeats inevitable" (74). Any theory that pretends to understand and organize desire is a myth, a form of ideology created by desire to further its own ends. "The will-to-power mystique," Girard continues, "might be called the *ideology* of mimetic desire, if it is true that ideologies are actively engaged in furthering ends that are best furthered by not acknowledging their true natures" (74).

If Girard admires Nietzsche, it is because he had the courage to push his imperfect intellect to its most awful extremities. Nietzsche's madness symbolizes in Girard's mind the relentless commitment to a lie that becomes increasingly unsupportable as it grows more exaggerated. The madness of Nietzsche fuses inextricably with his genius. In "Dionysus versus the Crucified," Girard traces the collapse of Nietzsche's Dionysian mania to the Christian revelation. The essay is remarkable because Girard acknowledges for the first time the role played by Nietzsche in his own theories.

Girard's article revolves around the voice of the madman in *The Gay Science* and the famous passage in *The Will to Power* that formulates the difference between Dionysus and the Crucified. Two Nietzsches emerge, manifesting Girard's double attitude toward the thinker.[9] One Nietzsche shares Girard's insights: "Nietzsche clearly saw that pagan mythology, like pagan ritual, centers on the killing of victims or on their expulsion . . ." (819). The voice of the madman in *The Gay Science* declares that mankind has murdered God, exposing the anthropological understanding that collective murder lies at the heart of religious and social structuration. In this insight, Nietzsche is rivaled only by the Freud of *Totem and Taboo*, who claims that the sacred is rooted in the collective murder of a real victim whom we call God.

The other Nietzsche represents most perfectly the inner compulsions that have led so many intellectuals to adopt "inhuman standards." For Girard, fragment 1052 of *The Will to Power* cuts to the heart of Nietzsche's immorality. There Nietzsche confronts the wisdom of Christ's teachings and rejects them in favor of Dionysian mania, providing modern thought with its most violent and unjust model:

> Dionysus versus the "Crucified": there you have the antithesis. It is *not* a difference in regard to their martyrdom—it is a difference

9. If one assesses the bulk of Girard's writings, little ambivalence about Nietzsche may be found, for Girard comes out against Nietzsche at every turn. I use the idea of two Nietzsches as a rhetorical device to examine two sides of Girard's thought. Girard sees Nietzsche as the first thinker to understand the essential choice, "Dionysus or the Crucified," between the all-out violence of paganism and the nonviolence of Christianity. The problem, of course, is that Nietzsche made the wrong choice. Moreover, the emergence of the nuclear age has made the choice of purifying violence through violence impossible, which explains, according to Girard, why Nietzsche appears so very brutal to us today and why he can no longer be considered a *maître à penser*.

in the meaning of it. Life itself, its eternal fruitfulness and recurrence, creates torment, destruction, the will to annihilation. In the other case, suffering—the "Crucified as the innocent one"—counts as an objection to life, as a formula for its condemnation.— One will see the problem is that of the meaning of suffering: whether a Christian meaning or a tragic meaning. In the former case, it is supposed to be the path to holy existence; in the latter case, being is counted as *holy enough* to justify even a monstrous amount of suffering. The tragic man affirms even the harshest suffering: he is sufficiently strong, rich, and capable of deifying to do so. The Christian denies even the happiest lot on earth: he is sufficiently weak, poor, disinherited to suffer from life in whatever form he meets it. The god on the cross is a curse on life, a signpost to seek redemption from life; Dionysus cut to pieces is a *promise* of life: it will be eternally reborn and return again from destruction.

Girard's reading of fragment 1052 explains that the difference between Dionysus and the Crucified is not their martyrdom but their respective interpretations. Whereas Christ condemns violence, Dionysus instigates "holy lynchings." The Crucified is the emblem of Christianity's condemnation of mankind's "violent nature." Dionysus, according to Girard, says "Yes!" to the harshest cruelty and suffering.

No one will deny the enormous ethical force of Girard's claims for Christianity, and clearly Christ's message against persecution lies at the heart of any defense that may be made for the West. It is not at all certain, however, that Nietzsche refuses the content of that message. In fact, he applies it in two startling and contradictory ways. On the one hand, the death of Dionysus Zagreus in Nietzsche's philosophy symbolizes the human tendency toward evil and violence, as does the death of Christ in Christianity. The difference is that Nietzsche is reluctant to perceive the symbol as an absolute condemnation of life and human society. He chooses Dionysus Zagreus as a symbol because mankind arises from his ashes. Nietzsche accepts, even affirms, the harsh suffering of the victim, but in no way does his affirmation preclude the struggle to overcome persecution. The show of violence is a sign of weakness in Nietzsche's mind because it implies that one can be goaded, and it must be overcome. The imperative to give style to one's character requires self-discipline, and in such self-discipline lie both the aesthetic and the ethical dimensions of Nietzsche's thought. Weak character hates and feels demeaned by discipline. Strong character attains beauty, order, and ease. It constrains itself in matters of revenge and resentment. "For one thing," Nietzsche explains in *The Gay Science*, "is needful: that a human being should *attain* satisfaction with himself, whether it be by means of this or that poetry and art; only then is a human being at all tolerable to behold. Whoever is dissatisfied with himself is continually ready for revenge, and we others will be his victims, if only by having to endure his ugly sight" (233). Whatever Nietzsche's own ability to repress violent emotion, his philosophy is designed to pass beyond human rivalry, and it requires that he reject resentment.

On the other hand, Nietzsche's embrace of Dionysus possesses a personal dimension that contradicts his philosophical disgust with human cruelty, for his choice of Dionysus encourages suffering. The difference between Christ and Dionysus is, as Girard explains, one of interpretation, but it is not the difference between victim and victimizer. Nietzsche affirms the necessity of suffering, not the right of victimizers to create suffering. Indeed, Nietzsche's relation to Judeo-Christianity emerges only when we understand that Dionysus represents first and foremost the victimary attitude. That Nietzsche is able to sign himself as either "Dionysus" or "The Crucified" exposes an identify between the two images that cannot be blamed entirely on insanity. Girard reads the oscillation as a sign of madness because he insists on the difference between Christ and Dionysus even more strongly than does Nietzsche. Untypically, in this instance, Girard reads Nietzsche's attack on Judeo-Christianity literally, as a philosophical argument, and not as a manifestation of resentment. But it is precisely at this moment that Nietzsche should be read not philosophically but in terms of his resentful desire to usurp Judeo-Christianity.

Nietzsche indeed proclaims his preference for victimizers over victims. But what does it mean to label oneself a victimizer in Judeo-Christian culture? It means finally to name oneself as the outcast of that culture, and Nietzsche's identification with the outcast exposes his desire to steal the position of the victim from

Judeo-Christianity. Such a strategy may seem an extreme measure to attain notoriety, but Nietzsche was faced with the dilemma of trying to appear truly unique and original in a world where anyone could attain significance merely by proclaiming his or her persecution at another's hand. Possible models might have included Socrates, whose image of martyrdom had already been assimilated by Christianity along with Platonism, or Jean-Jacques Rousseau, who invented a secular version of the victimary attitude called Romanticism when he proclaimed himself the unanimous victim of high European culture. Rousseau's self-confessed desire to be as self-sufficient as God already foreshadows Nietzsche's desire to achieve the status of the one unique individual in Western history. Nietzsche could have embraced the image of Christ crucified, but this choice would have meant adopting the position of an imitator, unless he could displace Christ and take his place on the cross. Nietzsche attempts this path whenever he signs himself "The Crucified," but each model is finally inadequate to his desire for uniqueness, and he makes a point of rejecting them with great pomp and circumstance.

Every model provides a direct access to the position of the victim, but Nietzsche's desire for originality and uniqueness requires that he take a less direct path. His resentment begins by placing him in a victimary attitude, and he struggles to preserve that position of significance by proclaiming with wild enthusiasm his antipathy to the majority. He takes on the image of Dionysus, the unjust, the drunken, and the violent, to perpetuate his opposition to traditional religious values. But even the choice of Dionysus betrays the desire to be a victim, for Dionysus remains of all the Olympic gods the most marginal and least acceptable. Such titles as *The Antichrist* and *Ecce Homo* appear to be as discordant as "Dionysus versus the Crucified," but each epithet exposes Nietzsche's wish to usurp the victimary attitude of Judeo-Christianity rather than to eliminate its values. Nietzsche stood not against valuation but for revaluation.

Judeo-Christian culture responded to Nietzsche's rhetoric by fulfilling his most precious desire. Nietzsche is named, following his own wishes, as the Antichrist, and as the solitary and grand opponent of Western Christianity. Moreover, thanks to his sister, he became associated with the Nazis, who now serve as the modern symbol of human brutality and perversion. If the Nazis symbolize everything that the West now wishes to reject, then Nietzsche makes a good candidate for the high priest of Judeo-Christianity's satanic alter ego. Increasingly, Nietzsche stands out as the one against the many, and to this position Western thought has given a singular interpretation: to be the one is to be the victim.

Everywhere is the evidence that Nietzsche achieved the special status in the Western thought that he so anxiously desired. The slogan "God is dead" has attained a popularity that remains untouched by the vulgarity of its applications, most notably because its essential vulgarity helps to heighten Nietzsche's opposition in the popular mind to the dominant values of the West. Within intellectual circles, Nietzsche is either ferociously denounced or strongly defended, but neither reaction alters his marginal status. His detractors call him a proto-Nazi or a madman and demand his expulsion from the philosophical canon. His proponents, especially of late, do not contest his madness, but defend it as an example of fierce individuality, as a harbinger of the counterculture, or as a call for a titillating freedom from rationality. Nietzsche's defenders and detractors end by sharing the same vision of their subject. The preferred image of the broken Nietzsche, sitting in a catatonic stupor, his eyes vacant and moustache overgrown, presents the same model of weakness and impoverishment to modern thought that Nietzsche himself ascribed to the icon of the crucified Christ.

Girard senses that Nietzsche is a victim of himself and of modernity, but it has never softened his attack on the Antichrist. Rather, Girard remains with the philosophical issues, and he understands the competition between Nietzschean and Christian philosophy only too well. In fact, he bases his attack on the opposition invented by Nietzsche. Nietzschean thought is "pagan" insofar as it views life as a means to knowledge. Christian thought condemns life. "Since all human culture is grounded in this collective violence," Girard writes, "the whole human race is declared guilty from the standpoint of the gospels. Life itself is slandered because life cannot continue and organize itself without this type of violence" (823). Note that Girard is repeating Nietzsche's view of Christianity not to debunk it but to explain why this world fails.

In Girard's estimation, pious efforts to exonerate Nietzsche or to represent him as a teacher of ethics are misguided. Such efforts must fail, however, not because Nietzsche's madness cannot be separated from his genius but, apparently, because the knowledge of desire cannot be achieved by the human intellect without the intervention of sublime wisdom. Yet Girard's work constantly returns to the idea that the message of Christ has so far managed only to hobble our murderous drives, menacing to turn them into "a fierce monster that now threatens to devour us all" (828). We cannot reach the truth of desire and violence without Christ, and our nature may make it impossible to grasp his message. The dark unintelligibility of desire promises to cast in shadow the light of Christ. The conclusion of Girard's "Dionysus versus the Crucified" ends with the words of Nietzsche's madman proclaiming the distance between our deeds and our consciousness of them. Human beings by definition suffer a fatal birthright of ignorance with regard to their own violence, and as such, the murderers of God do not understand their own act: "This deed is still more distant from them than the most distant stars—*and yet they have done it themselves*" (835).

Although many would call Girard an extremist, he is not a nihilist. The ending of "Dionysus versus the Crucified" demands comparison with the last words of *Le Bouc émissaire*, Girard's book on primitive mythology and the Bible, where a different message is given. The words present a warning, fatalistic in meaning but not deprived of hope. Human society is in crisis, but it can be saved through forgiveness: "All violence from now on reveals what the passion of Christ reveals, the idiotic birth of bloody idols, of all the false gods of religions, of politics, and of ideologies. The murderers nevertheless believe that their sacrifices are virtuous. *They too know not what they do, and we must forgive them.* The time has come for us to forgive each other" (295; my emphasis). The similarity between the two conclusions is all the more startling because their messages are so contradictory. One denies that we might understand our nature; the other offers the possibility of survival in forgiving ourselves through others. Apparently, the guilt that Christianity casts on life can be abated if we forgive the murderers and affirm everyone's potential for violence.

Girard's comparative reading of Freud, Dostoevsky, and Nietzsche, "The Underground Critic" in *To Double Business Bound*, reproduces more economically the same contradictory view of knowledge and desire. Once again, Girard begins by giving a pessimistic description of human desire: "The more desire learns about itself, the more self-defeating it becomes" (39). The essay then gives a detailed account of desire and concludes with an attack on those who would deny the value of the human. Girard's final remarks defend the great literary works against "waning dogmatisms" and ask that we give the floor to those writers "who are capable of going much farther than has ever been gone toward the understanding of the relations of desire" (60).

Girard's contradictory positions on desire are embodied in the shift between his two Nietzsches. One Nietzsche reveals the role of desire and violence in social organization; the other remains the dupe of his own desires and lives in the blackness of ignorance. Remarkably, the same opposition can be found in Nietzsche's own descriptions of the two kinds of willing. The contradictions, however, do not follow from madness or from some inherent limitation of the religious mind. There is no reason to follow current fashion and assert the mutual incompatibility of either desire and knowledge or religion and thought. Indeed, the greatest insights of anthropology have revealed that religion is a form of social thinking. The expulsion of religion today is based not on its supposed irrationality but on the ethical claim that religion incites rivalry and aggression. The movement of modern intellectual atheism derives in part from the perception that religion, more than anything else, excites violent opposition toward competing opinions and arguments. But there can be no reason for attacking religion alone on such grounds, especially when the current intellectual climate holds that any form of belief may provide the justification for argument and violence. The expulsion of religion for its apparent narrowness and intolerance repeats the crime of which modern thought accuses religion. The contradiction in Girard's theory of desire is rather a sign of his humanism. Where Girard might perfect his theology by positing the existence of grace to explain the occasions on which individuals, despite their nature, understand Christ's message of nonviolence, he becomes noticeably silent on religious issues and affirms instead the values of humanism and anthropological science.[10] The absence of a theory of grace returns Girard to the power of human understanding. Unlike the French Nietzscheans, however, he does not return because it is impossible to move beyond the self within language; rather, he returns because he does not wish in the final analysis to use his theology to negate humanism. In one of his most severe attacks on the French Nietzscheans, "Delirium as System," Girard faces a theory of desire not unlike his own. Deleuze and Guattari posit the existence of a truly unconscious and paradoxical desire, and Girard reacts fiercely against the idea that the relations of desire might be unknowable: "If true desire is unconscious and still crushed by repressive codings, even in capitalism, how do the two authors know it exists?" (84). The violence of Girard's opposition to the French Nietzscheans on this point exposes his own internal contradictions, but, more important, it serves to stress the crucial role that he wishes to give to human intelligence in the revelation of violent desires. Girard's religious thought provides a means to transcend human understanding, but he does not always follow its path. He seems to prefer balancing on the brink of contradiction to giving up the possibility of an anthropology, and in that preference he comes closest to being a disciple of Nietzsche.

In Nietzsche, the tragedy of mankind lies in the fact that imperfection should exist at all, that imperfection returns eternally,

10. Grace appears only as a metaphor in Girard's thought, and to my knowledge in only one place. At the conclusion of *Deceit, Desire, and the Novel*, Girard contends that "conversion in death should not seem to us as the easy solution but rather an almost miraculous descent of novelistic grace" (310).

not as an ineluctable blindness but as the thousand scandals to be overcome as individuals face themselves and each other. Nietzsche learns from Greek tragedy to affirm life in spite of suffering and cruelty. *The Birth of Tragedy* describes tragic drama as the mirror in which the Dionysian man contemplates himself, but the mirror is hardly narcissistic. Tragedy illuminates the absurdity of belief, the desire for revenge, and the bloody foundations of social existence. It portrays the human struggle to affirm life in spite of its horrors, and the beauty of this affirmation is the only hope for our future.

Tragedy discloses the truth of the human situation in the social world, and Nietzsche uses it as the basis of his psychology. The one significant idea that the existentialists took from Nietzsche, despite their odd emphasis on the absurdity of existence, was the profound impact of the tragic on the problem of knowledge. Knowledge in Nietzsche's philosophy is supremely relational, which does not mean that it is relative. Fear founds courage. Comedy insinuates itself into tragedy. Lies beget truth. The point is that knowledge exists not in itself but in relations. The tragedy of history, which envisions mankind's bloody past, impotent present, and tenuous future, promotes a deep pessimism, but it also teaches us to search for knowledge in life and not beyond it. Whence Nietzsche's happiest principle: *"Life as a means to knowledge"* (GS 255). The wisdom of tragedy is the necessity of not refusing that life.

The present generation of Nietzscheans denounces the search for a knowledge of humanity. For them, "man is dead," and the quest for knowledge cannot be separated from the thirst for power and blood. They point knowingly to Nietzsche's own critique of the will to knowledge and embrace a philosophical nihilism. Some go so far as to deny that Nietzsche ever harbored the desire to know anything, recalling his theory that truth is nothing but a figure of speech. Those who are honest enough to confess that Nietzsche believed in the possibility of knowledge also end by renouncing the search on the basis of modern theories of desire. Nietzsche may have believed in the philosophical possibility of knowledge, they admit, but his own desirous na-

ture placed it beyond his powers. Here Nietzsche's final madness appears as the prize given to one who dares to question his
own desires and unconscious strivings.

The opposition between knowledge and desire has become a
cliché of modern thought, and it is perhaps the greatest threat to
ethics today. It reproduces, even among atheists, the old Christian distinction between the worlds of the flesh and of the spirit.
At first glance, Nietzsche emerges as the greatest enemy of this
distinction. He fought courageously to bestow upon humanity
the strength of will and intellect necessary to acquire a knowledge of its own emotions. But Nietzsche's project fell short, not
because the search for knowledge necessarily ends in madness
but because he was unable to free himself from his resentful
desire to imitate Judeo-Christianity. In his imperative to overcome mankind, Nietzsche duplicates the same idea of human
inadequacy and weakness held by his rival. Nietzsche's call for
an overman and the Judeo-Christian belief in a messiah obey the
same impulse, the impulse to bring in a conscience other than
human to provide ethics with an intelligent foundation. Girard's
divine revelation of desire and violence also appears at moments
to rely on the tragic labor of human intelligence, but it risks
concluding, as does Nietzsche's work, at the point where the
self succumbs to its own scandalous nature. Nietzschean philosophy and Judeo-Christianity are finally inadequate for an understanding of ethics, although they may be necessary to its
evolution, because they place ethical models beyond the scope
of the human community and its representations. Even if such
models are only projections of internal social and ethical attitudes, as Durkheim argued, the essentially unconscious nature
of the projection stands in the way of the more advanced ethical
conception deriving its force from the broad awareness on the
part of the community that the human community is itself the
only solution to its problems.

Both Girard and Nietzsche discover the drama where the idea
of humanity confronts its tragic limitations. The modern perception of desire, whether it appears in the form of Freudian, mimetic, or resentful theory, has denied to human beings the

degree of self-consciousness necessary to conceive of an ethics. If we listen to these modern theorists of desire, mankind may only hope to attain a knowledge of ethics unconsciously, or as a consciousness other than itself. Perhaps the time has come to stop searching for this other consciousness and return to the study of humanity and its ethics.

7

The Ethical Unconscious:
From Freud to Lacan

Psychoanalysis has always been fascinated with the sublimation of aggression in language, and by extension with the sublimation of aggression in the subject, especially given Lacan's view that the subject is a signifier for other signifiers. Lacan's unique contribution to psychoanalysis has been to describe aggression and sexuality in terms of a language of the self, positing a fundamental similarity between linguistic structure and the unconscious. More specifically, Lacan argues that the status of the unconscious, which is structured like a language, is ethical, and consequently one may ask in what ways Lacanian theory does and does not elaborate the relation between psychoanalysis and ethics.[1]

Following the late Freud, Lacan places aggressivity in the forefront of psychoanalysis, and in this preoccupation with aggressivity lies psychoanalysis's greatest intimacy with ethics.

1. General references to Freud and Lacan will be given parenthetically in the text. They include Sigmund Freud, *The Standard Edition*, ed. James Strachey, 24 vols. (London: Hogarth, 1953–74); Jacques Lacan, *Ecrits: A Selection*, trans. Alan Sheridan (New York: Norton, 1977), *Encore* (Paris: Seuil, 1975), *De la psychose paranoïaque* (Paris: Seuil, 1975), *The Four Fundamental Concepts of Psychoanalysis*, trans. Alan Sheridan (New York: Norton, 1981), and *L'Ethique de la psychanalyse* (Paris: Seuil, 1986). Translations, unless otherwise indicated, are mine.

Moral philosophy has strived traditionally to resolve conflicts, and psychoanalysis, when it takes aggression as its object, allies itself with this tradition. Indeed, the transference of the analytic session, according to Freud, transforms "pathogenic conflict into a normal one for which it must be possible somehow to find a solution" (16:435). The analyst may thus "expect to lead the revived conflict to a better outcome" (16:438). Although Freud refers specifically to conflict, it is Lacan who gives aggressivity more substance. Indeed, in Lacan, aggressivity is constitutive of the subject. The theory of the mirror phase reveals aggression to be at the heart of subjectivity. A network of imaginary identifications captures each self and effects an aggressive disintegration of the individual at an early age. The subject is cut into *membra disjecta*, as illustrated by the mutilated and partial bodies found in fantasy and art. Lacan points to Hieronymous Bosch's paintings as "an atlas of all the aggressive images that torment mankind" (*Ecrits* 11). The fragmented nature of the subject also comes to light in fantasies of the fortified self, symbolized in dreams by images of castles, stadiums, and inner enclosures. The imaginary phase inserts the subject in a line of fiction that prefigures the later splitting of the ego as it accedes to language and falls under the sway of symbolic mediations.

More significant, however, the mirror phase situates the play of aggressivity in relation to primary narcissism. Later instances of intersubjective rivalry are referred to self-aggression because the narcissistic perspective maintains an identity between self and objects. The phenomenon known as transitivism, of which Freud's "A Child Is Being Beaten" provides a fine example, demonstrates the strictness of narcissistic identifications. "The child who strikes another says he has been struck," observes Lacan, and "the child who sees another fall, cries" (*Ecrits* 19). The subject's aggression toward an object similarly refers to an essential self-aggression.

The analytic session represents another kind of mirror phase, but exists to lay bare the fact of the patient's self-aggression. Analysands in Lacan's view strive to complete themselves by coming to grips with the aggression that threatens the unity of subjectivity. The flow of speech directed toward the analyst is the venom of aggressivity, whereas any pretense of altruism on the part of the doctor conceals intense desires and self-interests. The analytic session risks turning into a mock battlefield, where analyst and analysand seek to capture each other in an action of warfare against themselves. Lacan seems at first glance to push sexuality into the background. The sexual relation cannot be the end of analysis. Nor does Lacan find it inscribed in the unconscious.[2] The early paper "Aggressivity in Psychoanalysis" gives great prominence to aggression, and elsewhere Lacan admits that he has been accused of ignoring sexuality. The accusation arises in part from the emphasis on structure and language made so familiar by the formula "The unconscious is structured like a language." Yet the charge may also derive from Lacan's insistence on the aggression of subjectivity. The influence of Hegel and Kojève in Lacan's work encourages one to read him in terms of identification and of the struggle between master and slave; and even when one proceeds carefully, desire seems a question more of identity and aggression than of sexuality.

Freud's own attitude toward aggression has a complicated history. He resisted recognizing an aggressive instinct until the end of his life because he feared that it would monopolize the nature of instinct in general. Yet from the case study of Dora, where he recognizes aggression as integral to treatment, to *Jokes and Their Relation to the Unconscious*, where he links hostility and obscenity as the only true purposes of jokes, and finally to *Beyond the Pleasure Principle*, where the idea of the death drive reaches its perfection, aggression grows in importance for Freud and eventually moves to the center of his theory. In effect, the history of psychoanalysis may also be considered the history of Freud's discovery of an aggressive impulse, the death drive, and his attempt to reconcile it with sexuality. The history moves from Freud's early interest in the traumatic nature of sexuality to his recognition of the death drive—the moment when Eros and Death embrace. Lacan, who need only return to Freud, begins

2. See Jacques-Alain Miller, "Another Lacan," *Lacan Study Notes* 1.3 (1984): 1–3.

with this embrace. Freud's work opens with sexuality and tends toward a theory of aggression, whereas Lacan begins with aggression and identification and increasingly brings them into relation with sexuality. Lacan repeats Freud, but he differs in something essential: he repeats the path of subjectivity, stressing in his attempt to relate aggression and sexuality certain ethical implications only suggested by Freud.

Proton Pseudos

In the *Project* of 1895, Freud asks what special attribute of sexuality makes it alone subject to repression. The question engenders a search for memories, a quest for scenes, that leads ultimately to a primal scene.

In hysteria, Freud discovers, the patient displays an seemingly inappropriate response to a situation or sensation. She traces the origin of her compulsive behavior to a memory, but remembering the scene has no effect on her fears, nor does it seem to provide a sufficient cause for the symptoms. Hysterical repression takes the form of a *proton pseudos*, a series of false conclusions based on false premises, which serves to conceal from consciousness the traumatic scene responsible for the patient's illness. More specifically, before analysis, a scene A forces its way into the patient's consciousness and causes an affect, but the patient finds it ridiculous that A should be disturbing. Analysis uncovers a scene B that justifies the patient's response, but B has remained hidden in the unconscious. As Freud explains it, "B was appropriate for producing the lasting effect. The reproduction of this event in memory has now taken a form of such a kind that it is as though A has stepped into B's place. A has become a substitute, a *symbol* for B. Hence the incongruity: A is accompanied by consequences which it does not seem worthy of, which do not fit in with it" (1:349).

Freud notes that the normal formation of symbols occurs in the same way. Soldiers sacrifice themselves for a scrap of cloth on a pole, called a flag, and knights have entered into combat over a lady's glove. But the knowledge of symbol formation in hysteria is different: "The knight who fights for his lady's glove *knows* . . . that the glove owes its importance to the lady. . . . The *hysteric*, who weeps at A, is quite unaware that he is doing so on account of the association A—B, and B itself plays no part at all in his psychical life" (1:349).

It may be an understatement to conclude that the originary scene plays no part in the patient's psychical life, for it is precisely its repression that orients the individual's illness. The repression is incomplete, however, as repression always is. Although the second scene (A) is an interpretation of the repressed scene (B), it remains available to memory. The originary scene is repressed from consciousness, but its interpretation is not. The second scene signifies the earlier one, but also carries a later interpretation of the first, thereby accounting for the incongruity between the second scene and its effects. More precisely, the interpretation of the first scene is of a sexual nature, whereas the second scene appears to have no relation to sexual desires.

The case of Emma reported by Freud in the *Project* may serve to clarify the idea of the *proton pseudos* and to introduce the role played by aggression in symbol formation. Freud recounts that Emma suffers from a compulsion of not being able to go into shops alone. As an explanation, she reports a memory from age twelve, in which two shop assistants laughed at her and she fled with a feeling of fright. She also recalls that the two were laughing at her clothes and that one of them was sexually attractive to her. Further analysis, however, reveals an earlier memory. When Emma was eight years old, she entered a small shop to buy some sweets, and the shopkeeper took hold of her genitals through her clothing. Freud describes the incident as a "sexual assault," and it has an oppressive effect on Emma's conscience. Despite her first experience with the shopkeeper, she returned to the store a second time. Later she reproached herself for returning, as if she had desired to provoke an assault. Freud traces her present mental condition to the experience and reconstructs the course of events:

> In the shop the two assistants were *laughing*; this laughing aroused (unconsciously) the memory of the shopkeeper. Indeed,

the situation had yet another similarity [to the earlier one] she was once again in a shop alone. Together with the shopkeeper she remembered his grabbing through her clothes; but since then she had reached puberty. The memory aroused what it was certainly not able to at the time, a *sexual release*, which was transformed into anxiety. With this anxiety, she was afraid that the shop-assistants might repeat the assault, and she ran away.

(1:354)

Freud's description of memory focuses on the sexual content contributed to the first scene by the action of the second one. According to Freud, the sexual nature of the attack is at the age of eight beyond Emma's comprehension, but once she reaches puberty, her unconscious mind reinterprets the scene correctly without fully remembering it. In the end, her traumatic experience cannot be attributed to either scene; rather, it arises as a result of the interpretive activity linking the two scenes. Freud defines this peculiar function of memory as "deferred action": "Now this case is typical of repression in hysteria. We invariably find that a memory is repressed which has only become a trauma by *deferred action*. The cause of this state of things is the retardation of puberty as compared with the rest of the individual's development" (1:356). Deferred action (*Nachträglichkeit*) cannot be contained to a specific connection between memories. It operates within the first scene and wherever the subject judges her past actions according to a new knowledge. The knowledge carries with it responsibility, and eventually turns the individual's consciousness toward itself.

It has rarely been remarked, however, that deferred action is specifically sexual. It operates at every level of memory, connecting the two scenes as Emma's sexuality emerges, but also turning her consciousness inward. In this case, the deferred action pushes Emma's awareness of her sexuality backward in time and makes her more responsible for the sexual assault. She suffers from an "oppressive bad conscience" because she returned to the shop a second time. She feels guilty about playing the seductress for the shopkeeper. Jean Laplanche, in *Life and Death in Psychoanalysis*, interprets Emma's role as actively seductive. He argues that nothing prevents one from asking whether she had come to the shop on the first occasion to be attacked, having been "moved by some obscure sexual premonition."[3] Astoundingly, Laplanche fails to offer an analysis of deferred action. Rather, his reading is itself an example of deferred action applied by the analyst, for the question is not whether Emma is prophetic but whether she now believes that she originally went to the shop for a sexual experience. Undoubtedly, she would believe Laplanche's interpretation, for it reinforces her own interpretation and seems the only explanation for her present refusal to enter a shop alone. The analyst and patient end by agreeing that sexuality holds a privileged position in memory.

The similarity between Emma's bad conscience and Laplanche's interpretation suggests that psychoanalysis tends to reinforce the subject's self-victimization. It shifts responsibility from the victimizer to the victim of abuse, making her the prime mover in her suffering. The victimary tendencies of psychoanalysis are especially obvious in its theories of masochism, particularly in the view that creates an equation between the structures of masochism and female subjectivity. This equation is only valuable because women as a class are victims, not because it cuts to the truth of female character. On the one hand, the theory further suppresses women. On the other hand, it fails to note that masochism is a logical structure directed at restoring power and self-esteem to the victimized self, at transforming it from the passive to active subject, and that as such it belongs to the subject's actions of recovery and self-preservation. Ultimately, however, this defense can only become destructive and redundant, not unlike the activity of the child in the *Fort-da* game, where the recuperated mastery of the boy is an illusion of self-manipulation, not a genuine recovery of self-esteem.

The two scenes of Emma's seduction nevertheless share another similarity unnoticed by either Freud or Laplanche. Both

3. Jean Laplanche, *Life and Death in Psychoanalysis*, trans. Jeffrey Mehlman (Baltimore: Johns Hopkins University Press, 1976), p. 39. On the issue of the victimizing impulses within Freud's theory of hysteria, cf. Jeffrey Moussaieff Masson, *The Assault on Truth: Freud's Suppression of the Seduction Theory* (New York: Farrar, Straus and Giroux, 1984).

the shopkeeper and assistants behave aggressively toward Emma. Especially in the second case, the laughter of the shop assistants has an unmistakably hostile content that is all the more remarkable for the fact that Emma and Freud mistake it. For Emma, the sexual release aroused by deferred action overwhelms any other interpretation of the scene, including the meaning that most people would naturally give to it. Since Freud is searching for what Emma has already found, he follows her lead and accepts the sexual meaning.

Lacan's reading of the case, sketched in the seminar *L'Ethique de la psychanalyse*, is equally baffling. Like Freud, he views the convergence between the two memories as essentially repressive. In fact, Lacan attaches a special significance in this regard to the fact that Emma's second "assault" occurs in a clothing store. The old man in the candy store grabs Emma through her clothes, and the vestiges of the memory remain attached to clothing. But the fact that clothing creates the alliance of memories is belied by the fact that clothing also covers things up. The deferred action between the scenes takes on the quality of clothing one memory in the other, hiding the truth under what Lacan calls the *"Vorstellung* mensongère du vêtement," or the "deceitful representation of clothing" (90).

The lie of clothing is most instructive with regard to the action of deferral, but Lacan's insistence on the problem of deceit does not end by exposing the aggressivity of the early scene. Surprisingly, Lacan begins by giving more emphasis to the old man's aggression than Freud's text would actually seem to permit. He adds to Freud's account and goes to the trouble of imagining the encounter in great detail. Freud, we remember, writes that the "shopkeeper had grabbed at her genitals though her clothes" (1:354). But Lacan describes "an old man who pinched her I don't know where very directly under her dress" (90). Yet when he analyzes the incident in the clothing store, he takes it for granted that the sexual attraction that Emma feels for the clerk is an echo of the sexual feelings experienced during the pinch. Lacan exaggerates the aggressivity only to whisk it away. The translation from Lacan's imaginative version of the aggressive pinch to the sexual attraction of the later scene merely occurs, and with little reflection on the fact that the repression of aggressivity seems to undo those details that Lacan chooses most to emphasize. It appears that Lacan too follows the sexual inclinations of deferred action.

Freud does not ask Emma whether she had interpreted the original assault as sexual, but he might have, as he did in the case of another hysteric. Katharina, in the *Studies on Hysteria*, was attacked by her father, but she blots the scene from her memory. She suffers as a result from anxiety attacks accompanied by the vision of an awful face. At first she traces her seizures to a scene in which she discovered her father with her cousin. Eventually, Freud uncovers the seduction scene, in which the father comes to his daughter's bed in the night; and the inevitable question, the mark of deferred action, arises: "From the way in which she reported having defended herself it seems to follow that she did not clearly recognize the attack as a sexual one. When I asked her if she knew what he was trying to do to her, she replied: 'Not at the time.' It had become clear to her much later on, she said; she had resisted because it was unpleasant to be disturbed in one's sleep and 'because it wasn't nice'" (2:130).

Deferred action is not only Freud's discovery; it is his method of analysis. Deferred action serves both to infuse past scenes with a sexual content and to accord sexuality the principal role in the interpretive process. Psychoanalysis, at least in its early stages, proceeds in the same style, uncovering the sexual content in early life and establishing it as the privileged element in psychic development. The sexualizing impulses of deferred action leave little room for another form of interpretation, but they organize memories in terms of sexuality. As such, neither Emma nor Freud is able to recognize the violence in the two scenes, for any aggressivity is expressed through sexual symbolism.

Likewise, Katharina's "sexual attack" has principally an erotic content. First, the phrase "sexual attack" itself is recognized as violent only with difficulty, for the modifier "sexual" overwhelms the sense of the other term. The phrase enters the reader's consciousness in the same manner as it enters the hysteric's mind when she is in the throes of deferred action. Second, the erotic nature of the attack persists at a theoretical level. Freud's theory of anxiety at this time has a sexual orientation. Accordingly, "anxiety attacks" express ambivalence toward sexual experience. They express fear, but also simulate the agitation of sexual orgasm. Katharina's seizures are a fulfillment of her desire to be seduced by her father. "Go on, you silly girl, keep still. You don't know how nice it is," the father commands in order to pacify her during the attack (2:130). Her anxiety attacks obey his orders belatedly. Her vertigo and shortness of breath represent the victory of desire over repression.

Yet some elements of the experience remain untranslated by the sexualizing impulse of deferred action and continue to trouble the two hysterics. Emma refuses to go into shops alone for fear of being attacked again. Katharina's "anxiety attacks" are accompanied by the awful face, which she eventually understands to be her father's face in rage. It is not, however, the face that he makes upon being repulsed from his daughter's bed. Later, Katharina's mother discovers her husband's infidelities and enacts divorce proceedings against him. Katharina's story of her father's assault contributes to the case, and he becomes her enemy: "He kept saying that it was all my fault: if I hadn't chattered, it would never have come to a divorce. He kept threatening he would do something to me; and if he caught sight of me at a distance his face would get distorted with rage and he would make for me with his hand raised. . . . The face I always see now is his face when he was in a rage" (2:132).

In psychoanalytic language, Katharina's vision of the awful face and Emma's fear represent examples of ambivalence. But the present context reveals ambivalence to be the product of the incomplete action of deferral and its erotic impulses. The violence of the attack, now confused with sexual desire but not fully controlled by it, remains to disturb the hysterics. A more complete fusion of the violence and sexuality would define masochism, not hysteria, and in that case, Katharina's "anxiety attack" would be more pleasurable and the awful face more welcome. Emma in turn would not fear to go to shops alone, but would seek to be attacked, as Laplanche and her bad conscience charge that she had done originally.

Freud's contention that the awful face is the sign of ambivalence reveals his concern with the relation between sexuality and memory. Katharina's vision represents the face of repression itself. Later, after *The Ego and the Id*, we would say it becomes the face of the superego, the agent of the death drive, expressing its anger at the sexual pleasure of the attack. Freud begins by asking why repression acts on sexuality alone and discovers that desire is the one emotion capable of outwitting repression, of recollecting past events without having to remember them. Desire is interpretation, as Lacan says in *The Four Concepts*, but it is also its own interpretation; and as such, desire returns irrepressibly to desire (176).

The question arises whether sexuality defeats repression or cooperates with it in matters of aggression. The case of the *proton pseudos* introduces this question, but can do nothing to answer it. Nor does Freud find it adequate to the task of understanding the special relation between sexuality and repression. First, further thought leads him to subvert his analyses of hysteria. As he comes to believe more strongly in the existence of infantile sexuality, deferred action becomes possible long before the advent of puberty. Emma and Katharina are already sexual beings at the time of their assaults, and their inability to understand them is now ascribed to repression, not to incomplete sexual development. Freud increasingly turns his interest to the part played by the sexual impulses of childhood in the production of neurosis. Second, Freud determines that a fantasy of seduction, not seduction itself, lies at the basis of hysteria. This new hypothesis compels him to search for a scene of fantasy, in which the subject is not the object of love but a spectator of a scene, and in which the subject only fantasizes the seduction through a complex process of identification.

The Sexual Theories of Children

The primal scene represents another situation in which sexuality and repression collide, and psychoanalysis sets out from the premise that the primal scene is traumatic. Children who happen to witness the act of sexual intercourse between their parents experience conflicting emotions. According to psycho-analytic theory, the scene excites the child sexually, but also provides the basis for castration anxiety. The scene is first and foremost an arena of fantasy. Freud contends that evidence of primal fantasies is usually found among neurotics and probably exists among most people.

Although Freud now situates the beginnings of sexual excitation earlier in childhood, the role of deferred action does not change. It remains predominantly sexual and, as an agent of memory, would seem to have no more chance of representing aggression than it did in the case of hysteria. The significance of the primal scene pivots after all on its sexual content. It is a sexual scene that imposes itself on the child. In the case of the Wolf Man, Freud isolates deferred action as the means by which the child enters more fully into the scene of observation: "the scene of observation of the coitus . . . in its deferred action operated like a second seduction" (17:47). Deferred action plays an essential role in the activity of unconscious sexual fantasies. In fact, it seems tempting to equate deferred action with unconscious sexual fantasy itself, for deferred action represents the sexual theorizing of the unconscious in matters of the past. Speaking once more about the Wolf Man, Freud describes the child's sexual theories and their relation to deferred action: "the object of his observation was in the first instance a coitus in the normal position, which cannot fail to produce the impression of being a sadistic act, and that only after this was the position altered, so that he had an opportunity for making other observations and judgements. . . . This is simply another instance of *deferred action*" (17:45 n. 1).

The sexual theories of children do not differ from Freud's views, at least with regard to deferred action. Children re-create their past through sexual fantasy, and Freud seeks to prove the basis in reality of primal fantasies. Unable to demonstrate their reality, however, he proves it unnecessary to analytic theory by observing that primal fantasies have as much reality for the unconscious as genuine primal scenes. The tendency in fantasy to reconstruct the sexual history of oneself and of one's parents takes precedence over the incidental and haphazard events of childhood, and as such, Freud can rightly claim that primal fantasies belong to the phylogenetic memory. The proof discovers a justification in the unconscious both for the sexual theories of children and for those of psychoanalysis.

Nevertheless, Freud's discussion of the primal scene remains unique within psychoanalytic theory for its refusal to privilege sexual interpretation in one special case. As Freud remarks in the citation above, the observation of sexual intercourse by the child "cannot fail to produce the impression of being a sadistic act" (17:45 n. 1). The early article "The Sexual Theories of Children" provides the most complete description of the child's experience: "if, through some chance domestic occurrence, they become witnesses of sexual intercourse between their parents . . . children arrive in every case at the same conclusion. They adopt what may be called a *sadistic view of coition* . . . for the very reason that they have interpreted the act of love as an act of violence" (9:220–21).

From the outset, I should note that Freud does not mean to refer to sexual sadism in the foregoing passage. He often uses the word "sadistic" in place of "aggressive" and appears, as does Melanie Klein, to argue for the existence of a form of nonsexual sadism. Freud does admit, however, that the sadistic view of coition may contribute to a "subsequent sadistic displacement of the sexual aim" (7:196), but such is not his topic here. Rather, he is discussing the interpretive primacy given to aggression in the child's perception of the world.

Freud's account of children's sensitivity to violence is in fact astounding, especially given his belief in the interpretive superiority of desire and deferred action in general. Children, in Freud's estimation, sense an amazing variety of details. The child's "sadistic view" has great interpretive force, for it uncovers the unconscious motivations and unspoken discomforts of parents. The child's theory, Freud writes, "is correct up to a certain point; it has in part divined the nature of the sexual act and the 'sex-battle' that precedes it. . . . In many marriages the wife does in fact recoil from her husband's embraces, which bring her no pleasure, but the risk of a fresh pregnancy" (9:221). Consequently, the child receives the impression from the mother that she is defending herself against an act of violence. Furthermore, the child tends to situate local action in the context of the marriage. "At other times," Freud continues, "the whole marriage offers an observant child the spectacle of an unceasing quarrel, expressed in loud words and unfriendly gestures; so that he need not be surprised if the quarrel is carried on at night as well . . ." (9:221–22). Children soon become detectives to confirm their theories. The presence of blood in the mother's bed or underclothes proves that the father has made an assault on his wife during the night.

This last perception emphasizes the importance of aggression in the child's sexual theories. In *The Interpretation of Dreams*, one of Freud's patients confirms that the primal scene unfolds within a violent context. In recounting an anxiety dream about being pursued by a man with a hatchet, a twenty-seven-year-old patient recalls how his mother feared that he would be the death of his younger brother because of his proclivity to physical abuse. Freud continues, relating and commenting upon his patient's recollection by association: "While he still seemed to be occupied with the subject of violence, a recollection from his ninth year suddenly occurred to him. . . . While he pretended to be asleep . . . he had heard sounds of panting and other noises . . . and he had also been able to make out their position in the bed. . . . He had subsumed what happened between his parents under the concept of violence and struggling; and he had sound evidence in favour of this view in the fact that he had often noticed blood in his mother's bed" (5:584).

The patient's testimony is significant because it confirms Freud's suspicions that children interpret the act of love as an act of violence. It is disturbing, however, because their interpretation is so obviously wrong. Especially for young children, the view is strangely paranoid. Where Freud is seeking to demonstrate the sexuality of early childhood, he finds that children miss the point. They do not recognize sexual activity when it is taking place before their very eyes.

In place of the disposition to sexual interpretation, Freud discovers that children possess an almost paranoid tendency to interpret the world in terms of aggression. The sexual interpretation of the scene develops later, as Freud argues in the Wolf Man case, through the agency of deferred action. At that moment the primacy of the interpretation is reversed, and the child's perception of violence turns vague, remaining only as the obscure vestige of a mistaken view, the dim recollection of some fantastic theory. The sexual interpretation takes precedence, and one might further argue that the earlier aggressive interpretation only emerges through the aid of the erotic one. Freud contends that the death drive escapes detection unless it is represented through the agency of sexuality, which may explain why it took him so many years to accept the existence of an aggressive instinct. In *Civilization and Its Discontents*, he says of the death drive that "we can only suspect it, as it were, as something in the background behind Eros, and it escapes detection unless its presence is betrayed by its being alloyed with Eros" (21:121). Without an agent similar to deferred action, which alloys aggression and sexuality, the violence of the primal scene would be neither stored in the unconscious nor represented to consciousness.

Freudian theory repeatedly emphasizes the power of Eros over the death drive. Eros has libido at its command, whereas the death drive has no source of energy of its own. When the two drives fuse, Eros overwhelms the death drive, except in those instances when cunning Death twists the power of Eros against itself. In such cases, however, the erotic urges still demand satisfaction. Even when aggressiveness seems to surface without sexual purpose, in the blind fury of chaos, a degree of narcissistic enjoyment accompanies the satisfaction of the instinct, for the ego revels in the assurance of its omnipotence.

The children's theory of the primal scene bears no relation to the reality behind their observations. Yet it is not the fact that they mistake the act of love for one of violence that guarantees a correct interpretation later in life. Indeed, the question arises whether the sexuality of the primal scene is at all necessary. Since the scene of "attack" must be eroticized to be represented to consciousness, a similar process would occur if the scene were not originally sexual. Sexuality is the product of interpretation, and consequently it is not a required element of the scene.

It is the perception of aggression that fixes the child's attention. Would the scene have less impact if the father were actually beating the mother as the child believes? Not at all, for the action of deferral would still develop a sexual interpretation of the scene. In effect, we have returned to Freud's reading of the *proton pseudos*. It was Emma's unconscious association between the hostile actions of the shopkeeper and assistants that allowed deferred action to recover the first scene through a sexual interpretation of the second one. The recollection of the scene emerges as a sexual component is added, and the addition becomes the origin of the memory. The first and second scenes become sexual scenes, not aggressive ones, as the representation of sexuality represses the reality of violence and enters into the unconscious.

Consequently, the sexual interpretation of the primal scene is guaranteed not by its reality but by the nature of subjectivity and its essential relation to deferred action. Sexuality emerges as a drive only when the nonsexual activity of self-preservation becomes detached from its natural object. Lacan's theory that desire is a lack has this meaning. The disappearance of the object produces a moment of self-reflexivity during which sexuality emerges. The instant of self-reflexivity is an "autoeroticism," in which the subject replaces the lost object with a fantasy, thereby internalizing the object within the subject. Freud originally stresses the activity of internalizing the object in "Mourning and Melancholia," but later recognizes it as essential to all subjectivity, especially to the formation of the ego. Lacan's theory of the mirror phase begins where Freud leaves off, where the pen falls from his hand during the writing of the "Splitting of the Ego in the Process of Defence." The mirror stage identifies the phase during which the child enters into object relations, not through sexuality but through identification, and explains how the disruption of identification through separation from the object inserts the subject in a line of fiction, the configuration of desire and language, whose essentially divisive natures will henceforth dominate his or her life.

Not surprisingly, narcissism lies at the heart of the primal scene. The child's perception of the scene pivots on a narcissistic identification with the mother, against whom the child believes the father is directing his aggression. The violence is therefore aimed through primary identification against the child and provides the basis for castration anxiety: the drama where the child must decide between being the object of violence, through present identifications, or the violator, through a new identification with the father. The threat of castration reveals the double nature of narcissism. Indeed, narcissism is duplicitous from its inception in the myth of Narcissus to Lacan's theory of the mirror phase.[4] The child's narcissistic identification with the mother is transferred through his narcissistic concern for preservation to an identification with the father. Narcissism is active at every stage of the transference. It defines the movement from primary to secondary identification. But it is most contradictory at the moment before the allegiance to the mother is abandoned. As the identifications cross, children violate themselves. They are crucified, fixed at the crossroads, as the tale of Oedipus records. And healthy children will exist at cross purposes with themselves until they enter language. Only then will the violence directed against the self be distributed according to the oppositions of language. The Other is born. The Other loves, torments, and forsakes. *Eli, Eli, lama sabachthani?* Lacan establishes such exemplary self-aggression as the source of intersubjective violence, and thus emerges the necessity of the analyst's drawing out the analysand's aggressivity, of being an obstacle to the further establishment of secondary identifications between patient and doctor, and of keeping the speech of the patient flowing in a symbolic bloodletting of violence.

In subjectivity, self-aggression is primary, for the subject and sexuality emerge at the moment when aggression turns into self-aggression. I do not have the space here to illustrate this process on a theoretical plane; nor is the illustration necessary, as Laplanche describes it in great detail. The essential point

4. See my history of narcissism in *The Mirror of Medusa* (Berkeley: University of California Press, 1983).

remains that masochism is primary within the field of sexuality. The masochistic fantasy, in the foregoing example, occurs when children's identification with the mother allows the fantasies of their parents to assault them, to seduce them into the scene. As children identify with their mother, they introject the suffering object, fantasize the suffering object, make the object suffer inside them, and make themselves suffer.[5] In terms of the primal scene, therefore, only the presence of the suffering object is important. The scene serves to traumatize the child, introducing the moment of primary masochism, during which aggression becomes self-aggression and the "attack" is eroticized as it is repressed. Psychoanalysis sets out from the trauma of the primal scene because it alone explains the traumatic nature of sexuality, but the trauma makes no sense unless it is viewed within the context of another relation between sexuality and aggression: that sexuality represents aggression, and that behind the repression of sexuality lies another form of repression, in which sexuality and the unconscious cooperate to exclude the reality of violence.[6]

Encore at Last

In *The Four Concepts*, Lacan takes for granted that his readers understand the meaning of the phrase *"the unconscious is structured like a language"* (20). Yet he still makes an effort to dispute the charge that his view of the unconscious is not strictly Freudian and that he may have betrayed Freud in his embrace of linguistic structuralism. Lacan admits only one difference in em-

5. See Laplanche's explanation, p. 97.
6. Within a Lacanian register, the phrase "reality of violence" may cause some confusion. What I am trying to describe is the tendency on the part of the unconscious to represent violence in a sexual manner. It could be argued that violence therefore belongs to the Real—that which cannot be represented— since the Real serves as the zero point of death or what Lacan calls the "mystery of the unconscious" (*Encore*, p. 118). I am arguing, however, not for the (un)reality of violence in this sense, but for its status as an element opposed to sexuality, an element that the unconscious struggles to incorporate whenever it is encountered. This incorporation implies a representation of violence that represses it, but clearly not in the derogatory sense sometimes given to "repression." Rather, it defines the unconscious as ethical.

phasis: "If I am formulating here that the status of the unconscious is ethical . . . it is precisely because Freud himself does not stress it when he gives the unconscious its status" (34). He further suggests that it is linguistic structure that gives the unconscious its ethical status.

Lacan discusses the ethics of psychoanalysis at great length, but his most revealing statements appear in *Encore*. It is true that Lacan devoted his 1959–1960 seminar to *L'Ethique de la psychanalyse*, but he was reluctant to publish it. He seemed to fear that it was incomplete, an idea already expressed in the opening statement of the seminar, where he decides to leave open the question of knowing what will be included under the topic. In *Encore*, Lacan returns to the question of knowing, and his opening remarks there recall his *L'Ethique*: "It has happened that I have not published *L'Ethique de la psychanalyse*. . . . With time, I have understood that I could say a little more about it. And then, I perceived that what was directing my path was of the order of the *I want to know nothing about it*" (9).

The Ecstasy of Saint Theresa by Bernini appears on the cover of *Encore*. It is the supreme emblem of the "I want to know nothing about it," and as such it orients the reading of the seminar. Bernini's sculpture begins by situating wanting to know nothing in relation to a collision between sexuality and aggression, and it provides a version of the primal scene in which the unconscious relation between sexuality and violence reveals its ethical dimension. In fact, we must ask whether the Wolf Man had a similar image in mind when he described his vision of the primal scene to Freud: "He assumed to begin with, he said, that the event of which he was a witness was an act of violence, but the expression of enjoyment which he saw on his mother's face did not fit in with this; he was obliged to recognize that the experience was one of gratification" (17:45). The Wolf Man, Freud notes, changes his interpretation through deferred action, and Bernini's *Saint Theresa* provides a vivid image of the process. It is a superb illustration of the choice in identification that the little spectator (or any spectator) of the scene must make. The scene intrudes upon spectators, asking them to identify with either the dangerous ecstasy of Saint Theresa or the sexual glory of the infant angel. This is a choice after the fact, however, for the inclusion of the child in the scene demonstrates that the decision has been made. The child occupies the place of the father and takes up the golden arrow, remarkable in itself for its unnaturalness in comparison with the figures in stone. The arrow is placed after the fact in the hands of the angelic child. It is a symbol of power, but a symbol that can be removed from his possession, for it is not part of his natural substance.

The scene is principally one of intimidation, and it convinces the spectator aggressively and sexually in a way that the analyst refuses to convince his patient. The patient's demand to know what he wants is too heavy for him to bear, and he prefers to know nothing about it. He would prefer to faint in ecstasy at the analyst's feet and be convinced, as God convinces Saint Theresa: "The pain was so great that I screamed aloud; but at the same time I felt such infinite sweetness that I wished the pain to last forever. It was not physical but psychic pain, although it affected the body as well to some degree. It was the sweetest caressing of the soul by God."[7] The Wolf Man, for example, is in analysis because he has chosen to remain in the position of the mother. But to the patient's demand to take Saint Theresa's place, to want to know nothing, Lacan responds that he wants to know nothing about it. Although he is the subject who is supposed to know, he knows nothing in reality. Finally, it is the mutual want to know nothing, Lacan explains in *Encore*, that brings the analyst and analysand together again and again.

The doctor and patient both demand an encore, and this act of repetition would seem to strike to the heart of the ethics of psychoanalysis. For Lacan, the refusal to stop the flow of speech overwhelms each conclusion, each interpretation, with the demand for an encore of more interpretation. "The universe," he remarks, "is a flower of rhetoric. This literary echo could perhaps help us understand that the self can also be a flower of rhetoric. It grows from the pot of the pleasure principle, which Freud calls *Lustprinzip*, and which I define as that which is satis-

7. Cited by H. W. Janson, *History of Art* (Englewood Cliffs, N.J.: Prentice-Hall, 1974), p. 412.

fied by blablabla. This is what I mean when I say that the unconscious is structured like a language" (*Encore* 53).

On the one hand, the temptation exists to interpret the ethical orientation of the analytic experience in terms of pluralism. The analyst encourages freedom of speech, thereby confronting the subject's desire to have his or her freedom limited. (The greatest threat to analysis is simply to give patients what they want.) As such, the theory of the unconscious would seem the very expression of critical pluralism. The unconscious does not create boundaries between the outside and inside. It refuses to say "No!" It only replies "Yes!" and "Encore!" Lacan's own reluctance to publish his *L'Ethique* appears to obey this imperative and thus to swerve away from a more significant formulation of the relation between the unconscious and ethics. The seminar responds to each ethical theory, seemingly conclusive, with the encore of endless interpretation. Each theory is met with the humorously black and cynical phrase "One more time!" The ethical act comes to represent the play of purposeful incompleteness, what Lacan calls blablabla, in its refusal to convince, to name, to stop.

On the other hand, when Lacan endorses or is used to endorse the play of the signifier, as Jacques-Alain Miller asserts, it completely disorients the ethical path of the analytic experience.[8] The ethical aim of psychoanalysis is to save the patient from dependency, not to force independence upon him. Freud's phrase "Wo es war, soll ich werden" charts the path of the analytic experience. Lacan renders the line as "Wherever it was, I must go there" and discusses it in terms of Freud's ethical orientation.[9] Freud aims to progress from the repressed material of the unconscious ("Wherever it was") to a self free of depen-

---

8. Miller, "Another Lacan," p. 3.

9. For Lacan's commentary on the phrase, see *The Four Concepts*, p. 33, *L'Ethique de la psychanalyse*, p. 16, and "Compte rendu avec interpolations du Séminaire de l'Ethique," *Ornicar?* 28 (1984): 7–18, esp. 9–10. See also Catherine Clément, *The Lives and Legends of Jacques Lacan*, trans. Arthur Goldhammer (New York: Columbia University Press, 1983), pp. 145–46; Michel de Certeau, "Lacan: An Ethics of Speech," trans. Marie-Rose Logan *Representations* 3 (1983): 21–39, esp. 35; and Mikkel Borch-Jacobsen, "The Freudian Subject, From Politics to Ethics," *October* 39 (1986): 109–27.

dency, including the excessive defensiveness of the ego ("I must go there").

Nevertheless, the analyst's policy of nonintervention rings of an altruism that Lacan himself does not permit to exist. Lacan's anti-altruism risks distorting the sense given to the idea of the "ethical unconscious" by couching it not in terms of ethical behavior but merely in terms of "character" or "personality." Ethics would be but another way to refer to subjectivity. The analyst's altruism in Lacan's eyes conceals only his own unconscious desires, and as such every nonintervention must come to represent a strategy designed to intimidate. Psychoanalytic theory, when driven to this point, always risks becoming a mere echo of the unconscious, for like the ego, it is not the master in its own house. Either the unconscious has no ethical status, and psychoanalysts delude themselves when they pretend to speak about ethics, or the unconscious permits, indeed provides the source for, the ethical aims of the analytic experience. A third option is to abandon the current theory of the unconscious altogether.

Given that Lacan admits the ethical status of the unconscious, it seems odd that he hesitated to publish *L'Ethique de la psychanalyse*. "I prevented this *Ethique* from appearing," he confesses. "I refused because I do not seek to convince people who do not want anything to do with me. Il ne faut pas convaincre. Le propre de la psychanalyse, c'est de ne pas vaincre, con ou pas" (*Encore* 50). The last few phrases are difficult to translate because of the wordplay. I render them as follows: "One must not convince. The nature of psychoanalysis is not to vanquish, sexually or otherwise." The translation is inadequate, but it makes my point. The passage is central to the history of psychoanalysis because it situates the relation between aggression and sexuality in an ethical context. To convince is to collude with repression, and Lacan's pun on *con-vaincre* suggests that repression involves both aggression and sexuality. Yet it remains almost impossible to trace the relation between repression and aggressivity. When we enter the domain of language, where the convincing takes place, sexuality takes precedence over aggression. Emma, Katharina, and Saint Theresa are convinced in their ecstasy that no scene of violence ever existed. Freud and Lacan agree with them, positing the primacy of unconscious sexual fantasy. Only children, for a short period, miss the point. They interpret the act of love as an act of violence. Are they too repressed to see the truth, or not sufficiently repressed?

The child's vision of violence shares certain similarities with the paranoid worldview, for the paranoid also experiences the world as aggressive and threatening. Indeed, Lacan suggests that a dimension of the self is inherently paranoid. In his thesis on paranoid psychosis, *De la psychose paranoïaque*, Lacan explains that paranoia is a "syntax" of social relations viewed separately from the "naive realism" of its object (387–88). This syntax consists of the paranoid's exaggerated view of social tensions, and as such psychotic violence emerges not as an arbitrary action but as an attempt to represent the world. It is an attempt both to take revenge and to fit into society because the paranoid psychotic perceives violence as reality and reality as violence.

The reality of violence is an interpretation for both the paranoid and the child. In one case, it is linked to social perception; in the other, it appears in an individual who would seem to lack social awareness. According to Lacan, however, the violence of paranoid delusion corresponds to a special relation to objects, based on a regression to secondary narcissism. At this stage, the libido is freed from objects and invested in the ego by the introjection of objects as part of the self. In a limited sense, the paranoid and child share the same view of reality. They are both imprisoned in the glass house of the mirror phase, where violence and undifferentiation reign.

For Lacan, however, the primal scene is not merely the discovery of parental intercourse. It is the stage (*autre scène*) used by the child to advance through the oedipal drama of sexuality and into symbolic relations. The scene works to give meaning to the affects associated with castration, language, and various images. But Lacan does not explain that the scene works principally to replace aggressivity with sexuality by establishing the identifications that lead children to represent their perception of aggression as a sexual episode. Neither Freudian nor Lacanian analysis can conceive of sexuality as repressive.[10] At most, sexuality plays the role of an obstacle or an impasse in the individual's attempts to chart the limitations of his or her own desire. Freud reveals in *On the History of the Psycho-Analytic Movement* that "the theory of repression is the corner-stone on which the whole structure of psycho-analysis rests" (14:16). It goes almost without argument that the repressed is sexuality. From the inception of his project, Freud links sexuality and repression in a special relationship. In the desire to polemicize, some analysts have noted that the contribution of psychoanalysis has been mistaken by modern thought: modern thinkers have accepted Freud's theory of repression but have repressed sexuality. They are repulsed, it is argued, not by the dynamics of the unconscious, whose formal structure they now identify with a variety of problems, but by Freud's insistence on sexuality, evident in the almost tyrannical correspondence posited between sexuality and any symbolism. In the spirit of polemics, I would respond that repression has not been accepted either by modern thought

10. It may be objected that Michel Foucault conceives of sexuality as repressive. In *The History of Sexuality: Volume 1*, trans. Robert Hurley (New York: Vintage, 1980), he argues that the discourse of sexuality emerging in the modern age is repressive and hardly an escape from "Victorianism," since the language of sexuality is an ordering of the drives. But Foucault does not mean that sexuality is itself repressive. Rather, the discourse of sexuality remains repressive of a pure sexuality that lies undiscovered beneath the crushing weight of pages and pages of writings on sex. Furthermore, *The Use of Pleasure*, trans. Robert Hurley (New York: Pantheon, 1985) reveals that sexuality and pleasure remain for the subject of ethics the objects of mastery and ascetic practice.

Nevertheless, Foucault's *The Use of Pleasure* does present an interesting reading of Greek homosexual ethics that has bearing on the relation between violence and sexuality. According to Foucault, sexuality was interpreted by the Greeks only in terms of an event in which someone was "penetrated." Each sexual act, therefore, requires an active and a passive agent. As long as the political hierarchy is not transgressed, sexual intercourse presents no problems. For example, when males penetrate females or slaves, the political hierarchy remains intact. But male homosexual desire represents an ethical crisis because it necessitates that the equality of the partners be disturbed: the penetration of one party by his social equal introduces a moment of violence that destroys political stability. That the Greeks conceived of some forms of sexuality as a form of violence is contrary to the theories of psychoanalysis, of course, but it also presents interesting parallels to children's sexual theories.

or by psychoanalysis. The emphasis in psychoanalysis on the return of the repressed defines the essential dynamics of repression itself, exposing the fact that repression is by nature an idea that undoes itself. The more psychoanalysis turns its attention to this dynamic, the more repression turns into representation. The unconscious does not repress as much as it represents. And what is repressed—or, more precisely, represented—is not sexuality. The repressed is more strictly speaking sexual, by which I mean that the repressed does not have to be sexuality but that it must be fused with sexuality.

Psychoanalysis has never reached this formulation, although Lacan offers a clue to it in *The Four Concepts* when he insists on the "affinity between the enigmas of sexuality and the play of the signifier" (151). This new view of the unconscious ventures from Freud to Lacan and beyond to the domain of ethics. The concept of a "beyond" has a special status with regard to ethics. Indeed, there can be no ethics without moving "beyond." But we need not conceive of the place of ethics as a transcendental zone; it may refer, in opposition to traditional thought, to the most human and earthly impulses, those that structure through the pleasure principle both nature and culture. In Freud, however, the "beyond" describes the passage from the demands of the pleasure principle to the necessity of death. This fearful necessity assumes, even though Freud struggles against the idea of a death instinct, an unconscious dimension, and it restricts rather than encourages human ethics. Freud's *Beyond the Pleasure Principle* is the place where aggressivity catches up with sexuality and unravels the interpretive knots and temporal twists of deferred action, making the avoidance of violence an ethical impossibility. The book is Freud's least psychoanalytic and least ethical work because it makes aggression and not sexuality the interpretive mode of the unconscious.

In Lacan, it is also difficult to conceive of the sexualizing impulse of the unconscious as already being "beyond" aggressivity; one is tempted to read Freud's ethical itinerary, "Wo es war, soll ich werden," not as reducing the conflict between the ego and the unconscious but as bringing the ego to the place of unconsciousness and death. In neither Freud nor Lacan can

the idea of the unconscious be securely united with ethics, unless ethics is radically redefined as the particular desire of an
individual or reduced to a mapping of the boundaries, in the
form of desire and law, of the unconscious. In psychoanalysis,
the unconscious is largely a place to go beyond and not a place
that is already beyond. [11]

A theory of the ethical unconscious, it follows, fits only with
difficulty into psychoanalytic thought. The idea of the ethical
unconscious means that ethics holds sway within the desire of
individuals and their communities and that the unconscious
creates the necessary space to reorient the aggressive impulses
detrimental to human relations. It means in the last analysis that
Eros may win out over the death drive and that the sexualizing
impulse of deferred action is the method of its victory. The
unconscious represents cunning Death as Eros and makes it
play the awkward role for as long as possible. The unconscious
exercises its will through the providence of representation, of
language, which clarifies and reorients the meaning of Lacan's
famous phrase. The unconscious is structured like a language in
its capacity to represent the world, and this linguistic structure
defines its ethical status. The unconscious reproduces the same
gap between sign and object that modern literary critics find in
language, but here the gap reveals itself to be a safety margin, a
necessary distance, a "beyond," maintained for the sake of self-
preservation. The unconscious represses aggression through
the agency of sexuality; no matter how obvious the violence,
when the unconscious acts upon it, we are convinced of its
sexual nature. The aggression is contained by representation.
Although it remains in view, it is hidden in plain sight.

Bernini's *Saint Theresa* is such a cover story. But it represents a
cover-up not on the part of Lacan, nor on the part of psychoanalytic thought in general, but on the part of the unconscious. It
illustrates admirably why the idea that repression acts only on
sexuality is itself a manifestation of repression. The complaint

11. On the idea of the "beyond" and ethics, Lacan makes two rather enigmatic
statements in *L'Ethique de la psychanalyse*. He remarks that the reality principle "is
something beyond" (91) and that "ethics begins beyond" (92).

by non-Freudians against the pansexualism of psychoanalysis is, as Freud always preached, a product of repression, but no more so than was his own preoccupation with sexuality. Both gestures find their source in the unconscious, which prefers love over violence, and life over death. The preference confounds for the better the radical insight of a child's sexual theory and the delusion of a saint.

8

The Ethics of
Sexual Difference

Feminist criticism today comprehends a diverse field of ideas and interests, disabusing one of the thought that it might represent a unified or single theoretical camp. Indeed, the disunity of feminist criticism is itself a matter for varying opinions, and feminist thinkers have reacted to the problems of internal debate with both enthusiasm and dismay. Some women believe that their political cause is compromised by internal debate because dissent allows men to dismiss the importance of feminist literary theory, just as they have dismissed generations of women. Other women see dissent as the sign of a healthy pluralism not permitted to them in the male world and essential to a future of political openness and change. The future of sexual difference, they argue, depends on the recognition of all differences.

One tendency, however, does appear to mark much feminist literary criticism. Feminist critics tend to assume that literature is a social institution, although the nature of the institution is still open to debate. What is at stake in feminist writing is not simply literature or criticism as such but the ethical and social consequences of women's exclusion from the world of literature in particular and the world of men in general. The result is a powerful dialogue between life and literature. When feminist critics make statements about a literary text, they insist that their remarks carry immediate import for the social world. We are in the habit of speaking of the politics of literature in such cases, but feminist theory has revolutionized the notion. No one writing currently, whether from a Derridean or Marxist perspective, has produced anything that expresses the degree of political pertinence immediately recognizable in even the most naive piece of feminist criticism.

Despite the claim that all criticism is political, the perception is trivial in most instances, either giving a false sense of importance to literary theory or reducing the idea of politics to its most banal and detached expression. What makes feminist criticism different? And what is the source of the feminist's power? It has little to do with conventional political power, for rare is the woman who holds a major political office. Rather, feminism represents a minority or marginal form of politics. It taps the moral sentiments of its age by showing to what degree the rights and opportunities prized by male society have not been made available to women. By drawing attention to their marginality, women exercise a sense of contradiction that becomes a critical and moral force. Indeed, moral outrage is the underlying emotion of feminist literary criticism, especially in England and America, and its cry of outrage brings a coherence to all of its concerns. Feminist criticism relies on moral anger, but it would be an error to believe that its anger is unconscious. Feminist critics are aware of their moralism. "When I talk about feminist criticism," Carolyn Heilbrun remarks, "I am amazed at how high a moral tone I take" (*FC* 129).[1]

Feminist criticism has trouble defining itself without exposing its ethical principles, and consequently those feminist critics who try to escape from moral feelings have experienced little success. In "Toward a Feminist Poetics" (*FC* 125–43), for example, Elaine Showalter works to distinguish feminism's ethical

1. The anthology edited by Elaine Showalter, *The New Feminist Criticism: Essays on Women, Literature, and Theory* (New York: Pantheon, 1985), contains a great number of seminal essays on feminist theory. Hereafter, I will refer to the anthology parenthetically as *FC*. References in general to frequently cited texts will be given parenthetically.

and aesthetic concerns by dividing feminist criticism into two types: the feminist critique and gynocriticism. The feminist critique represents an ethical and defensive rereading of literature that exposes sexual biases, prejudices, and codes with a mind toward social reform and action. Its objective is to lead women out of the "Egypt of female servitude," and its language resounds with emotion over the ethical injustice of female inequality.

Gynocriticism, by contrast, is not supposed to be either defensive or moralistic. Rather, it is aesthetic. Showalter defines it as a writing concerned with woman as the creator of meaning; its topics include the psychology of female creativity, the problem of female language, and the trajectories of the individual or collective female literary career. And yet when Showalter defines gynocriticism, she fails to distinguish it from the feminist critique. The gynocritical studies that she praises explore the paradox of "cultural bondage," "disestablished groups," and "sisterly solidarity." This is the language of the feminist critique, not that of a politically disinterested exploration of woman as writer.

A true gynocriticism would require a different social environment, one in which the ethical agenda of feminism would already be a reality. There, working on the topic of "woman as writer" would be a critical pursuit like any other, and it would not require a special label like "gynocriticism." No one can blame Showalter for aspiring to this kind of political neutrality, but the desire for that state remains the driving force behind the feminist critique as she defines it. Only when success has made the feminist critique obsolete will gynocriticism lose its revisionary and defensive character. At that time, moreover, there will be no reason to distinguish between either gynocriticism and the feminist critique or gynocriticism and literary criticism as such.

That a "pure" gynocriticism encounters difficulties in the present climate does not mean that feminist literary criticism is destined to fail. It merely serves to expose the greatest asset of feminist criticism. Feminist criticism cannot avoid the fact that it has become the most obvious arena for the ethics of criticism.

Feminist theory has not yet made any substantial changes in the methodology of criticism; indeed, some feminists associate methodology as such with masculine authority. The contribution of feminism to literary study consists largely in its ability to reveal the importance of women in history and language as well as the injustice of their alienation from the basic rights given to men in Western society. The ethics of sexual difference has always been the implicit subject of feminist criticism, and critics from the most diverse camps are becoming more aware that women's studies may be used as a stage from which to issue ethical challenges. Luce Irigaray's *L'Ethique de la différence sexuelle* finally makes explicit the ethical orientation of her previous work; and Wayne Booth has recently tried to use feminist criticism to clarify his political and personal opinions. Booth's "Freedom of Interpretation: Bakhtin and the Challenge of Feminist Criticism" was written when he was president of the Modern Language Association. The essay is a political statement calling for the recognition of feminist concerns, but it also allows Booth to give special notice to his own brand of ethical criticism.[2]

That feminist criticism is timely and popular, however, may have already endangered its ethical project. Success for women has, in Betty Friedan's view, bred complacency. More significant is the ease with which men appropriate the issue of feminism. Feminist theory has become a stage for moral pronouncements in general, and its specific concerns risk dilution. One must be delicate in describing this problem because it has many sides. On the one hand, for example, the appearance in a man's book of the obligatory chapter on women's issues smacks of tokenism. It serves as a symbolic act to protect the male author against the accusation of sexism, and it may contribute nothing

---

2. Wayne C. Booth, "Freedom of Interpretation: Bakhtin and the Challenge of Feminist Criticism," *Critical Inquiry* 9 (1982): 45–76. While feminists have welcomed Booth's statements, his essay is awkward in many ways. He ignores the literature of feminism, as if women have made no contributions to issues of interpretation, and uses his spouse as a character in his morality play, in which she appears as the patient homemaker, doing the ironing, as he engages in intellectual pursuit.

to the goals of feminist criticism. On the other hand, many would claim that even the most insincere cases of tokenism contribute to the profile of feminist criticism and help it gain strength. For example, the inclusion of a single woman author on a core syllabus may be tokenism, but it means that students will encounter at least one example of feminine writing. But the problem of tokenism runs much deeper. Feminist criticism depends on what I have called a marginal politics; it exercises the greatest force when its statements call attention to the injustice of women's marginality, and its ability to influence is substantially increased when those statements are made by women—in short, by the marginal group itself. Men have been excluded from women's discussion groups not only because their presence may potentially threaten women's ability to raise their special issues but because feminist politics has the greatest influence when it stays in the hands of women. Consequently, some feminist critics cling to their marginal status and oppose anything approaching pluralism. Gayatri Spivak has objected that "to embrace pluralism . . . is to espouse the politics of the masculinist establishment. Pluralism is the method employed by the *central* authorities to neutralize opposition by seeming to accept it. The gesture of pluralism on the part of the *marginal* can only mean capitulation to the center" (*FC* 13).

Here is a paradox that threatens feminist criticism in general. The uniqueness of its project depends on its marginality; therein lies its ethical justification and its hopes for the future of women. But the progress of this same project demands that marginality and difference must be increasingly broken down in order to bring women into an equal sphere with men. Annette Kolodny has compared the risks of taking on the masculine establishment to "dancing through the minefield" (*FC* 144–67). But feminist criticism is engaged in a double dance: it both pirouettes through the minefield of male resistance and balances on the taut line dividing the contradictory desires for marginality and equality.

Before beginning to describe this double dance, I need to make two statements. First, for the male critic entering the field of feminist theory, where moral outrage against men finds vigorous and justifiable expression and where his presence may not be welcome, the phrase "dancing through the minefield" takes on a wholly different meaning. There is no justification that will not be rejected by those who believe that men can have no share in feminist criticism. Nevertheless, joining the waltz of feminist theory is essential for the critic interested in the ethics of criticism precisely because of its privileged relation to ethics. Second, although it is an obvious perception by now that the central conflict of feminist criticism lies in the contradictory impulses toward difference and equality, the significance of this dispute for the ethics of criticism is not obvious. The same controversy animates a variety of critical problems, including Girard's theory of desire, Derrida's idea of differance, Foucault's late critique of Greek sexuality, and de Man's rhetoric of marginality. Feminist criticism, however, appears to possess the greatest awareness of the stakes at issue in this conflict, perhaps because it refuses to deny its political agenda, whereas other forms of literary criticism often distance themselves from life and society with their inaugural gesture. Carolyn Heilbrun and others claim that feminist criticism is capable of bringing spirit back to literary studies; perhaps it can also clarify some of the choices central to the ethics of criticism.

Sentimental Power

Oscar Wilde remarked that all bad art springs from genuine sentiments. Does it follow that bad criticism also springs from genuine feelings? If this statement were true, feminist criticism would be bad criticism, and indeed it fails to conform to the Arnoldian standard of disinterestedness so prevalent in this century. For feminist criticism is nothing but interested. The interested nature of women's writing, however, gives it an attentiveness and capacity of self-awareness as rare in literary theory as its commitment to social change.

The attention of feminist studies is largely directed toward the issue of the persecution and exclusion of women, although not entirely, since much of women's theory conserves the compassion toward suffering people traditionally associated with the feminine conscience. The interest in the maternal metaphor in modern feminism has the effect of preserving this ethical attitude. Some have argued that the idea of women's unique sensitivity to suffering is a cliché to be discarded, but we must be careful not to reject a valuable attribute merely because it has become familiar. Nancy Chodorow's work in *The Reproduction of Mothering* is invaluable in this regard.[3] Chodorow explains that mothering evolves as an emotional attitude that can be taught to both sexes. The question of whether mothering is a female characteristic is less important than the possibility that its insistence as an attitude opens for family life and humanity in general. In family life, the idea of mothering contributes to the forms given to parenting. More generally, feminine sympathy enriches the notion of social character, and both men and women can appropriate the attitude when they exercise their own characters.

Indeed, much of the current writing on women's popular literature—that of Nina Baym and Jane Tompkins, for example—holds women's maternal instincts and hatred of violence in great esteem. Jane Tompkins's "Sentimental Power: *Uncle Tom's Cabin* and the Politics of Literary History" analyzes Stowe's epic novel of feeling, attributing its unique place in literary history to its capacity to reorganize culture from the female point of view. Here again the importance of literature as a social institution asserts itself, for Tompkins demonstrates how women's popular literature strives to influence the course of history. The pivotal point of this reorganization is the recognition of persecution: the novel's sentimental power derives from the suffering and death of an innocent victim.

What is striking about Tompkins's analysis is her ability to account for the power of Stowe's work on an ethical plane, and the discovery of the ethics of the suffering and excluded is soon extended to Stowe's novel itself and eventually to the position of women in history. Paradoxically, *Uncle Tom's Cabin* becomes the innocent victim of literary history. Even though it teaches one to recognize the moral tragedy of racism and prejudice, it falls

---

3. Nancy Chodorow, *The Reproduction of Mothering: Psychoanalysis and the Sociology of Gender* (Berkeley: University of California Press, 1978).

victim to men's prejudice against women writers and disappears from our literary canon. Tompkins's efforts to restore the novel to its rightful place repeat Stowe's ethics. More significant for feminist criticism, Tompkins extends Stowe's ethics to the exclusion and suffering of women, and her analysis of Stowe's Indiana kitchen offers a vision of what this ethics promises for women and men. Like the kitchen, the new society created by the insistence of women's point of view will be a center of harmonious activity controlled by women, and men will be "incidental," like Simeon Halliday, standing in his "shirt-sleeves before a little looking-glass in the corner, engaged in the anti-patriarchal activity of shaving" (*FC* 100).

Stowe's novel was capable of bringing about enormous social change because it forcefully identified the victims of the institution of slavery. To change the situation of women, feminist criticism similarly begins by giving voice to women's suffering. The image of the suffering and excluded woman takes as many forms in feminist literary theory as it does in society. Feminist criticism has been so successful in its illustration that I need list only a few instances here. Christine Rochefort calls women's literature a "literature of the colonized." Hélène Cixous, in "The Laugh of the Medusa," provides many descriptions of women's troubling situation.[4] They are the "repressed of culture." Women have been driven away from writing; "they have been driven away as violently as from their bodies" (245). Nina Baym's "Melodramas of Beset Manhood: How Theories of American Fiction Exclude Women Authors," as its title indicates, traces the expulsion of women's writing from literary tradition (*FC* 63–80). Rare, indeed, is the work of feminist criticism that does not give illustration to woman's persecution.

Feminist criticism would justify its existence if it catalogued only the injustices against women. Violence against women is a reality and demands everyone's attention and care. Yet many women theorists have not been satisfied with merely illustrating

4. Hélène Cixous, "The Laugh of the Medusa," in *New French Feminisms: An Anthology*, ed. Elaine Marks and Isabelle de Courtivron (Amherst: University of Massachusetts Press, 1980), pp. 245–64.

female victimization; they explain that the process of identifying victims may lead to a general identification with the victimized that scandalizes feminism in its most valued pursuits. Feminist theory ventures beyond a catalogue of women's suffering by demonstrating an awareness of the psychological dangers created by the state of suffering. In "Toward a Feminist Poetics," Showalter explains that suffering may become a "literary commodity" that both men and women consume. Those feminist writers whose purpose is to discover a new world often begin by reclaiming the suffering of the past. When feminist criticism becomes nothing but an ideological critique, Showalter argues, it "has a tendency to naturalize women's victimization by making it the inevitable and obsessive topic of discussion" (FC 130). Women risk making a career out of being betrayed by men, and Showalter finds that "this comes dangerously close to a celebration of the opportunities of victimization, the seduction *of* betrayal" (FC 131). Showalter ends the essay by analyzing her own struggle, as a "Minority Professor," with the contradictory desires for marginality and equality: "There have been times when the Minority wishes to betray the Professor by isolating herself in a female ghetto; or when the Professor wishes to betray the Minority by denying the troubling voice of difference and dissent. What I hope is that neither will betray the other, because neither can exist by itself" (FC 141).

Showalter is wrong that neither the oppressing Professor nor the oppressed Minority might exist by itself within one individual, although she is right to hope that she does not lose the equilibrium between them. More often than not, oppressors have little sympathy for their victims, and genuine persecution sometimes causes victims to lose sight of everything but their own suffering. By and large, feminist theory has not fallen victim to such oppositional thinking. Indeed, it is startling to find such balance in the thought of a truly persecuted group, especially when modern criticism, which cannot be said to be persecuted in any manner, flees on nearly every front to a rhetoric of marginality to exonerate itself from its own violence. Being a victim has become fashionable in literary theory because the position is not easily attacked. Paul de Man prefers a theory of rhetoric that mourns for the critic's blindness instead of risking the aggression of insight. Michel Foucault's early work seeks identification with the madmen, deviants, and excluded of history instead of proposing a historical system. Jacques Lacan threatens to make the death drive the motor of the unconscious, making everyone its necessary victim. René Girard describes human beings as the victims of their own desires, promising them hope only if they identify with the figure of Christ, whose innocent self-sacrifice distinguishes him as the only victim worthy of emulation.

If modern literary theory truly values a victimary rhetoric, it remains a mystery why theory is so often associated with intellectual terrorism. Could it be that modern theorists identify with those who suffer in a desire to avoid violence, but forget that the victim and victimizer are related roles? Jean Bethke Elshtain's essay "Feminist Discourse and Its Discontents" exposes the dangers of an excessive identification with the victimized and explains some of the presuppositions underlying the almost universal preference for the identification.[5] Elshtain finds it troubling that "some feminists who set out to describe in order to condemn may, in their descriptions, embrace the terms of their own degradation" (136). They are motivated, she claims, by the ease with which the voice of the victim is accepted: "The presumption is that the victim speaks in a pure voice: I suffer therefore I have moral purity and none can question what I say" (136). Elshtain's reading is not a nihilistic critique of the "slave morality" in the Nietzschean vein but a perceptive analysis of how modernity's valuable sensitivity to suffering may nevertheless be perverted.

Feminist critics are not alone in being led to embrace suffering to gain moral superiority. But they seem more aware than many of the temptation. Bonnie Zimmerman's description of lesbian literary criticism, "What Has Never Been: An Overview of Lesbian Feminist Criticism," is firmly disposed toward a "radical

---

5. Jean Bethke Elshtain, "Feminist Discourse and Its Discontents: Language, Power, and Meaning," in *Feminist Theory: A Critique of Ideology*, ed. Nannerl O. Keohane, Michelle Z. Rosaldo, and Barbara C. Gelpi (Chicago: At the University Press, 1981, 1982), pp. 127–46.

politics of marginality." She believes that the "otherness" of lesbian experience must be accented, arguing that heterosexism is primarily a form of exclusion that denies the lesbian difference. Moreover, she expresses little desire to bring lesbian critics into the mainstream, but grants that lesbianism has a "unique and critical place at the margins of patriarchal society" (*FC* 204). The worth of lesbian criticism for Zimmerman cannot be thought apart from its marginality, for the "value of separatism is precisely this marginality" (*FC* 214–15). Most significant, she does not define marginality as a position imposed by male oppressors; rather, it is necessary for the lesbian to marginalize herself: "Those critics who maintain a consciously chosen position on the boundaries (and not one imposed by a hostile society) help to keep lesbian and feminist criticism radical and provocative, preventing both from becoming another arm of the established truth" (*FC* 215).[6] The radical politics of marginality sacrifices its proponents to be provocative; it is self-victimizing and therefore potentially victimizing, for the moment that the self-victim provides a radical critique of others' tendencies to victimize her, she becomes their oppressor. Zimmerman nevertheless seems aware of the relation between the victim and victimizer. Despite her allegiance to marginal politics, she confesses that the lesbian essence, in which she believes, is dangerous, resembling a "curious revival" of the nineteenth-century belief in female moral superiority. As a remedy, she proposes that women remain sensitive to the "dynamic between oppression and oppressing," although such sensitivity is ultimately incompatible with a truly radical politics of marginality (*FC* 216).

The difficulty with the politics of marginality remains that it may create a victimary mythology in order to reign over its victimizers. Men have a history of persecuting women; this history must end. But if this history is attributed to unchangeable differences between men and women, feminism risks creating a reverse mythology. The world that this mythology demands would be something like Stowe's Indiana kitchen, where men

6. Cf. Josette Féral's belief that women must choose marginality in "The Powers of Difference," in *The Future of Difference*, ed. Hester Eisenstein and Alice Jardine (Boston: G. K. Hall, 1980), pp. 88–94.

still hold weapons, but turn them benignly against themselves. We may all, men and women alike, desire such a world, but a real world it is not. It is nevertheless a fact of politics that minority groups must often risk essentialism to spark political events. The modern critique of ethics points to the fact that ethical systems often open with an unethical gesture. It condemns ethics as such for its tendency toward essentialism and false opposition. But the most successful ethics is one that strives to compensate for the violence in its past, and only a criticism that believes more in essentialism than it claims moral philosophy does will reject ethics out of hand for essentialism.

Whether the time has come to ask feminist criticism to call for this corrective action is not an easy question, and the call, when it arises, will have to come from within feminism itself. If feminism dismantles its own political rhetoric prematurely, it may lose its voice and its cause. Yet it will encourage attack, if it does not provide a place for the Simeon Hallidays of the world.

Some women have already called for the next stage in feminist rhetoric. Others have tried, either implicitly or explicitly, to provide models for a nonsexist personality. In almost every case, the models attempt solutions to the oppositions created by the contradictory impulses toward difference and equality. Heilbrun's early *Toward a Recognition of Androgyny* uses the literature of androgyny to break down conventional attitudes toward sexual identities.[7] She searches through literary history for women who are strong and men who are gentle. Most important, she argues that the complete human being brings together a harmonious mixture of those traits often divided according to feminine and masculine ideals. Whether androgyny genuinely exists may not be as important as its message. The concept of androgyny supports a political and ethical agenda that would erase those oppositions standing in the way of sexual equality. It is in effect a hypothetical basis for social action.

The fight for sexual equality is first and foremost an ethical issue. The goal in fact exposes the ethical orientation of feminist

7. Carolyn Heilbrun, *Toward a Recognition of Androgyny* (New York: Knopf, 1973).

theory as such. But equality defined from an ethical standpoint has nothing to do with natural differences; the ethically minded person may recognize that sexual distinctions exist, but understands that they should not be allowed to become the reason for prejudice. Yet sexual difference holds a fascination for human beings: their identities cannot be thought apart from their sex, and sexuality itself serves as a primary force in bringing differences in gender to consciousness. The struggle for sexual equality must therefore confront the "reality" of gender, but feminists have felt uncomfortable basing their fight for equality solely on ethical principles. Heilbrun's idea of androgyny is a case in point. Androgyny is a "theory" that represents the desire to find a motivation other than ethical upon which to found sexual equality, and yet it cannot escape its ethical content.

Feminism for and against Psychoanalysis

The argument between feminism and psychoanalysis presents the most dramatic illustration of the ethics of sexual difference. Modern feminism cannot divorce itself from Freud because psychoanalysis invented the twentieth-century myth of the self. More important, psychoanalysis encourages the belief that anatomy is destiny. The feminist critique opened by attacking Freud because women thinkers saw him as the greatest obstacle to their desire to explain that men and women are equal. Such early opponents of Freud as Kate Millett and Betty Friedan were usually content to develop an ethical argument against psychoanalysis. They demonstrated Freud's outmoded attitudes toward women and exposed the ideological content of psychoanalysis.

But Freud's biological theories appeared more concrete than the ethical claims of feminism. The science of sexuality claimed to have biology on its side, and the feminist's ethical critique seemed weak by comparison, especially in an age when ethical arguments seem hopelessly out of date. If biology was to be surmounted, the feminists seemed to think, they needed an argument with not only ethical validity but scientific power. Suddenly, feminists became more interested in psychoanalysis.

Juliet Mitchell's role in this project has been to eliminate the opposition between feminism and psychoanalysis by attacking the biological basis of gender.[8] Mitchell bases her work on the theories of Jacques Lacan, whose revision of Freud acts to destroy the humanistic basis of ego psychology and the importance of biology. For Mitchell and Lacan, sexuality is a language. The terms "masculine" and "feminine" await the child when s/he enters the symbolic order of culture, and s/he gains a sexual identity by taking a place within the symbolism of social relations. "Masculine" and "feminine" are terms whose relation is marked as differential by another term, "the phallus," and as a linguistic marker of difference, the phallus bears no relation to the male penis. Differences in anatomy, according to Lacan and Mitchell, do not determine gender identity.

Mitchell's argument tries to free sexual identity from biology, breaking the hold of anatomy on women's destiny. Despite Nancy Chodorow's disagreements with Mitchell, her work on mothering has the same effect because it wishes to demonstrate that gender identity is an acquired characteristic. Analogously, Heilbrun's idea of androgyny—the notion that human beings are bisexual by nature, and only acquire fixed sexual identity within society—serves to justify the ethical claim that men and women are equal. Now human biology, as defined by psychoanalysis, appears to share the feminist's ethical principles, for it also refuses to fix identity. Paradoxically, then, revisionary psychoanalysis provides feminism with a scientific basis for its struggle toward sexual parity. To change human anatomy would seem an onerous task. But if social language establishes male and female identity, perhaps the possibility of social change does exist. Marxist feminists find the shift in emphasis from anatomy to language especially attractive, and one understands at once the importance of Marx in Mitchell's project. Might women not strip away the corrupting influence of the symbolic order and restore the primitive equality of the sexes?

Unfortunately, Lacanian psychoanalysis does not readily admit this solution. According to Lacan, no human being can be-

8. Juliet Mitchell, *Psychoanalysis and Feminism* (New York: Pantheon, 1974).

come a subject if she or he remains beyond the division of the sexes. The revisionary position of Mitchell does not rely on biology, but sexual difference exists nevertheless. Sexual difference remains a fact of existence, for each individual is subject to its laws in language. Anatomy controls no one's fate, but fate remains. Now language is destiny. Thus, Jacqueline Rose, a Lacanian, attempting to characterize woman's place in the symbolic order, offers only a minor consolation to feminism: "woman is not inferior, she is *subjected*" (44).[9]

Not satisfied with the dream of equality of the Anglo-American feminists, and not able to support woman's subjection by language, the French feminists take what appears to be another direction. They continue to rely on psychoanalysis, but return to the body as a means of staking out the difference of women. The body, for them, represents what cannot be categorized by language; it lies beyond the definitions of language and fails to align itself with the binary oppositions of linguistic and ethical systems. In this view, the languages of society have too long subjected women because of their difference; male society fears feminine difference, and its enslavement of women represents its attempts to control what it cannot understand.

Hélène Cixous's "The Laugh of the Medusa" returns with insistence to the idea that women and their writing defy conventional categories of description. The world of women stands beyond knowledge as such; it is a world of pleasure and sensation that cannot be limited: "A world of searching, the elaboration of knowledge, on the basis of a systematic experimentation with the bodily functions, a passionate and precise interrogation of erotogeneity. This practice, extraordinarily rich and inventive, in particular as concerns masturbation, is prolonged or accompanied by a production of forms, a veritable aesthetic activity, each stage of rapture inscribing a resonant vision, a composition, something beautiful" (246).

Women write literature in secret, just as they masturbate, and their writing captures their ecstasy. Cixous claims that "there

9. Jacqueline Rose, Introduction II, in *Feminine Sexuality*, ed. Juliet Mitchell and Jacqueline Rose (London: Macmillan, 1982), pp. 27–57.

has not yet been any writing that inscribes femininity," and stakes as her project the task of putting woman into the text (248). Cixous's project is paradoxical, however, because she believes in feminine writing (*écriture féminine*), but refuses to offer a definition of it. Nor will she define feminism, but shies away, as do most French feminists, from any movement that would determine itself by opposition to another term. But her refusal of definition makes sense only in an ethical context, for she allies definition and male violence. For Cixous, sex equals politics, and masculine sexuality is responsible not only for violence but for the political systems that enslave women. Indeed, Cixous describes male anatomy as the model for political dictatorships: "Though masculine sexuality gravitates around the penis, engendering that centralized body (in political anatomy) under the dictatorship of its parts, woman does not bring about the same regionalization which serves the couple head/genitals and which is inscribed only within boundaries. Her libido is cosmic, just as her unconscious is worldwide" (259). Anatomy becomes destiny again, but not to subjugate women. Feminine sexuality is superior because it refuses tyranny; it keeps in touch with the unconscious, "that other limitless country," where possibilities are open and equal. Feminine writing is true poetry because only poetry gains strength through the unconscious, the place where the "repressed manage to survive" (250). "Men say," Cixous notes, "that there are two unrepresentable things: death and the feminine sex" (255); indeed, that woman is an "impossible subject" means that she cannot be subjected, for to fly beyond representation is to be free.

Consequently, the practice of feminine writing always refuses to neutralize woman's difference through language. Women's "vatic bisexuality," in Cixous's mind, stirs up, pursues, and increases the number of differences, thereby throwing into confusion those who would try to systematize them. Most significant for the ethics of criticism, feminine writing prefers "love" to the exclusions and aggressiveness that it associates with male theory and politics. As Cixous wishes feminine writing to be practiced, it "will surpass the discourse that regulates the phallocentric system; it does and will take place in areas other than those subordinated to philosophico-theoretical domination. It will be conceived of only by subjects who are breakers of automatisms, by peripheral figures that no authority can ever subjugate" (253). Cixous's manifesto gives privilege to marginality and otherness, for they alone provide an antidote to political repression and violence. Her ethics seeks the other in the other. Indeed, such is her definition of love. Love merges with literature in feminine writing: "When I write, it's everything that we don't know we can be that is written out of me, without exclusions, without stipulation, and everything we will be calls us to the unflagging, intoxicating, unappeasable search for love" (264).

The heart of ethics is the desire for community. Traditionally, ethics has struggled to represent the other as the same to break down the prejudices brought about by the thought of otherness and to make community possible. To accomplish the task, moral philosophy invented the concept of equality, which does not necessarily imply reducing the other to the same but rather posits a hypothetical sameness that allows us to conceive of different people as being equal to ourselves. French feminisms, however, seek an alternative to this view. Cixous, for example, bases her ideas on the concept of "other love." Luce Irigaray rejects the notion of sexual equality altogether.[10] She believes that the ideal of sexual equality causes women's otherness to be absorbed into masculine discourse. She designates as "feminine" an economy founded not on sameness but on otherness.

The "feminine," however, does not seek to steal power through its otherness; only men, as Irigaray explains in *This Sex Which Is Not One*, struggle toward a phallic "seizure of power" (130). The French feminists, like their Anglo-American counterparts, define their project in opposition to aggression, and the concept of "other love" emerges as an extreme instance of the

10. See Luce Irigaray's arguments against equality in *This Sex Which Is Not One*, trans. Catherine Porter (Ithaca: Cornell University Press, 1985), pp. 129–30. Other important works include *Speculum of the Other Woman*, trans. Gillian G. Gill (Ithaca: Cornell University Press, 1985), and *L'Ethique de la différence sexuelle* (Paris: Minuit, 1984).

compassion traditionally associated with women. A danger lies in sentimental power, however, if we must mark women as other to arouse sympathetic attitudes. It is one thing to identify with another's difference; this is essential to sympathy itself. It is another thing to represent oneself as different. Although most individuals desire to be different from others, a threshold exists where difference begins to provoke anxiety in either individuals or their neighbors. Excessive difference excites anxiety because it marks the extremes of social life, where an individual threatens the community with violence or the community threatens to destroy the individual. It is perhaps an ironic indication of the importance of community that we tend to define the first as tyranny and the second as sacrifice.

To view Irigaray's rejection of sexual equality and adoration of otherness as unethical, however, would be to misunderstand her project. The ethics that she appears to reject still exists within her thought; she has merely shifted it to another location. Pluralism, although often misunderstood today, refers not to undecidability but to the Kantian ideal that accepts the diversity of human beings on ethical principle. When Irigaray dispenses with the idea of sexual equality, she would appear not to support pluralism, and yet the body of woman becomes nothing other than the terrain of diversity and multiplicity.

In *This Sex Which Is Not One*, Irigaray discovers a country where pluralism exists, and its borders are the female sex organs. The male sex organ is one; it is singular and hierarchical with respect to his body. Contrariwise, the female sex organs are not one; they are "plural": *"woman has sex organs more or less everywhere"* (28). Furthermore, woman's multiplicity means that she is in touch with herself. Women turn to themselves, Irigaray insists, murmuring to and caressing themselves. Their discourse may appear hysterical to men, but in reality their speech indicates their intimacy with themselves. Most important, for Irigaray, woman's plurality means that she can be fulfilled without the aid of men. The desire of women may be interpreted by men as an insatiable hunger, "a voracity that will swallow you whole," but Irigaray attributes it to another sexual economy, one that upsets "linearity" and "diffuses the polarization toward a single pleasure, disconcerts fidelity to a single discourse . . ." (30).

Irigaray's earliest work often verges on mysticism in its description of women's sexual economy and special consciousness. In *L'Ethique de la différence sexuelle*, Irigaray argues that an explicit relation exists between mysticism and sexual ethics. She describes the ethics of sexual difference as an ethics of female flesh that allows the possibility of bringing together spirit and body. Woman's pleasure is never an instance of power or separation, but an instance of dispersal, a liberation of being by affective emotions, in which sexuality and ethics merge in transcendence. Woman's otherness places her close to the alterity of God, and in the way of flesh Irigaray finds an ethics faithful to a new incarnation that refuses the sacrificial substitutions and violence of traditional religions. In short, women's hysteria and refusal to submit to a single discourse demonstrate their mystical nature.

The mystery of woman remains a source of terror for men because it escapes all rational logic. Irigaray argues that men fear women's heterogeneity. She explains that men have always interpreted women's multiplicity not as a mystical fullness but as incompleteness; their sex appears to men as fragmented or in shards, as if the female organs were merely remnants of the perfect organ. The point remains that male thought reduces women and does violence to them, and indeed, Irigaray sees male and female relationships as fundamentally violent. Once more, politics and anatomy come together to expose the violence of male desire. Men disrupt women's autoeroticism with a violent break-in: "the brutal separation of the two lips by a violating penis, an intrusion that distracts and deflects the woman from this 'self-caressing' she needs if she is not to incur the disappearance of her own pleasure in sexual relations" (24). The imperatives of male rivalry dominate heterosexual relations, Irigaray contends, "the 'strongest' being the one who has the best 'hard-on,' the longest, the biggest, the stiffest penis, or even the one who 'pees the farthest' " (25). Male desire works to force entry, to penetrate, and to appropriate, whereas female desire has no violent aims. Men and women, for Irigaray, are strangers to one another's desires. Their only meeting place is reproduction, where man and woman may finally caress one another through the mediation of the child.

I hope that both Irigaray and Cixous are wrong in their claims about the respective natures of men and women. Perhaps we can do away with the perception that male desire is essentially violent without losing the idea that women are compassionate. Passion should in fact lay the foundation for compassion between men and women, and rare is the man, I think, who values passion for long when it is not accompanied by compassion. Feminism is responsible for changing the attitudes of men toward the sexual act, and the appearance of greater sensitivity in men to women's pleasure enriches their lives together. But the existence of greater masculine sensitivity may require a change in women's attitudes as well. For a man sensitive to the history of masculine persecution of women, the charge that his desire, by nature, vandalizes his partner or destroys her pleasure may itself be a subtle form of victimization. The solution is for men and women in relationships to be aware of their own rhythms and identities and not to confuse them with political generalities, if they are not to bruise one another with accusations.

In the meantime, feminist criticism does have the immediate value of introducing, through the issue of sexual difference, a means of developing an ethical critique of violence. Indeed, the issue of sexual inequality has no meaning outside of an ethical context, and consequently, the debate over the value of psychoanalysis for feminism robs women thinkers of their greatest asset. It leads feminists to abandon a strong ethical position for a weak and murky scientific argument. There is ultimately no point in debating whether language or anatomy is destiny, for both theories venture toward the same ethical vision, and in spite of themselves. Mitchell's revisionary reading of psychoanalysis gives privilege to the preverbal period of subjectivity because this time lays the hypothesis for her Marxist dream of social equality. Cixous and Irigaray stress female anatomy, but end by representing woman's body as the means of escaping from the male language of oppression. Julia Kristeva's notion of the "semiotic" also privileges bodily images, fluidity, and heterogeneous discourse in order to counter the "symbolic" distinctions upon which repressive systems are constructed.[11] The ethics of the female body and its preverbal discourse provide feminism with a response to those forms of violence that are justified by the perception of sexual difference. It is not sexual difference, however, that needs to be either accepted or rejected; we need to reject the prejudices that rationalize aggression and exclusion on the basis of those differences.

Symbolic Wounds

The Romantic interest in suffering has ensured a diverse representation of the poet's agonies for our day, but the extent to which the image of the *poète maudit* constitutes a theory of personality has not been adequately studied.[12] Freud, in particular, takes inspiration from the Romantic poetics of suffering and adopts its metaphors under the guise of science. The idea that the self emerges on a battleground pervades psychoanalysis, but it was in *Moses and Monotheism* that Freud found his ideal metaphor. Here Freud describes the self as a fortress whose walls are constructed of scar tissue, of the "scars of repression" that force instinctual drives to seek increasingly new paths in their assault on the ego.[13] To each new assault, the apparatus of repression responds by closing the wound, only to await the next invasion and the next coagulation. How does one imagine the self? Is it a corpus of flesh plagued by open and festering sores and hardened by scabs, scars, and shards of skin?

That the female sex has been seen as a wound acquires new meaning if seen within the context of the Romantic view of

11. Important works for feminist theory by Julia Kristeva include "Women's Time," in *Feminist Theory*, trans. Alice Jardine and Harry Blake, pp. 31–54, "The Ethics of Linguistics," in her *Desire in Language*, trans. Thomas Gora, Alice Jardine, and Leon S. Roudiez (New York: Columbia University Press, 1980), pp. 23–35, and "Héréthique de l'amour," *Tel Quel* 74 (1977): 30–49. For a discussion of Kristeva, see Chapter 2.

12. I explore this topic briefly in *The Romantic Fantastic* (Ithaca: Cornell University Press, 1984).

13. Sigmund Freud, "Moses and Monotheism," *The Standard Edition*, ed. James Strachey, vol. 23 (London: Hogarth, 1953–74), p. 127.

personality. The Romantics created a dynamic relationship between selfhood and its wounds. In effect, they discovered that suffering could be a commodity, as Showalter would say, and they exhibited their wounds like old war horses for the purpose of poetically creating themselves. Feminist theorists, especially in America and England, have deployed their critical powers against the Romantic poetics of suffering. They openly detest the masculine perception that women are masochistic or that their sex is a wound. Feminists seem to recognize the risk of adopting the image of the suffering woman and contradict the idea that the voice of the victim is always pure. The image of the suffering woman loses its romance in the context of genuine suffering, and it is perhaps the experience of authentic persecution that allows some feminist thinkers to resist the temptation of the poetics of suffering.

And yet, if women have been hurt by men, and they have, what better way to demonstrate it than to display their wounds? If one subscribes to the metaphor that men penetrate women in the sexual act, it means that their sex may be wounded. Although French feminists have also reacted against the romanticization of persecution, some have described the sexual act as a "break-in." Irigaray and others openly detest the idea that woman is wounded or that her sexual organs might be considered wounds, but they end by viewing heterosexuality as an action that wounds women by interrupting their "self-caressing." A subtle translation begins to occur. If woman's sex reveals her pluralistic nature, it also exposes her status as a victim. Woman is open, but woman is wounded.

That some women theorists have adopted the masculine image of their sexual organs will astonish us only if we forget the crucial role played by marginality in feminist ethics. To direct attention to the margins, women need to conserve the image of their suffering. This tactic is not a sham in any manner of speaking, as long as it has a legitimate political basis. The tactic becomes suspect only when it increases the suffering of women and contributes to the prejudices responsible for their oppression. A fine line exists between these two positions, and the best feminist thinkers keep watch over it. But the advantages both in political and personal terms may sometimes be too great to resist. That the sexual act wounds women remains an extraordinarily provocative image. It provides an avenue to the conscience of men. Moreover, the traditional masculine fascination with the otherness of the female organs can be used to an advantage by presenting men with their own fears, fantasies, and prejudices. Ironically, anatomical description has become a major trope in feminist writing, whereas one rarely finds it in any literature or criticism other than that of pornography. These descriptions either present women's genitalia as a symbolic wound or as a mysterious and dangerous object. In the first case, the writer stresses woman's difference as victim; in the second case, her difference engenders an aura of power. In both cases, the distance between victim and victimizer grows dangerously close.

Sarah Kofman's *The Enigma of Woman* works to transform marginality into power, and consequently she strives to enhance the mystery of the female organs.[14] She finds in Freud's "On Narcissism: An Introduction" an exception to his usual oppressive descriptions of women and an incentive for her own celebration of women's uniqueness and power. Whereas Freud most frequently emphasizes the natural inferiority of woman's sex, the text on narcissism assigns women a remarkable autonomy shared only by beasts and birds of prey. But Kofman argues that Freud cannot sustain the effort for long. By the conclusion of the essay, he begins to cover over the libidinal superiority of women by representing them not as "great animals" but as "hysterics," thereby returning to his usual choice of images. Freud's essay

14. Sarah Kofman, "The Narcissistic Woman: Freud and Girard," *Diacritics* 10.3 (1980): 36–45. This essay is extracted from *L'Enigme de la femme* (Paris: Editions Galilée, 1980), translated by Catherine Porter as *The Enigma of Woman* (Ithaca: Cornell University Press, 1985). I use the version printed in *Diacritics* because Kofman's exposure of woman's sex in the opening sequence is especially audacious. The book, however, displays the translation by which Kofman ascribes the image of a "cavity filled with pus" to the vagina. Freud uses the image in an analogy between psychoanalysis and surgical intervention, in which he compares psychoanalytic treatment to scraping out a cavity filled with pus. It is Kofman who applies the metaphor to the female sexual organs. See *The Enigma of Woman*, pp. 46–50.

presents not a case of penis envy, Kofman claims, but one of a momentary venus envy. Freud wishes that he could possess the superior energy and autonomy of the narcissistic woman. Crucial to Kofman's interpretation is her image of the feminine sexual organs. She adopts the Freudian view of the castrated woman, but not to display her suffering. Rather, the presence of the castrated woman petrifies men by providing them with the image of their most dreadful nightmares. The castrated woman assaults men's narcissism, while her narcissism remains uninjured because she has nothing to fear. Indeed, Kofman's essay strives both to incorporate the image of the narcissistic woman and to present it to her readers. When part of the essay appeared in translation in *Diacritics*, it was accompanied by a line drawing of a female nude, conveniently placed next to Kofman's initial exhibition of the vagina: "that 'pus-filled cavity' which threatens to contaminate and infect man" (36). The rest of the essay merely gives representation in one form or another to men's apparent fear of this opening image. For example, Kofman explains that Freud, unlike Nietzsche, fears woman's voluptuous feelings of her own force. Freud's retreat from the *unheimlich* place of women, as illustrated in "The Uncanny" where he describes his flight from a group of prostitutes, stands for all men's terror. Freud's theories pretend to show women a redemptive path, but in reality he draws them with him into retreat. Similarly, Kofman criticizes René Girard's assault on Freud's theory of narcissism because it tries to expose Freud's momentary belief in women's narcissistic superiority as a myth. Like Freud, Kofman argues, Girard flees from the power of woman, and she points to Girard's use of Latin and German words for the vagina as the proof of his terror.

Kofman prefers Freud to Girard because psychoanalysis allows her to represent women as "great animals," whereas Girard does not believe in the metaphor. But Kofman misreads Girard at a fundamental level when she argues that he attacks female narcissism to preserve male superiority. For Girard, narcissism does not exist for either men or women. The coquette uses a strategy to enflame men's desires: she fascinates men by desiring herself in the presence of her lovers, literally dividing herself into a desiring subject and a desired object. But "co-quette" is only a word for Girard, and it refers to no specific gender. Girard argues that Proust's male dandies and snobs use the same strategy, and he works to expose the mythological nature of such narcissistic strategies by pointing to Freud's metaphors. In short, men and women are not birds or beasts of prey. If Girard's reading has a moral, it is not that women do not have enough power or sense to overcome selfishness, but that narcissism uses false accusations to create the differences that make prejudice and sexism possible. In this respect, Nina Auerbach's admirable *Woman and the Demon: The Life of a Victorian Myth* gives a feminist perspective that improves greatly on Kofman's essay.[15] Auerbach exposes repeatedly how images of women's demonic or animal nature justify mistreating them.

Kofman's theories partake of a certain intellectual terrorism on many levels. While presenting herself as a deconstructive theorist, she in fact works to reverse the hierarchies of power and not to neutralize oppositions. Kofman, of course, draws on the theories of Derrida, but the alliance has been over-emphasized because she clings to differences, refusing to defer them in a deconstructive gesture. Whereas Derrida wants women to be indifferent to men, Kofman wants women to frighten them. In Derrida's language, then, Kofman remains a "feminist." In *Spurs: Nietzsche's Styles*, Derrida sets down the lines of his attack against the feminist movement.[16] He argues that only men believe in castration and that those women who believe that women are wounded by men subscribe to a male myth. Feminism becomes nothing but the operation of a woman who aspires to be a man. Feminists, Nietzsche said, lack style (spurs), and Derrida agrees. Kofman's narcissistic woman may seem indifferent to men. Indeed, she presents herself as truly autonomous. But her indifference does not preclude the desire to toy with men by presenting them with their own frightening myths. Woman's power, as Kofman defines it, consists in the

15. Nina Auerbach, *Woman and the Demon: The Life of a Victorian Myth* (Cambridge, Mass.: Harvard University Press, 1978).
16. Jacques Derrida, *Spurs: Nietzsche's Styles*, trans. Barbara Harlow (Chicago: At the University Press, 1979).

ability to terrorize men with the spectacle of otherness. Kofman would reverse the years of male victimization of women by transforming the myth of sexual difference into a means of ensnaring men in their own violence. In effect, Kofman plays the "coquette" because she desires to possess the power that narcissism brings, but, paradoxically, she must remain an orthodox Freudian, believing in castration and narcissism, to accomplish her goal.

In short, Kofman fights in every instance to emphasize woman's difference. In place of Nietzsche's superman or overman, Kofman would substitute her "superwoman." Women may have suffered at the hands of men, her reasoning asserts, but their persecution proves their superiority. And, in fact, men are really terrified of women because they secretly resent their inherent strength. One day the "slave morality" of men will collapse, and women will rise up to take their rightful place as masters. Given their interpretation of Nietzsche, it grows easy to understand why Derrida and Kofman play the coquette, but the benefits of coquetry to feminism remain perplexing.

Gayatri Spivak focuses on another aspect of woman's difference. For the last few years, Spivak has been constructing an extraordinary political allegory that plays out the relations between the violence of male literary critics and the suffering of Third World women, feminists, and herself. She employs many deconstructive tactics, but there is nothing coquettish about her theories. Indeed, she focuses in great detail on women's suffering as a means of establishing their difference. Her objective, however, is to demonstrate that suffering transforms women not into "superwomen," as Kofman claims, but into "superobjects." Two essays in particular draw the lines of her argument.[17] The first, "'Draupadi' by Mahasveta Devi," concludes with an image of a woman naked and brutalized. The second, "French Feminism in an International Frame," begins with a

17. Gayatri Chakravorty Spivak, "'Draupadi' by Mahasveta Devi," in *Writing and Sexual Difference*, ed. Elizabeth Abel (Chicago: At the University Press, 1980, 1981, 1982), pp. 261–282, and "French Feminism in an International Frame," *Yale French Studies* 62 (1981): 154–84.

quotation from the work of a woman Sudanese sociologist who describes a clitoridectomy, as performed in the Sudan:

> In Egypt it is only the clitoris which is amputated, and usually not completely. But in the Sudan, the operation consists in the complete removal of all the external genital organs. They cut off the clitoris, the two major outer lips (*labia majora*) and the two minor inner lips (*labia minora*). Then the wound is repaired. The outer opening of the vagina is the only portion left intact, not however without having ensured that, during the process of repairing, some narrowing of the opening is carried out with a few extra stitches. The result is that on the marriage night it is necessary to widen the external opening by slitting one or both ends with a sharp scalpel or razor so that the male organ can be introduced.
> (154)

In this passage, Spivak confesses, "I found an allegory of my own ideological victimage" (155). Spivak's statement of her victimization, which she places immediately after the vivid description of the clitoridectomy, tells of being forced to choose English Honors and to become a professor of English in the United States. Apparently, such persecution entitles Spivak to speak on behalf of the feminists and Third World women who suffer oppression. Spivak's other essay, which is really a translation with preface of a short story by Mahasveta Devi, creates a similar allegory between the institution of literary criticism and the victimization of women, but it gives a clearer indication of how to interpret the relation between Spivak's argument and her portrayal of the female sexual organs. The story puts two characters in confrontation. Senanayak is an army officer who captures Draupadi (also called Dropdi) and orders her to be raped and brutalized. Draupadi is a member of the revolutionary forces, although Mahasveta Devi makes a point of saying that her name is not included in the list of insurrectionists. But Spivak insists in her preface that Senanayak represents the First World scholar in search of the Third World, here represented by Draupadi. Senanayak, it seems, is also a literary critic and a "pluralist aesthete." He enjoys interpretation, makes literary allusions, and displays interest at least in theory in the otherness of those whom he is exploiting. But he destroys them nevertheless.

Moreover, as Spivak portrays the army officer, he appears to suffer from a split consciousness. One wonders whether Spivak intends to present Senanayak as some sort of alienated consciousness, as an ideological victim, caught between the First and Third World, just as Spivak claims to be. Repeatedly, her allegory groups herself, her readers, and Senanayak together in a collective "we." Indeed, Spivak's allegory never dispels the confusion over Senanayak's character, for her objective remains to demonstrate how Senanayak's conscience allows Dropdi to destroy male authority in the story's final scenes. There Dropdi achieves the reversal of power by turning Senanayak against himself, after becoming, in Spivak's words, a "superobject."

What does it mean to be a "superobject"? A brief plot summary may explain. The morning after her brutalization, Dropdi tears her clothes with her teeth and strips herself naked. Fear and commotion spread through the camp as Dropdi approaches Senanayak. She walks "toward him in the bright sunlight with her head high. The nervous guards trail behind her" (282). Senanayak is stupified by her naked presence and cannot talk. "Draupadi stands before him, naked. Thigh and pubic hair matted with dry blood. Two breasts, two wounds" (282). Senanayak asks where her clothes are, and Dropdi shakes with "indomitable laughter," her ravaged lips bleeding as she howls. Then, "in a voice that is as terrifying, sky splitting, and sharp as her ululation," she cries, "You can strip me, but how can you clothe me again? Are you a man? . . . There isn't a man here that I should be ashamed. I will not let you put my cloth on me. What more can you do? Come on, *counter* me—come on, *counter* me—?" (282). The final image of the story completes the reversal of power: "Draupadi pushes Senanayak with her two mangled breasts, and for the first time Senanayak is afraid to stand before an unarmed *target*, terribly afraid" (282).

No doubt, "Draupadi" presents an extraordinarily powerful expression of a woman's moral anger. Whether the story supports Spivak's allegorical attack on literary criticism is another matter. Some may find offensive, even victimizing, her identification between Senanayak and the literary critic, and we may question whether the analogy between physical violence and literary interpretation is at all legitimate. Spivak's essay does not distinguish between forms of ideology and acts of brutality, betraying its debt to Rousseau's belief that writing makes violence possible. But if we adhere to such analogies every person becomes a victim of culture, and the idea of the victim, so important for both Spivak's argument and feminism, loses all meaning. It is not impossible to suspect the equivalence between social ideology and murder without condoning either one.

No reason exists, however, to suspect Spivak's feminist interpretation, for it is easy to see Mahasveta's tale as an allegory for women's outrage against male brutality. Dropdi's moral power, her only power, consists in the ease with which she can now be destroyed by Senanayak. Hers is a moral victory over tyranny, but her moral superiority depends on having turned Senanayak against himself. She accomplishes this effect by exhibiting her wounds to the officer, and the tale turns our attention to his reactions. Dropdi's final epithet, "unarmed *target*," conveys the officer's subjectivity, not Dropdi's, for his hesitation comes from his realization that Dropdi is a pure target and that he has become an instrument of destruction.

Spivak nevertheless distorts this crucial fact by interpreting "unarmed *target*" as "superobject."[18] The stress should lie on the word "unarmed," but Spivak's desire to empower the victim by changing her into a "superobject" betrays Dropdi. The guards in

18. Spivak also describes Dropdi as "a palimpsest and a contradiction" and these terms expose a desire to empower the victim (268). The notions of palimpsest and contradiction are consistent with the term "superobject" and also with the epic on which Mahasveta bases her story. Indeed, the figure of Draupadi in the original epic defines the idea of "superobject" better than her namesake in Mahasveta's tale. There when the enemy chief tries to strip Draupadi, she prays to the incarnate Krishna, and the chief finds that her *sari* is infinitely long. He pulls and pulls on the cloth, but Draupadi cannot be stripped. Here is an example of a "superobject," and it clearly owes its superiority to divine intervention. A "superobject" is not an object at all, but something mysterious and supernatural. Spivak tries to transform Dropdi into such a "superobject," and therefore insists that she is "a palimpsest and a contradiction." The force of deconstruction depends on exposing layers of meaning and their contradictions. For deconstruction appropriates instances of textual ambiguity and presents them as an obstacle to understanding and literary interpretation. "Superobject" is an example of a self-contradictory term, but there is nothing undecidable about an "unarmed *target*."

the camp fear that Dropdi might be a "superobject." Senanayak fears that she might be a "superobject." In her rage, in fact, Dropdi demands to be the object of their violence, but she walks a fine line, for when her aggressivity surpasses a certain threshold, Senanayak will reciprocate in kind, that is, as soon as Senanayak can forget that Dropdi is an "unarmed *target*" and can justify thinking of her as a "superobject," he will also justify killing her. The term "unarmed *target*" means that Senanayak is concerned that he will endanger himself by killing Dropdi. The term "superobject," by contrast, conveys Senanayak's fear of Dropdi without the mediation of his conscience.

Some might argue, however, that Spivak does succeed in capturing the essence of Mahasveta's story, and there are reasons to agree, especially if we stress the final paragraph of the tale: "Draupadi pushes Senanayak with her two mangled breasts, and for the first time Senanayak is afraid to stand before an unarmed *target*, terribly afraid" (282). At this point, Dropdi is clearly the aggressor, and one wonders whether Mahasveta's inclusion of the words "unarmed *target*" represents an attempt to compensate for Dropdi's aggression by reasserting her absolute passivity. The final lines in fact shift attention from Dropdi to Senanayak, marking him as her object. Most important, the scene satisfies a sense of "poetic justice," for the reader sees Dropdi take her revenge on Senanayak, who now appears not as a brutal persecutor but as "terribly afraid." The scene would have been more effective for a feminist reading if Mahasveta had dropped out the last lines and concluded with Dropdi's final words: "Come on, *counter* me—come on, *counter* me—?" (282).[19] It would then be the reader's task to imagine Senanayak's re-

---

19. A question on a question: what is the significance of the question mark in Dropdi's last words? Does it signify her desire to be "countered" and her disappointment over Senanayak's hesitation? In this case, her final gesture is a measure of her frustration, in which she takes Senanayak's place to accomplish the expected violence against the victim. Or does the question mark expose Dropdi's impending collapse? The question would be a sign of stress, of her inability to force Senanayak to use violence against her, and of her recognition of her self-defeating situation. In this case, her final gesture would contradict the sense of her final words. In both cases, the reader's interpretation must confront the issue of Dropdi's subjectivity.

sponse and the emphasis would have remained with Dropdi alone. The tale would be more Dropdi's story and less the narration of Senanayak's split consciousness. But poetic justice demands that the reader see Senanayak punished in some form so that his brutality may be forgotten. Dropdi must win her self-respect so that we can justify and forget her suffering.

Spivak's allegories also feed our sense of poetic justice. They are narrations telling how persecuted women win out in the end because their persecution makes them strong. But some situations of victimization simply cannot be overcome by self-assertion. Some situations create victims. In short, real victims exist. "Draupadi" translates victimization into power, reading like an Ovidian transformation of being. But how many human beings can be expected to rise phoenixlike from such brutal persecution? Spivak undercuts her position by making persecution necessary to female power. Indeed, her allegory creates a direct equation between the suffering of women and the power of revenge. This is why she relies on the exhibition of the female sex as a wound. Its image makes legitimate the protests that follow.

Both Spivak and Kofman desire the conventional shock of portraying the female organs. They use such exhibitions to offer a political challenge, in which women either take the image of their victimization and confront men with it, or contest the prejudicial image of women's weakness by showing that they too can be aggressive and vulgar. Both alternatives evolve by assuming the pure voice of the victim, and in both cases, exhibitionism is a show of power. But, for Spivak and Kofman, the tactic has more impact in terms of personal than political power. Spivak's confession of her ideological victimage allies itself with the image of the clitoridectomy, and the essay effectively transfers to her discourse the power of sentiment that this image invokes. Similarly, Kofman's "male" description of a vagina appears quite extraneous to her argument, until we realize that it prefigures her desire to ensnare both Freud and Girard in their own rhetoric. The positions of Spivak and Kofman are nevertheless distinct in an important respect. Spivak speaks out against the barbaric practices and oppressive ideologies that persecute First and Third World women. Kofman, however, refuses to contribute to the feminist critique. She prefers representing women as "great animals" to challenging the mythological and prejudicial content of Freud's metaphors.

Humanity and Feminism

Ethics concerns the habits, haunts, and character of human beings. We may enlarge the scope of ethics to include a greater variety of living creatures within our conception of the human being, but ethics cannot endure without the idea of humanity.

The concept of humanity has nevertheless presented enormous difficulties for feminists. It is easy to understand the reason. Humanism makes its claims in the name of man, and "man" has frequently excluded "woman." The French feminists, in particular, have justified the rejection of the ideas of "truth," "man," and "self" because far too often they refer to "man's truth," "the male sex," and "masculine personality." Humanism, as defined by men, has been responsible for the most inhumane treatment of women, and the rejection of feminism by Kofman, Cixous, and others remains a condition of their hatred of humanism. Like humanism, they contend, feminism clings to traditional philosophical oppositions, and oppositional thinking belongs to a male history of rivalry, violence, and exclusion.[20]

The response of French theorists to humanism nevertheless raises some contradictions. They are right to stand guard over the human tendency to justify aggression and prejudice on the

20. Alice Jardine argues that definitions of feminism in terms of identities and differences are troubling because they "homogenize, colonialize, and neutralize the specificities of struggles . . ." (15). She defines "gynesis" as a "woman process" that is never stable and has no identity. Gynesis confronts the void left by women's rejection of those concepts and truths determined by male violence, vaguely aware that this void must "be spoken differently and strangely: as woman, through gynesis" (154). Women's departure from male concepts also engenders a different approach to ethics. According to Jardine, women are best served not by a humanistic ethics, but by an *ethos unheimlich*, an uncanny ethics, that "involves, first and foremost, a relinquishing of mastery, indeed a valorization of nonmastery. And, as we know, a lack of mastery has, historically, always connoted the feminine" (154). See Jardine, *Gynesis: Configurations of Woman and Modernity* (Ithaca: Cornell University Press, 1985). Cf. Judith Kegan Gardiner, "On Female Identity and Writing by Women," in *Writing and Sexual Difference*, ed. Elizabeth Abel, pp. 177–92. Gardiner also argues that "female identity is a process" (183).

basis of concepts such as "truth," "self," and "man." But they do
not strengthen their critique of violence by pretending to weakness and nihilism. Without the concept of humanity, their critique of mastery and aggression has no purpose, for the elimination of violence as such is disastrous unless we understand the
relation between violence and humanity. Competition, striving,
and pursuit define the human species, and a general fear of
violence risks prohibiting the activities through which men and
women guarantee their survival and propagation. Aggression is
not always evil. But it is the responsibility of human beings to
react against those forms of violence that endanger their ability
to live together in their strange states of harmony and chaos.
The preservation of humanity requires that we believe in the
value of community and come to an understanding of those
actions that endanger our existence together.

Refusing the idea of humanity too often conceals a detestation
of life and human pursuits, rationalized by disillusionment and
crushed idealism. But nihilism is only a stage in moral development. Ethical nihilists believe that every action has violent consequences, including the belief in good and evil, and they prefer
passivity as a result. Unfortunately, they soon discover that passivity leads to crises of conscience as much as action. Decision
cannot be avoided, but if one wishes to avoid as many decisions
as possible, two unpleasant alternatives exist. One either
chooses passivity with a vengeance or activity with a vengeance,
and here the key word is "vengeance," for both choices avenge
themselves on the world of violence, not by adopting a critical
attitude toward violence but by extending its grasp. In the case
of the passive choice, the disillusioned determine to define their
circumstances in the most unsystematic and unconscious manner. They hibernate to escape from life, and all choices made by
them are attributed to the other within them, their unconscious
self for example, toward whom they can take only the attitude of
an unknowing and obedient child.[21] In the second case, the

21. Such is the result of Alice Jardine's thesis, which, ironically, unravels its
own hopes for success. Consider, for example, Jardine's description of how
gynesis works: "gynesis must . . . operate differently. Indeed, can we say that it
operates at all?" (*Gynesis* 236).

believers in nihilism create a meaningful universe to fill the nothingness surrounding them, but it is a universe of violence and excessive willfulness. Such is the world of Nietzsche's Homeric contest, affirmed by Kofman, where the strong consume the weak to prove themselves the stronger. Both attitudes end by accepting inhumane notions of humanity, for human beings are neither passive nor active with a vengeance.

International feminism encompasses the extremes of modern theory's embrace and rejection of humanity, but it consistently approaches the issues from a humane perspective. Anglo-American feminists such as Heilbrun, Showalter, Elshtain, and Kolodny remain clearly within the tradition of liberal humanism, although expressing their dismay with how its ideals have been practiced. Irigaray, Cixous, and Spivak offer strong attacks on humanism, but they conserve a sense of humanity, if in the name of woman only. In this sense, feminism need not fear the accusation of disunity, for it has been elaborating, through diverse measures, an ethical project more harmonious than any on the current scene. It is a project in which the ethical questioning of violence and exclusionism finds a renewed vigor. Although the history of women's sentimental power has its troublesome aspects, it is reassuring that we continue today to find in the name of woman the strongest expressions of our humanity.

9

The Ethics of Nuclear Criticism: Conclusion

The danger of ethical criticism is its tendency to think about moral philosophy or about an ideal form of criticism instead of about literature. Literary criticism of any kind risks substituting its own interests for those of literature, but ethical criticism has been especially susceptible to the problem. Traditionally, ethical criticism has tried to avoid the question of literature in two ways. Either it limits the value of literature for moral thinking in the manner of Plato, or it stands in for literature by affirming, in a Nietzschean gesture, the essentially fictive nature of all moral discourse. Either literature cannot compete with moral philosophy, or everything is only literature, but this "only literature" refers to the idea that meaning in general is fictional, mythic, or deceitful. This either/or position, ironically, leaves little space for a literary ethics; indeed, the antipathy between literature and ethics emerges as a phenomenon too little questioned by moral philosophers and literary critics alike. Not to think about literature, modern theorists assume, is the only way to think critically and ethically. To think about literature is to deny the possibility of thought. The objective of critical theory would seem to be not to think about literature.

But how *not* to think about literature?

This question, perhaps the master question for the ethics of criticism, requires a context with some finality, and the current scene provides none better than that of nuclear criticism. For nuclear criticism is obsessed with the ends of literature, ethics, criticism, and humanity. As an invention of literary theory, however, nuclear criticism confronts an awesome problem of self-definition, and not merely because it is the latest phase in critical fashion. Rather, its self-definition goes awry because it finds itself obstructed by the apparent incompatibility of literature and ethics. For nuclear critics, by definition, attempt to think about the relation between literature and life, and insofar as they remain within the tradition of critical thought as we know it, they do not have the resources necessary to the task.

Definitions: From Apocalypse to *Hamlet*

The Summer 1984 issue of *Diacritics*, which introduced the phrase "nuclear criticism" to the reading public, provides a working definition in which the obstacle between literature and ethics found throughout modern theory may be tested.[1] There are two forms of nuclear criticism, according to the editors. The first form applies "literary critical procedures to the logic and rhetoric of nuclear war" (1). The second interprets canonical texts through the perspective of the nuclear age (1). The definitions rely on two local assumptions and an overarching ethical imperative. The first definition assumes that "the terms of the current nuclear discussion are being shaped by literary or critical assumptions whose implications are often, perhaps systematically ignored" (2). The second arises from the feeling that a certain amount of criticism and critical theory "recounts an allegory of nuclear survival" and that other critical and canonical texts conceal "unknown shapes of our unconscious nuclear fears" (2). But the general imperative for expounding a nuclear criticism is ethical: "critical theory *ought* to be making a more important contribution to the public discussion of nuclear is-

---

1. Unless otherwise indicated, parenthetical page numbers refer to the special issue, "Nuclear Criticism," *Diacritics* 14.2 (1984).

sues" (2; my emphasis), and "critical theory *must* play a role in analyzing the mechanisms by which nuclear narratives are construed and enacted" (3; my emphasis).

Despite their apparent unfamiliarity, both definitions of nuclear criticism continue the long tradition, from Plato to linguistic pluralism, of dividing literature and ethics, and they run as a result into the difficulties raised by that division for the relation between literature and life. If nuclear critics have difficulty defining their discipline, it is not necessarily due to faulty thinking about the nuclear problem, although one may question whether a tradition that has defined literary issues as largely disinterested can now successfully contribute to political arguments that are highly interested. To suppose that professional readers of literature have expertise in nuclear policy merely because they have a good sense of grammar ignores that we have generally formulated our theories of rhetoric in purposeful isolation from political and legal issues. Rather, the contradictions of nuclear criticism derive from a certain kind of thinking about literature and criticism. It is not the unconscious fear of nuclear devastation that shapes our present crisis in criticism. Nuclear criticism is only the most recent development in what is now a long-standing practice of associating literature and violence, and it uses this all too conscious tradition of fear to imagine the nuclear catastrophe. Thus, the first definition of nuclear criticism dwells on the relation between literature and war, and the second one creates an analogy between theory and war. Both definitions end by giving literature and its theories a marginal status with regard to human interests, and as such they represent a flight from politics and social life disguised as an embrace.

First Definition.   That nuclear critics view atomic war as a possible object for literary analysis exposes their urgent desire to enter current discussions of the nuclear age. This large ethical imperative is admirable, but it relies on assumptions about literature and theory that undercut its effort. The first definition, by applying literary criticism to the logic and rhetoric of nuclear war, launches its ethical project by assuming a strong resemblance between literature and war. This resemblance is only implied, but it exposes the explicit connection established by many critics today between literary language and violence. Indeed, this connection leads to the familiar presupposition found among nuclear critics that war is mainly textual. The assumption remains that nuclear war cannot be extrinsic to literature, and this idea divides the aesthetic interests of literature from its ethical ones because it insists that the letter is violent.

Nietzsche originally suggested that violence and power follow linguistic laws, but the idea was implied as early as Plato's attempts to free society from aggressive competition by controlling literary expression. Today, few people outside the field of literary criticism take the position that violence is linguistic, but many nuclear critics do assume, unfortunately, that language establishes the basis for aggressive and willful actions. Michael McCanles's "Machiavelli and the Paradoxes of Deterrence," for example, examines the problem of nuclear dissuasion as largely a matter of language. McCanles correctly describes "human textuality" not only as an "extension of war" but as a "displacement of it" (19). Yet he soon begins to take for granted that power equals the language of power, although he identifies with precision the linguistic strategies and rhetoric of deterrence. The "deployment of armies," he writes, "remains a mute language, void of meaning and therefore impotent, until they are transcoded into discourse, and thereby given both a meaning and the power to threaten" (12). McCanles's idea that military maneuvers are but an extension of diplomatic display leads to his belief that literary criticism has a role in nuclear deterrence, but he accomplishes this lofty role for criticism at the expense of literature. For McCanles concludes that a literary rhetoric empowers military arms, and not that weapons provide the basis for threats.

Derrida argues an even stronger case for the relation between war and literature in his example of nuclear criticism, "No Apocalypse, Not Now (full speed ahead, seven missiles, seven missives)." The essay pivots on the relation between "missives" and "missiles," leading Derrida to exclaim that writing "includes the power of a death machine" (29). Throughout the essay, Derrida deploys his missives on nuclear war, and although he sometimes claims that they are "tiny inoffensive missiles," the critical zeal of their launch betrays his belief that the letter has a cutting edge. Here Derrida's usual hesitation about power seems to dissipate, and he refuses to acknowledge the limitations of students of literature in the discussion of nuclear issues. Rather, the fact that the humanities are "incompetent" makes them more competent to enter the debate, since nuclear war is a "phantasm," a "hypothesis," a "fabulously textual" nonevent. Nuclear war exists only as a fable because it has no precedent and has never happened, and everyone, according to Derrida, has equal expertise in the matter of fables.

Derrida's purpose, however, is not to prove the competence or incompetence of the humanities to solve nuclear problems but to write a piece of nuclear criticism. In this respect, his essay is too deconstructive to succeed, if nuclear criticism designates a new approach to a new problem. Derrida's description of nuclear war as fabulously textual and massively real at the same time exposes the extent to which his version of nuclear criticism relies on the same laws and ethical presuppositions as deconstruction. The essay recuperates deconstruction for nuclear criticism only by declaring that the "hypothesis of this total destruction watches over deconstruction, it guides its footsteps; it becomes possible to recognize, in the light, so to speak, of that hypothesis, of that fantasy, or phantasm, the characteristic structures and historicity of the discourses, strategies, texts, or institutions to be deconstructed. That is why deconstruction, at least what is being advanced today in its name, belongs to the nuclear age. And to the age of literature" (27). The passage reveals admirably what deconstruction has often assumed: that the fabulously textual and the real are identical insofar as neither offers humanity a reprieve from violence. The age of literature is the nuclear age because "nuclear war is the only possible referent of any discourse and any experience that would share their condition with that of literature" (28). Quite simply, "literature has always belonged to the nuclear epoch," for literature expresses the sublime death of knowledge and the humanities whose equal in destruction can be found only in the apocalyptic nuclear vision of total global annihilation, or the revelation that reveals nothing (27). According to Derrida, "'literature' is the

name we give to the body of texts . . . most radically threatened
. . . by the nuclear catastrophe," for the preoccupation of literature with the nuclear is analogous in his view to its "absolute
self-destructibility without apocalypse, without revelation of its
own truth, without absolute knowledge" (27).

In the same way that Heidegger launched the "destruction" of
metaphysics and classical ontology against humanism, Derrida
directs "deconstruction" against the idea of humanity.[2] In neither case, however, do Heidegger or Derrida, especially the former, actively seek to destroy humane values. What we witness,
however, is the triumph of a point of view in which such values
no longer exist. The idea of a point of view needs to be taken
seriously, for it exposes the distance covered by the metaphors,
the transports, of nuclear destruction and its implications for
humanity and the humanities. This is not to dispute Derrida's
idea that philosophy, and especially moral philosophy, tends to
take an outside point of reference, be it metaphysical or religious, from which to guarantee the unity of its discourse; it is,
rather, to assert that there is a choice involved in that point of
view, and the proper view is the human one. Although Derrida
has struggled against metaphysical positioning by inventing a
radical form of inclusiveness in language, most often characterized by the phrase "il n'y a pas de hors-texte," his statements
come from an outside point of reference nevertheless. But not
until now has the location of his viewpoint been so unabashedly
clear. If, as Derrida claims, the hypothesis of total nuclear
destruction watches over deconstruction, his language crosses
over quite literally from beyond the pale. Instead of choosing
the point of view of a human being, Derrida decides to write
from the vantage of a postnuclear landscape in which humanity
has accomplished its end; and the agent and expression of that
end remains literature.

Having found the proper context of deconstruction, then, "No
Apocalypse, Not Now" exposes the source of Derrida's insights

2. Cf. Martin Heidegger, "Letter on Humanism," *Basic Writings*, ed. David
Farrell Krell (New York: Harper and Row, 1977), pp. 189–242, and Jacques
Derrida, "The Ends of Man," *Margins of Philosophy*, trans. Alan Bass (Chicago: At
the University Press, 1982), pp. 109–36.

as never before. The essay emphasizes at every turn the destruction implicit in deconstruction. Its opening sentence, *"At the beginning there will have been speed,"* places the deconstruction of the nuclear epoch within the logos of John and its preoccupation with beginnings, but the apocalyptic tense of Derrida's prophecy, its future perfect, originates from the book of endings, Revelation. The essay insists on one of Derrida's favorite topics, "the beginning and the end of the book," now properly revealed as an apocalyptic theme. The image of language, upon which Derrida fixes, also expresses the unity of beginning and end in violence, for the "word" issues from someone whose mouth holds "a sharp double-bladed sword" and who announces: "I am the first and the last" (31). The duplicity and violence of language described by deconstruction find an apt image in the double-bladed sword, for Derrida imagines the word to be double-edged as well. Finally, the essay ends by asserting the elite position of Derrida himself as the apocalyptic messenger of Alpha and Omega. By taking the form of the seven missives on missiles, Derrida's essay ironically imitates the seven letters of Revelation, delivered by the visionary Saint John the Divine, and purposively revels in satirical correspondences between Saint John and Saint Jacques. The last word of the essay, "John," names the messenger who delivered the seven letters to the seven churches of God, concluding in Derrida's often repeated gesture of signing off his writings with a pun on his own name.[3]

The resemblance between nuclear war and literature may be only a metaphor, but it remains a controlling metaphor for the way that critics think about literary language and violence today. The link established between literature and war would be insignificant if it were not enthusiastically promoted as well by the principal thinkers of poststructuralism. A thorough list of statements would require too much space and would take us far afield from the ethics of nuclear criticism, but a few samples may demonstrate to what extent the image of nuclear war provides

---

3. For Derrida's practice of signing off his essays, see "Signature Event Context," *Margins of Philosophy*, pp. 307–30, esp. p. 330, and "Ellipsis," *Writing and Difference*, trans. Alan Bass (Chicago: At the University Press, 1978), pp. 294–300, esp. p. 300.

only a new metaphor for the old practice of marking literature with the frustration felt by those who desire to act morally within society. Roland Barthes: "This Hunger of the Word, common to the whole of modern poetry, makes poetic speech terrible and inhuman." Harold Bloom, who finds that poetry is repressive: "The trope-as-defense or ratio between ignorance and identification might be called at once a warding-off by turning and yet also a way of striking or manner of hurting." Jacques Derrida, who insists that writing carries death: "What writing itself, in its nonphonetic moment, betrays, is life." Paul de Man, for whom literature is like the smile behind which we hide rage or hatred: "texts masquerade in the guise of wars or revolutions." Michel Foucault: "We must conceive discourse as a violence we do to things." J. Hillis Miller: "all imitation is subversive."⁴ For the poststructuralists, it appears, "literature" is the name that we give to the impediments, violence, and deceits that make human life unbearable.

Second Definition. By interpreting canonical texts from the perspective of the nuclear age, the second description of nuclear criticism presumes that the nuclear has a theoretical status. It assumes that placing literature in the context of nuclear war will bring an added dimension to it. The approach is extrinsic because it is radically contextual. Without worrying about the fact that this second approach contradicts the first—that nuclear war cannot be both intrinsic and extrinsic to literature at the same time, that it can make no sense for an extrinsic criticism to place a language that is essentially nuclear (i.e., literature) in a nuclear context—the gesture of granting a methodological or theoretical status to nuclear war is highly questionable. A critic may examine the influence of the Napoleonic Wars on Jane Austen's *Pride*

4. References are, respectively, Roland Barthes, *Writing Degree Zero*, trans. Annette Lavers and Colin Smith (Boston: Beacon, 1967), p. 48; Harold Bloom, *Poetry and Repression* (New Haven: Yale University Press, 1976), p. 10; Jacques Derrida, *Of Grammatology*, trans. Gayatri Chakravorty Spivak (Baltimore: Johns Hopkins University Press, 1976), pp. 25, 292; Paul de Man, *Blindness and Insight* (1971; revised, Minneapolis: University of Minnesota Press, 1983), pp. 11, 165; Michel Foucault, "The Discourse on Language," *The Archaeology of Knowledge*, trans. A. M. Sheridan Smith (New York: Pantheon, 1972), pp. 215–37, p. 229; and J. Hillis Miller, "Tradition and Difference," *Diacritics* 2.4 (1972): 6–13, esp. 9.

and Prejudice, but what does it mean to commit the anachronism of applying nuclear issues to *Hamlet*? Is nuclear war a methodology or a discursive practice with its own specific rules of formation? Can one interpret from the perspective of nuclear war in the same way as one does from a Freudian or Marxist perspective?

If literature somehow remains innocent of nuclear war, literary criticism works to remedy the problem. Nuclear criticism exists to draw literature into the nuclear age; it insists on interpreting the canon from the perspective of global destruction. Here nuclear criticism reveals its greatest paradox. It enters the public discussion of nuclear war on the side of peace and proposes aesthetic values as an antidote to those of violence. But it insists on bringing literature into the war zone to make its point. Literary theory begins to resemble nuclear war in its assault on literature, and critics confess their own underlying guilt about theorizing by revealing a secret equation between critical method and nuclear violence. More than one critic of late has alluded to the similarities between the paranoia of theory and nuclear terrors and has expressed the wish for the apparent serenity of aesthetic reflection.

Mary Ann Caws's "Singing in Another Key: Surrealism through a Feminist Eye," for instance, succumbs to the temptation of representing critical method as nuclear violence. Although finally a statement on the importance of human community, the essay nevertheless puts under suspicion the language of theory in the manner now typical of feminism's distrust of warring male discourse. Caws argues that surrealism, like feminism, "works its recreative techniques to bring back together what was lost, but in different combinations, toward a new full providence" (62). Yet the world of discourse that she describes has been contaminated by nuclear energy: "Even if the energy released in our *proliferating textual universe* is only mental, that very universe had its erstwhile apparent *explosion* of its myth by intertextuality, leading to the challenge of our authorial control and critical vision as they are in fact *uncontrollable* and their results *unpredictable*, of our own safe tenets as they were felt *to leak*, our own ironic elements as they *contaminate*" (61; my emphasis). Surrealism invents correspondences to create a community of objects and humans, whereas theory achieves a collective sense only through the negative image of nuclear proliferation and contamination. Although Caws favors community, a division exists in her mind between literature and theory.

The antagonism between literature and theory is an old story for literary criticism, and it is certainly not the invention of nuclear criticism. But interpreting works from the perspective of the nuclear age tends as a method to exacerbate the tension between literature and theory, and the metaphor of nuclear war becomes a convenient image with which to express one's critical inadequacies, hesitations, and guilty conscience about the problems of ethical criticism.

Although not exclusively devoted to nuclear criticism, René Girard's "Hamlet's Dull Revenge" clearly demonstrates the effect of the nuclear metaphor on the antagonism between theory and literature.[5] The presence of nuclear issues literally divides the essay along two contradictory poles. On the one hand, Girard seems to disparage the ethical impulses that cause critics to impose strict meanings on literary works. On the other hand, he insists that the nuclear age, as a context, presents an ethical imperative requiring that we "read *Hamlet* against revenge" and international warfare (200). In the first case, Girard manages to denigrate the critical temperament by resuscitating the notion of Shakespeare's two audiences—the idea that the bard wrote his works to reach two types of spectators—in the form of the poststructuralist ideal of undecidable textuality. According to Girard, Shakespeare writes with a "mixture of forcefulness and ironic nonchalance that constantly verge on the parodic, without actually turning into an obvious parody" (171). In ironic fashion, Shakespeare "keeps destroying with one hand what he

---

5. René Girard, "Hamlet's Dull Revenge," *Stanford Literature Review* 1.2 (1984): 159–200. Subsequent references will be given parenthetically in the text.

In this connection, consider the words of Robert Wilson, head of the bomb project's nuclear physics division: "You can't play Hamlet and fight a war at the same time" (*New York Times*, July 16, 1985).

is building with another," and such undecidable language makes it impossible for the ethical critic to render an interpretive decision without committing an act of violation (169).

Not unlike J. Hillis Miller's notion of the linguistic moment, in which poetic language achieves the heights of self-referentiality and undecidability, Girard's idea of Shakespeare's writing seems to encourage a particular ethics of reading. Girard has two specific targets in mind. He attacks the Freudian interpretation of *Hamlet* as a specious form of rhetoric and likens it to Polonius's diatribes about Hamlet's mad love for Ophelia. His other target is the moral tradition in Shakespeare criticism that wishes to differentiate between good and evil characters. According to Girard, Shakespeare is more interested in the undifferentiation of the revenge process than in the moral differences of character portrayal. In revenge, Girard concludes, character differences disappear, and *Hamlet* insists that the rites of vengeance make it difficult to distinguish between Hamlet the elder and Claudius. Hamlet's enterprise is sick precisely because he must participate in an act of revenge that accepts his father's goodness and Claudius's evil, whereas Hamlet cannot in fact perceive that difference. This undecidability thwarts ethical critics, forcing them to obscure Shakespeare's insights about violence in order to make critical decisions. Indeed, the ethical dimension of Shakespeare's work, in Girard's eyes, may only be described as a process of *"equalization in villainy"* (161). Shakespeare asserts negatively "the basic identity of all men" by insisting on their equal proclivity for evil, and this assertion characterizes his poetic genius. Shakespeare "can juxtapose two more or less incompatible views of the same characters. He does not choose between the two and the results show that it is better for a playwright not to choose. This paradoxical practice, far from diminishing, increases his effectiveness as a playwright" (162).

Only the most attentive reader, according to Girard, understands Shakespeare's double goal. The rest of the critical community works feverishly to limit Shakespeare's poetic powers. These critics ignore the lack of character differences in Shakespeare and try to recuperate a moral. They focus, for instance, on Richard III's death, but Girard contends that "if we look closely we will see that this demise represents neither the victory of right over wrong which the old tradition of optimistic humanism demands, nor the triumph of wrong over right which our perverse and inverted pessimism now seems to require" (166). Shakespeare's plays thwart ethical conviction and rational persuasion, exposing mob actions as a "kind of moral or even physical lynching, fundamentally irrational and arbitrary in spite of the superficially rational and moral motivations which are exhibited by the lynchers" (166). What characterizes Shakespeare's writings is not the moral duty of demystification but a double textuality that means different things to different people: "The most reflective part of the audience will perceive as ironic a handling of the material which will actually reinforce the more vulgar pleasure of the unreflective crowd" (169). Whereas the "knowledgeable few" with a "certain ethical sensitivity" will perceive "equalization in villainy," the majority will derive a vulgar pleasure from the ethical differences of the characters and the spectacle of violence that they encourage. In short, ethics must be reinvented as a form of linguistic pluralism, in direct antagonism to the old binary form of morality, if ethical and aesthetic sensitivities are to exist in concert, and even then only elite readers may be expected to understand. But if they, in turn, create a moral difference between themselves and the vulgar mob, they fall back into the sickness of revenge, victimizing the ignorant in a ritual scapegoating that eventually becomes a form of self-victimization. In the final analysis, then, equalization in villainy is the only form of ethical representation possible in both society and literature.

The second half of Girard's essay, however, seems to reverse some of these principles, and the upset occurs in the context of nuclear criticism. Girard invites Shakespeare critics to bring Hamlet into the nuclear age and to understand that his dilemma defines the modern space of nuclear politics. Hamlet rests his finger on the button, Girard argues, but perceives that he will be the victim of any act of violence. His tactics in fact delay the act of revenge for as long as possible, postponing revenge without giving it up. Such is the no-man's-land of sick revenge, and "like Hamlet," Girard argues, "we are poised on the brink between total revenge and no revenge at all, unable to make up our mind, unable to take revenge and yet unable to renounce it" (195). Only Shakespeare critics fail to perceive this dilemma, for they vie to solve the "Hamlet problem" and to cure Hamlet's sensible hesitation so that he may commit the act of violence. Girard taunts them with a fable, arguing that should our critical literature on *Hamlet* fall into the hands of some future people ignorant of our race, it could only convince them that "our academic tribe must have been a savage breed, indeed. . . . The only way to account for this curious body of literature is to suppose that, back in the twentieth century no more was needed than some ghost to ask for it, and the average professor of literature would massacre his entire household without batting an eyelash" (196–97).

Given Girard's previous discussion of Shakespeare's double goal, a question nevertheless arises. If the good dramatist must harbor such double goals, must the good critic respect them? Or is the good critic destined to be a bad dramatist in the desire to read *Hamlet* against revenge? Except for the negative ethical ideal of equalization in villainy, Girard cannot conceive of a situation in which aesthetic and ethical purposes may combine. His characterization of Hamlet attempts to harmonize them, but he ends unwittingly by producing a sweet version of the character and a truncated version of the play. One cut is particularly stunning, given Girard's interest in scapegoats. To convince his readers that Hamlet hesitates because he understands the truth about revenge, Girard ignores the murder of Polonius in act III. Indeed, Polonius emerges as the scapegoat of Girard's reading. His sexual theorizing reminds Girard of Ernest Jones, and his platitudes ring of deconstruction. But Polonius is also a scapegoat in the play. Indeed, a Girardian reading of *Hamlet* could be expected to stress that Hamlet calls Polonius a "capital calf" three scenes before he stabs him. And after slaying the old man, Hamlet confesses that he thought that Claudius was hidden behind the arras. The sacrificial substitution between Polonius and Claudius is all the more compelling because Hamlet's reference to the "capital calf" occurs after Polonius brags of playing

Julius Caesar on the stage: "I did enact Julius Caesar; I was killed i' the Capitol; Brutus killed me" (III, ii, 105). For Shakespeare's *Julius Caesar* stands in Girard's reading as one of the most powerful demonstrations of ritual scapegoating in all of literature. If a substitute "Claudius" is murdered in act III, Hamlet's delay becomes less tenable, and the play loses vitality as a model for ethical inaction in the nuclear age.

Even though Girard's reading against revenge is a dazzling display of ethical criticism, he does not allow literature to have an ethical purpose. He argues in favor of literary knowledge, granting it a scientific status, but the possibility of literary ethics remains questionable in the final analysis.[6] Literature partakes of moral insight only when it reproduces the divine revelations of the Bible. If literature follows its own inclinations, it falls prey to the blind requirements of desire, envy, and hatred. Much like Derrida, Girard often emphasizes the death carried by literature and the danger of theorizing about it, following the long tradition in the West of relegating literature and its theory to the margins of culture.

For the poststructuralists, those who love literature apparently live in a no-man's-land between literature and ethics, a postnuclear landscape strewn with the remains and prophecies of nuclear destruction. Past and future merge in the living ruins of the present. The ruins become a text that has no message other than the inevitability of human violence and death. Either literature, whether an oracle or monument of the nuclear holocaust, is contaminated by the images of atomic war, or literature is the victim of nuclear violence. The nuclear critic desires to give up both war and theory that we might find literature. But such desires are hopeless if literature is allied to war.

6. The division between ethics and literature has existed in Girard's work from its inception. In *Deceit, Desire, and the Novel*, for example, Girard argues for two different forms of literary expression: the *romantique* (or romantic) and the *romanesque* (or novelistic). Despite the etymological similiarity of the terms, Girard argues that the former reflects the trappings of desire and is overly aesthetic, whereas the latter reveals desire and is implicitly moral. See *Deceit, Desire, and the Novel*, trans. Y. Freccero (Baltimore: Johns Hopkins University Press, 1965).

The Nuclear Unconscious

Nuclear criticism assumes that unconscious fears of atomic devastation shape the present crisis in literature and critical theory. Indeed, the idea of unconscious activity remains central to the struggles of the nuclear age, for critics insist that unknown drives and impulses feed the arms race. More important, for the literary critic, the rhetoric of nuclear arms discussion always tends toward unconsciousness. According to many nuclear critics, strategic rhetoric moves in Orwellian fashion toward an obfuscation of its motives. In "The Nuclear Sublime," Frances Ferguson conceives of the sublimities of nuclear war as the most recent version of the unthinkable and provides a genealogy of the idea from Longinus, through Kant, to Mary Shelley's gothic sublime. To experience the sublime is to be possessed by something bigger, more powerful, and more threatening than any human being. It is to be trapped in a space that you cannot think your way out of. The nuclear sublime, Ferguson suggests, realizes this psychology of the unthinkable with a vengeance, portraying a claustrophobic world, in which individual freedoms are severely limited by the daunting presence of unknowable fears.

Critical theorists have felt trapped for some time, and the nuclear landscape lends a startling geography to their sense of claustrophobia. For some nuclear critics, these terrors are essentially psychological. Like the unconscious itself, the age of nuclear proliferation crams everything into its space, refusing to exclude anything and quelching all individual claims for the uniqueness of personal domain. In "Baltimore in the Morning . . . After," Dean MacCannell argues that the proliferation of nuclear weapons is directed not against an enemy but against one's own society, in the "realization of a collective unconscious desire" (34). Here nuclear destruction represents the ultimate technological fulfillment of Freud's *Todestrieb*. For Girard, similarly, the psychology of human society relies on the unconscious mechanism of collective victimization, but its full revelation leaves "the human community deprived of sacrificial protection" (191). The unconscious nature of violence guarantees the persistence of hatred, yet revealing the mechanisms of hatred does not result in a form of consciousness that has the power to surmount violence, and so unconsciousness remains all-embracing.

Other critics blame language for the spread of unthought. Like the prison-house of language, the nuclear world permits no escape from its ever-enclosing confines. The opening definition of nuclear criticism in *Diacritics* encourages the idea that literary assumptions shape current nuclear discussions but remain *systematically* ignored (2). It follows that literature plays the role of the unconscious in nuclear rhetoric. Michael McCanles also posits that words lead us into self-binding structures (19), and Derrick de Kerckhove's "On Nuclear Communication" maintains that the bomb has become a powerful unconscious symbol, informing our feelings and attitudes (78).

The idea of a nuclear unconscious, then, brings together the two most powerful images of enclosure to emerge in the last century. It combines into a provocative icon those theories of language and the unconscious most enthusiastically embraced by poststructuralist critics. The nuclear unconscious resembles language in its capacity for infinite digression and opaqueness, and it carries with it as well the deep power of death that Freud isolated in *Beyond the Pleasure Principle* as a feature of the unconscious. Language and unthought join forces as weapons of death in the service of nuclear devastation. There is no thinking about the bomb, but no way to stop thinking about it. There is no speaking about the bomb, but we cannot avoid talking about it symptomatically with every word. Like Freud's sublime *Ananke*, the nuclear unconscious speaks one final truth: "*the aim of all life is death.*"[7] No wonder, as Frances Ferguson notes apropos of Frankenstein's monster, we feel that our skin is too tight. Frankenstein supposedly brings the monster to life, but

---

7. Sigmund Freud, "Beyond the Pleasure Principle," *The Standard Edition*, ed. James Strachey, vol. 18 (London: Hogarth, 1953–74), p. 38. Interestingly, in contrast, see "Why War?" *The Standard Edition*, vol. 22, pp. 197–215, where Freud discovers an aesthetic and ethical perspective on warfare. The essay argues that civilized human beings have developed a "*constitutional* intolerance of war" based both on their disgust with its violence and on the fact that war causes a "lowering of aesthetic standards" (215).

the monster grows acutely aware that his master has brought only death to life. Similarly, our masters of suspicion have continually brought death to life, and it sometimes seems that our release will arrive, like the monster's, only with a final flight into some arctic void, either to escape the claustrophobic world of human beings or to embrace the negative freedom of suicide.

The idea of the nuclear unconscious has bleak consequences to say the least, but it is useful in posing a final question of self-definition to critical theory. To what extent has the nuclear metaphor become only another means of representing the dominant theories of modern literary study? (Indeed, the description of nuclear criticism provided by *Diacritics* merely repeats the latest phrases of critical theory in the context of nuclear politics: "use value," "mimetic rivalry," "the power of horror," "the interpretation of origin," "the role of gender," "rhetoric," and so on.) To what extent has the claustrophobia of current criticism found its ideal image? And what value can literary theory have for the understanding of the current scene, if its interest is only to convert the nuclear problem into an image of itself? Can theory be political, if it insists on importing into the present discussion of nuclear issues not openness and insight but definitions of thought and language that deny the possibility of insight and education? This is not to assume that sentimental humanism will provide the faithful cure for nuclear war. It is, rather, a question for modern theory. Has the marginalization of literary study through time become a habit that threatens to cripple it permanently for any significant contribution to human life?

The Finally Human

Nuclear criticism does have one advantage that has lately been absent from literary theory: it contains the potential to read literature not against human interests but for them. Whereas poststructuralist theory has been defined principally as linguistic, in direct opposition to psychological and anthropological issues, nuclear criticism exposes the fact that the most abstract of theoretical designs and the most simple of literary ventures conceal human interests. The central human issues, for nuclear critics, are the value of the human community and the danger of its destructive tendencies. Nuclear criticism may therefore serve a double purpose. It provides a means of reading the ethical preoccupation of those literary artists and critics who declare most zealously their antagonism to ethics, and it asserts those principles of human community and opposition to violence so vital to the discussion of nuclear issues.

Despite Derrida's claim, for example, that ethics originates as a violent gesture, his writings on nuclear criticism work to establish a parallel between his theory of differance and nuclear deterrence. He cites the wisdom of deferral through linguistic tactics, and one senses that he sometimes associates the play of language in dissemination not with nuclear proliferation but with a kind of playing against time. Given the right context, it would not be difficult to trace to what extent all of Derrida's writings strive—and not merely for philosophical reasons—to answer the question, "What links writing to violence?" The question marks the point where Derrida begins to contribute to the ethics of criticism and enters into the tradition of moral philosophy, for an ethical argument must result from Derrida's claim that writing is linked to violence.[8]

More important, Derrida's "No Apocalypse, Not Now" makes a tangential contribution to the ideals of humanism, seemingly breaking away from his long-standing practice of critiquing the tradition of humanity and the humanities. He opens the essay by referring to "what is still now and then called humanity" (20) and admits that "the stakes of the nuclear question are those of humanity, of the humanities" (22). Derrida's opening of the question of humanity is not a temporary breakdown in defenses, a sentimental moment born of the pressure of the nuclear question. The "now and then" of humanity reads in the same way as the phrase does elsewhere in his theory. In "Differance," Derrida announces: "I shall speak then of the letter *a*, this first letter which it seemed necessary to introduce now and then in writing the word 'difference'" (131).[9] Writing difference

8. See Chapter 4.
9. Jacques Derrida, "Differance," *Speech and Phenomena*, trans. and ed. David B. Allison (Evanston, Ill.: Northwestern University Press, 1973), pp. 129–60.

with an *a*, "now and then," means understanding that the structure of difference always and already engages in the process of deferral. Similarly, writing about "what is still now and then called humanity" means that we write always and already about humanity.

It seems that the claustrophobia of the nuclear unconscious reveals a specifically human content, and it eventually yields the sense that we are "finally human," as Wallace Stevens writes, "Natives of a dwindled sphere," in which "each person completely touches us / With what he is and as he is, / In the stale grandeur of annihilation" (cited by Mary Ann Caws, 69–70). Nuclear criticism, in fact, returns with insistence to the idea that nuclear war makes human community more apparent than ever. When Derrida reveals that nuclear devastation watches over deconstruction, he represents the bomb as the outer limit of human existence. Derrick de Kerckhove also argues that our "growning awareness of the planet's mortality is synonymous with the growth of its unified identity" (79). For de Kerckhove, the bomb becomes a principle of equality, for it says "the same thing to everybody" (81). Similarly, Girard describes the "modern space" of nuclear war as resembling a tribal village, where strict principles of reciprocity govern to preserve the community. The inevitability of this "modern space" orients Girard's desire to found a criticism that reveals the self-defeating nature of human aggression and the value of reverence and communion. Mary Ann Caws refers to this collective mentality as the spirit of Melusina, the threshold person, who contradicts warring impulses with the music of "slow rhythms, loving digressions and deflection, savoring deferral" (66). Born of literature, Melusina opposes to the glitter of nuclear weapons the harmonies of the body and social existence: reproduction, childbirth, and mothering.

The metaphor of nuclear war creates a sense of human community by virtue of exploring its loss. Indeed, according to de Kerckhove, the bomb instills the feeling that Yeats called "the emotion of multitude," a sense of "the magnitude of the human dimension on the planet and of the magnitude of the threat which is now forced upon it" (79), and he further compares the emotion of multitude to the sensation reported by many astronauts as they witness the unity of the planet from space. Nuclear criticism portrays total destruction and asks that we imagine in its absence what we might have had. It walks in the night to remember the day, choosing nuclear devastation over the astronaut's human elation. That nuclear criticism expresses the values of human life and peace only with negative representations indicates to what extent the spirit of modern disillusionment, which mocks sentiment and optimism as unintellectual and naive, has contaminated our positive images of life. The truth remains, however, that the thinking behind images of nuclear catastrophe is no less sentimental and no less naive than that of sentimental humanism in its inability to see the diversity of human behavior. The sentimentalist may be naive in singing songs of Melusina, but critical theorists are just as unintellectual in chanting Dies Irae.

If the dwindled sphere of nuclear criticism has any lesson, it is not one unique to its specific concerns. The value of nuclear criticism remains its ability to reveal that literary criticism in general holds to a set of ethical principles involving human community and its violence, despite various attempts on the part of criticism to seclude itself in a purely aesthetic realm. These ideas are not the particular province of those critics who call themselves ethical; they are the unspoken ethics of criticism, and they derive from the persistent cares and desires of people who write, read, and live together. They are human concerns, focused on the eminence of human society and the forms of violence that threaten community, and they represent the only space from which people cannot free themselves and still exist. The human space is often heavy with the stale grandeur of annihilation. More often it is simply mundane, as it should be, sounding of human language, conversation, and noise. Both aspects constitute the world not as seen from above but as seen by human beings, a world in which ethics and aesthetics, life and literature, and human beings cannot escape one another.

Nuclear missiles now have the capacity to penetrate the atmosphere, and it is tempting to accept their bird's-eye view of the planet. But literature provided a human view of the world long before our rockets reached their orbits. It has persistently given us a view of the whole of humanity, not with the false serenity of a mile-high vantage point, which presents the world as a ball of clouds, earth, and ocean, but with a distinctly human viewpoint, sometimes too peaceful, sometimes too violent, for any one human taste. The nuclear metaphor communicates in its care for life the wholly negative image of planetary death that literature has forever balanced with an ethical and aesthetic image of human life. To be human is to tell stories about ourselves and other human beings.

The finally human is literature.

Index

Library of Congress Cataloging-in-Publication Data

Siebers, Tobin.
    The ethics of criticism.

    Includes index.
    1. Criticism—Moral and ethical aspects.   2. Literary
ethics.   I. Title.
    PN98.M67S54   1988   174'.98   87-47820
    ISBN 0-8014-2128-4